THE ROMANTIC
COMEDIANS

ELLEN GLASGOW

THE
ROMANTIC
COMEDIANS

Afterword by Dorothy M. Scura

University Press of Virginia
Charlottesville and London

THIS TRAGICOMEDY of a happiness-hunter was written, as an experiment, for my own entertainment. Usually my characters, even the least of them, are born of unrest; but life had no sooner pushed the figure of Judge Honeywell into my mind than his biography bubbled over with an effortless joy. Although the style is that of the vignette, and necessarily circumscribed, I feel that the technique I used was the only possible choice. Yet the word "choice" is incorrect, since the act of elimination was absent from the beginning. At the risk of appearing over-enthusiastic about my own, I may confess that, in my opinion, this novel is one of those happy marriages of form and idea that could not have been different.

In my work as a whole *The Romantic Comedians* has, and I think merits, a special, if narrow, niche of its own. It was the first of three comedies, or tragicomedies, that I had placed in my Queenborough in Virginia. All through my social history of the Commonwealth, I had written of places under their actual names, and in at least two of my books, *The Voice of the People* (second part) and *The Romance of a Plain Man*, parallel studies of the emergence of the plain man from obscurity, I had portrayed, with scrupulous exactness, the Richmond scene from the year 1875 until the end of the century.

But for this trilogy I felt that I required the distilled essence of all Virginia cities rather than the speaking likeness of one. The last thing I wished to do was to transfix the wings of my comic spirit and pin them down to an existence in fact. It is true that those of my fellow-citizens who have read my novels appear to recognize not only the place, but, with far less reason, or, indeed with no reason whatever, the people as well. They have, with a charitableness for which I am grateful, either ascribed the actuality to me or ascribed me to the actuality whenever they have felt so disposed. Nevertheless, I hasten to explain that my new freedom includes neither moral nor literary licence. All I ask for my background is the saving grace of anonymity. All I ask for the author of this trilogy is that inalienable right of calling things by their wrong names which is common to all mankind, though it would appear to have reached its highest expression in the Southern breed. For the rest, it is only fair that a writer who is not writing history should be permitted to furnish his own scene and arrange his own chiaroscuro, undeterred alike by nature and circumstance. In my social history, for example, I had been careful to call every spade a spade and every molehill a molehill; but in this comedy of manners, I have not hesitated to call a spade a silver spoon or a molehill a mountain. When I was writing *The Romance of a Plain Man*, I verified, with exhausting, and I now think unnecessary, fidelity every detail of my setting; and my realistic conscience sternly forbade me to turn a maple into a mulberry tree. But in *The Romantic Comedians*, I have not failed, whenever I have needed shade, to make two trees grow in my Queenborough where only one was planted before me in Richmond.

For I had come at last to perceive, after my long apprenticeship to veracity, that the truth of art and the truth of life are two different truths. In any case, I had wearied of external verisimilitude when it conflicted with the more valid evidence of the imagination. Sound psychology, I found, was more important, and incidentally more interesting, than accurate geography. And more important to the novelist than any science, or all the sciences together, was the discredited art of the novel. Thus, when the final volume of my social chronicle had gone out into an indifferent world, I turned, with a fresh impulse and a heightened sense of conversion, to *Barren Ground* and my new creed in fiction. . . .

After I had finished *Barren Ground*, which for three years had steeped my mind in the sense of tragic life, the comic spirit, always restless when it is confined, began struggling against the bars of its cage. It was thirsting, as I was, for laughter; but it craved delicate laughter with ironic echoes, and it moved always upon the lighter planes of reality. As far back as I could remember, there had seemed to be a dual nature in my image-making faculty. Tragedy and comedy were blood brothers, but they were at war with each other and had steadily refused to be reconciled. My perverse imp of humour was not sufficiently robust to thrive either as parochial relief or as the boisterous offspring of realism. Its native element was the air, not the earth, and I had learned long ago that its flight could not be broken to the pace of pedestrian facts. Since it wore a semblance that we have agreed to call "un-American" when we mean civilized, it settled finally in that vague penumbra of consciousness which embraces two hemispheres—the world of fantasy and the world of matter. . . .

This trilogy was begun in the summer of 1926, and thus *The Romantic Comedians* is not yet old enough to rise as a ghost from the grave and reproach me whenever I turn and look backward. Even that younger writer of eleven years ago, who fraternized so cheerfully with the comic spirit, is not nowadays a dead person. I not only recognize this book as my own, but I still feel that, good or bad, it was the best I could do with the material at my command, and I should not wish to change it if I were permitted to take it apart and put it together again. A few sentences, not more than two or three, have been altered in the revised version.

Judge Honeywell is a collective portrait of several Virginians of an older school, who are still unafraid to call themselves gentlemen. Nothing was taken entirely from my acquaintances; it was a matter simply of contours blended and characteristics exchanged. Yet none of this, it is needless to say, was a voluntary process. The man himself was complete and alive in every part when he first entered my mind. Not until I had known him more intimately was I able to perceive a familiar outline or attribute. But I had wanted a subject for comedy, and now, in my need, one was proffered me directly from the background and atmosphere in which I had always belonged. Even the bare structure of events was one that I had often dissected and ana-lyzed. Given such a man, freshly widowed and cherishing the memory of a frustrated passion, placed romantically between the old love, which was safe, and the new love which was hazard-ous, with public opinion firmly pushing him toward the past, and awakened impulse violently thrusting him toward the future —given all these ingredients of drama, the situation would in-evitably spin its own tragicomedy.

A few of the other characters, also, were partly suggested by "real" persons. Mrs. Upchurch, the repository of common sense, I had known all my life in various fashions of dress and identity. Mrs. Bredalbane (Heaven be praised for her!) was a living proto-type of the recalcitrant Victorian crossed on the recalcitrant Vir-ginian. I was brought up to regard her less as a literary inspira-tion than as a warning example. In my early youth her defiance and her fateful doom (for she left more than her double in the actual Queenborough) were described in the sepulchral whispers of legend wherever groups of aging gossips were gathered. For my immediate generation, she, or her sisters in unrefined con-duct, had cast the flush of romance over the exciting spectacle of sin. I was the witness, too, of her more or less victorious return to society, after the post-war psychology had worked as yeast in genteel convention; and I observed, not without satirical hu-mour, that the youth of the period "regarded her scarlet letter less as the badge of shame than as some foreign decoration for distinguished service." Why is it, I speculated, while I brooded over this drama, which I now recognized as a morality play, that happiness-hunters travel perpetually on roads that are circular and lead back again to the beginning? Mrs. Bredalbane alone seemed to prove that much can be done with the pleasures of living, if only one approaches them with a mind swept clean of prejudice and illusion. As a twin sister, she was, wilfully or providentially, the antithesis of all the virtues that Judge Honey-well cherished:—moderation, dignity, reserve, equanimity.

Among my acquaintances in Queenborough there appears to be a general impression that Amanda Lightfoot was snatched bodily, with every feature and contour and posture exact, from our own social circle. But I have never, I repeat, borrowed wholly from life. Every novelist, I suppose, except the happy romancer, is assailed with letters from persons he has never seen, many of them unknown to him even by name, who have recognized themselves or other members of their family or their friends or even their enemies, in his narrative. Such wide response proves, no doubt, the substance and vitality of fiction; but all the figures that are instinct with animation, that have solidity and roundness, have been touched and moulded, I am convinced, by the imagination. Just as Mrs. Bredalbane incarnated the rare Victorian revolt against duty, so Amanda embodied submission to the awful power which governed that interesting era. And since Amanda's personality was not bold and hearty, but flat and mild, she existed in Queenborough and elsewhere, more as a pattern of pure womanhood than as a being invested with the tribulations of flesh. Because her attitude was general, as well as commendable, she will be easily recognized by all those women who have survived the severe discipline of the Great Tradition. But she is, as such women have always been, more active by nature than one would imagine from the unbreakable glaze of her femininity.

In Annabel, I was portraying youth in arms against life. This is the aspect of youth with which I have always felt a sympathetic alliance, not modern youth alone, but perpetual youth, in its spirited challenge to circumstances and its light-hearted revolt against the conspiracy of the years. Not a few readers have condemned Annabel (assuming illogically, after the habit of readers, that only "sympathetic" characters are worth writing about) because they disapproved of her attitude toward that other happiness-hunter, Judge Honeywell. Yet this verdict, I think, is unjust. The truth is that, in this novel, reckless youth, like reckless age, was little more than the result of a single troubled epoch in history. The upheaval of the post-war decade had disturbed the steady stream of experience, and from the shaken depths embryonic fragments of impulse had floated to the surface of consciousness. Everything was becoming—or so it seemed at the moment—nothing was finished, except the Great War and the Great Tradition. There was no immunity from discontent. The invincible good sense of Mrs. Upchurch was stirred if not shaken away from its anchor of pragmatic morality. Although she distrusted temperament, and was vaguely suspicious of any aspect of pleasure that was not profitable as well, she began, in spite of her disillusioned intelligence, to wonder about the past and to speculate, even more darkly, over the ways of the present. To Mrs. Bredalbane, a confirmed hedonist, who was regarded in her earlier years as an anachronism left over from the dissipated eighteenth century, the new freedom had promised all the comforts of faith without its irksome restraints. Even Altrusa, the coloured cook, who was predestinarian in religion, but had a firm hand with a crisis, was not insensible to the sudden swing from Negro spirituals into the syncopated riot of jazz.

All these people were drifting figures in a scene and a situation which were as fluent as time. Yet none of them moved in a vacuum; all were linked together not only with one another but with the dramatic unities which they observed and obeyed. Their origin is obscure to me, yet I cannot find among them a formalized or flat character. When I first saw them, they were full, round, animate, and capable of extension. There is space between them and their background; my arm stretched easily about them and felt them to be solid. For me at least (and I am writing as an author), this whole group, from Judge Honeywell to Altrusa, appeared to have created themselves out of chaos. Any novelist of experience knows the difference between the artfully invented puppet, which smells a little of clean sawdust, and the subconsciously created human being, who speaks and acts in response to the springs of character and is controlled by some arbitrary power that we call destiny. And all these imaginary persons contained, strangely enough, an almost equal endowment of reality. Judge Honeywell, the protagonist, was scarcely more convincing to me than was Altrusa, who existed only in a few paragraphs of the story. Yet I do not mean to imply, in this candid confession, that only *The Romantic Comedians* among my novels has seemed to me to create a world of its own that expanded in time and space. This is equally true of *Barren Ground*, of *The Sheltered Life*, of *They Stooped to Folly*, of *Vein of Iron*, and of *Virginia*. But in most of my other books, I have felt that some few major characters were composed of a richer substance or were more self-contained than the rest.

This small social unit, which existed in its own special interdependence, was related also to the mood and the mental climate of the post-war decade. Everywhere in the world outside old cultures were breaking up, codes were loosening, morals were declining, and manners, another aspect of morality, were slipping away. A whole civilization was disintegrating without and within, and violence alone was strong enough to satisfy a craving for the raw taste of life, for the sight and savour of blood, for the brutal ferocity of lust without love. In Queenborough, where lip-homage was still rendered to the code of beautiful behaviour, the long reverberations of violence were felt chiefly under the surface. An increased momentum, a shriller vehemence, a wilder restlessness—these were the visible manifestations of a decayed and dissolving social order. The comic spirit, an enemy to unreason in any form, was still urbane, though its irony was suddenly spiced with malice.

There is always the risk in analyzing one's own work that too much stress may be placed upon merely technical values. I doubt whether the natural novelist ever thinks, before a book is finished, in the terms of a formula. If theory enters the act of creation, it is wrapped up in some unconscious assimilation of knowledge. A novel designed according to the strictest laws of proportion and harmony would be as vacant as a temple the deities have rejected. A rich and vital work can spring only from a rich and vital consciousness of reality; and so it would seem to follow that the pure novel is the result, less of logical means than of the process known to the Aristotelian philosopher as "fortuitous spontaneity." Nevertheless, it is still possible to examine the completed work and to ascertain the method, either deliberate or intuitive, by which it was fashioned. For more than thirty years, I have studied different methods of fiction and problems of technique, yet whenever I sit down at my desk and take up my pen, I detach my mind from the working of every literary formula. Life and life alone is the power that controls the slowly evolving situation. In the present work, I kept steadily in view one or two evident points. Since I had never written a comedy of manners, the trilogy I had undertaken would be more or less in the nature of an experiment; yet I felt instinctively, and my reason confirmed this impression, that the form demanded a brief time-sequence, a limited scope, and a touch that was light, penetrating, satirical. The comic spirit may be wistful, but it is never solemn; a heavy-footed comedy, or tragicomedy, is doomed to disaster. Although the theme accumulated its own dramatic values, I worked with infinite patience over pattern and texture, until at last the adapted style seemed to me to fit the subject as easily as the glove fits the hand. What I needed, I felt from the beginning, was a style that was neither soft and spongy nor so hard and brittle that it would flake off into epigrams.

My one regret, if it may be called a regret, is that, to the hasty reader, the ironic overtones may seem occasionally to deny the tragic mood of the book. For there is tragedy in the theme, though it is tragedy running, like the "divine things" of Nietzsche, "on light feet." When I have said that there was no selection of medium, I mean simply that my selection was not deliberate, but unconscious. I knew, of course, that the theme must move swiftly, with its own laughing cadences, toward an end of gay disillusionment, while "all the tender little leaves of April were whispering together." It was, indeed, this concluding paragraph that accented the rhythm and placed the final tone of the book.

Although the setting is Virginian, the characters belong to no particular age or place. In Judge Honeywell, I have tried to isolate and observe the pulse of life, not the pattern of declining gentility, but the universal hunger for a reality that is timeless. If his happiness contained, like love, the seeds of decay, it created, like love also, the illusion of its own immortality. For, as one critic has remarked, "the story is the illusion of perpetual youth, and Judge Honeywell is man eternal."

Ellen Glasgow

PART
ONE

F O R thirty-six years Judge Gamaliel Bland Honeywell had endured the double-edged bliss of a perfect marriage; but it seemed to him, on this sparkling Easter Sunday, that he had lived those years with a stranger. After twelve months of loneliness, one impulse of vital magic had obliterated the past. As he arranged his tribute of lilies over Cordelia's grave, he tried with all the strength of his decorous will to remember her features and mourn for her as sincerely as she deserved.

"I am a bird with a broken wing," he sighed to himself, as he had sighed so often into other ears since the day of his bereavement. And while this classic metaphor was still on his lips, he felt an odd palpitation within the suave Virginian depths of his being, where his broken wing was helplessly trying to flutter.

It is astonishing, he reflected, with the slow but honourable processes of the judicial mind, what spring can do to one even at sixty-five—even at a young sixty-five, he hastened to remind himself. Beyond the impressive marble angel, the sky was of a glimmering April blue; fresh young leaves were sprinkling the gnarled old trees in the cemetery; a joyous piping and twittering of birds enlivened the feathery crests of the evergreens; and in his soul as well, beneath the gloom of his sorrow, there was this miracle of budding and piping and twittering, as if winter woods had awakened to spring.

Standing there, with his head bowed reverently over the grave, he searched his memory in vain for a living image of his Cordelia. To mourn was distressing, but to endeavour to mourn and fail was worse than distress. Yet to the casual passer-by, ignorant of this April burgeoning within, he was merely an inconsolable widower of fine presence at the grave of his happiness. Through jewelled branches, the sunshine wove a golden filigree from his silken grey head to the wide black band on the sleeve of his coat. Tall, lean, angular, a little dry and inelastic in thought, a trifle stiff when he moved, he had remained sprightly in speech while he became ceremonious in manner. Behind rimless glasses, his benevolent brown eyes were visited in moments of wistful longing by the bright flicker of youth. Over his full yet austere lips, with their splotches of dusky red, the ends of his still dark moustache tapered down into his trim silver beard. For the rest, his features conformed to the aristocratic Honeywell pattern. The beetling grey eyebrows, the thin Roman nose, the mottled stains under the eyes that flowed into the sallow flush of the high cheek-bones, the corded folds of the throat where his beard ended,—all these marks of character were subdued to the family inheritance of prudence, integrity, and reserve. Polygamous by instinct, like other men, he had confined his impetuous desires within the temperate zone of monogamy, where sober habit had preserved both his health and his appearance.

In the eighteen eighties, when his opinions were formed, he had determined to become one of the advanced minds of his age; and at sixty-five, he considered that he had kept well abreast of his time. An upright, even a religious man, with a rich Episcopal flavour of temperament, he was disposed to encourage liberty of thought as long as he was convinced that it would not lead to liberal views. Though he had lived all his life in Queenborough, where society had never outgrown an early stage of arrested development, his reputation as a lawyer had extended beyond his native Virginia, and many well-spent summers abroad had cultivated in him what he was fond of calling "an international attitude of mind." At least he had not, like the community of which he was a part, lost the faculty of self-criticism, and stiffened into a gelatinous mould of complacency. Southern in sentiment, yet not provincial in thought, he had attached himself to the oppressed minority which represented, he felt, the urbane and unprejudiced South.

In his ardent though fastidious intercourse with life, he had seldom failed to respect women, even those who had shown themselves to be unworthy of the sentiment. For a man who had been desperately in love with one woman and safely married to another, he felt that he had withstood all the grosser temptations. Sex as a topic for speculation was little more than a virgin wilderness in his mind, except those well-cultivated fields of sex that have yielded such abundant harvests to history.

A devoted wife, he was musing sadly; for this was as keenly as he could force himself to regret the estimable but ashen old lady who had scorned the temporary repairs of the toilet. For thirty-six years he had been genuinely attached to her. For thirty-six years, partly for her sake, he had resisted temptation. It was a consolation to remember to-day that he had resisted even in the case of that alluring young French girl who had returned with them as a maid, and who, he had soon discovered, was far from being the serious person described, with Gallic inaccuracy, in the letters she brought. Well, even then, though not without a struggle, he had resisted.

Yes, the phrase slipped more easily than the thought in the groove of his mind, he was as helpless without Cordelia as a bird with a broken wing. Bending over her grave, on this flower-scented, thrush-haunted Easter Sunday, he passionately invoked, not the Cordelia of faithful wifehood, but the immortally young and fair Cordelia, fragrant as the rose of desire, whom he had married. For he needed youth. His sorrow needed the memory of youth to keep it alive. So urgent was this craving of the withered heart to be green again that he would have given all the thirty-six years, when Cordelia and he were one flesh and spirit, for a single hour of her lost rose-coloured innocence.

Not only one flesh and one spirit, but one presence as well. Except in his office and in his profound judicial decisions, he had barely possessed an inviolable life of his own. Even on his professional journeys she had accompanied him; and upon the rare occasions when the illness of one of the children had prevented her, she had never failed to greet him at the station upon his return. A remarkable character, a wonderful mother, he murmured softly, with his gaze on the Italian tombstone, where even the marble angel, he observed, with a wanton flight of fancy, wore the enchanting contour of youth. If only she had had a dozen children instead of the two who had married and gone to live in other parts of the world, her life, he felt, might have been as abundant and as satisfying as she had deserved. Yet with a dozen children on her hands, she could scarcely have taken such excellent care of him and his health. For thirty-six years, he had eaten only food that was wholesome for him; yet so skilfully was it prepared, under her vigilant eyes, that he could not have enjoyed it more had it been indigestible. From the day of her marriage she had trained herself to eradicate the taint of nervous dyspepsia that had been for generations the hereditary curse of his family; and as long as she had been his housekeeper, he had indulged his appetite with both pleasure and impunity. He remembered now, in one of those trivial but tender recollections which bring a pang, that after he had been made ill by mushroom sauce, Cordelia, who had a preference for it, had never allowed it to be served again at their table.

"You have to thank your wife for your health and happiness," Dr. Buchanan had said to him at the beginning of her last illness. "She has been a perfect wife to you, and has worn out herself in your service."

It was all true, he acknowledged gratefully. It was all true; and it made no difference evidently either to the doctor or to Cordelia that he had not wanted her to wear out herself in his service, that he had not, when all was said, wanted a perfect wife.

"Yes, a wonderful wifely devotion," he murmured under his breath, while he was attacked by a curious pricking sensation—could it be one of relief?—because he should never again be obliged to sit opposite to that unselfish solicitude.

He turned away to his car, walking stiffly because he moved with his stubborn muscles instead of his agile spirit. As he drove through the cemetery, several elderly ladies enfolded him in the benevolent look with which women of every age survey the spectacle of a mourning widower. Though he bowed with suitable deference, Judge Honeywell's glance travelled rapidly over them; for he had reached the romantic period of life when elderly ladies are depressing. Not only do women break sooner than men, he reflected, with the fortitude we reserve for the afflictions of the opposite sex, but they are disposed far more readily to settle into a rut at the end, and the only difference between a rut and a grave, as some one had observed before him, is in their dimensions. And if elderly ladies are depressing when they settle, they are, as he had reason to know, even more painful to behold when they refuse either to step into a rut or to stay there after they are once safely entrenched. For example, there was his twin sister, Edmonia Bredalbane, an intrepid woman of liberal views and loose behaviour. After one early scandal, she had indulged herself through life in that branch of conduct which was familiar to ancient moralists as nature in man and depravity in woman. Moreover, she had lost her character, not quietly, as was the custom in such matters, but with a loud explosion which had startled Queenborough and involved her innocent family. Deaf alike to the whispers of conscience and the thunder of tradition, she had declined to remain a picturesque ruin in company with other damaged virgins of quality. While the rumble of her fall was still in the air, she had detached her loosened foundations and sailed by the next boat for Paris: a city that was regarded in Queenborough as little better than an asylum for determined profligates of both sexes. There, according to transatlantic gossip, she had pursued the downward path with four lawful husbands and a long procession of anonymous but affluent lovers. As he advanced farther away from the discredited Victorian era, Judge Honeywell's opinions were less outraged by her open avowal of infidelity at a period when religious doubt was more condemned, as well as more distinguished, than it is nowadays. Yet even after a world war, which had shaken everything but the unalterable laws of biology, he could find no milder word than reprehensible for Edmonia's flourishing career.

In his melancholy review of her past, he had forgotten that

she was not only undesirable but imminent, and he was stung to resentment by the thought that she was probably awaiting him in his library, with the intention, no doubt, of remaining to lunch. A few days before, she had arrived in Queenborough, with her old effrontery but fortunately without her fourth husband. Ralph Bredalbane, an impecunious young mooncalf, who had been tracked down while he was suffering from the idealistic interpretation of war, had lingered on in Paris to enjoy his negligible share of Edmonia's tainted millions.

"That is what happens when a woman loses her modesty," Judge Honeywell mused, as his car passed through the gate of the cemetery. After all, the orthodox beliefs and the conventional standards were safest; and he recalled that his father, one of the last of the old school, had remarked at the close of his life: "If there is anything wrong with the Episcopal Church or the Democratic Party, I would rather die without knowing it."

TOO DEMOCRATIC to live contentedly in a street or even a road, the modern inhabitants of Queenborough preferred the grandiose style of an avenue or a boulevard.

The Age of Pretence, The Age of Hypocrisy, Age of Asphalt, Judge Honeywell reflected, while his car skirted a plebeian park, where the best taste of politicians was commemorated in concrete walks and triangular beds of canna. What, he wondered gloomily, was the peculiar merit in the middle-class mind? In what particular was the tyranny of the inferior an advance upon the tyranny of the superior? Beyond the few ancient elms, which had been threatened but not destroyed by the political axe, he could see the once aristocratic and now diminished length of Washington Street merging into the ostentatious democracy of Granite Boulevard.

The Easter stream, which he had left a little earlier at the door of St. Paul's Church, had subsided into rippling pools on the pavement. Here he caught the outline of familiar gestures, and recognized faces he had parted from after the morning service. Where else on earth, he sighed, could people know so little and yet know it so fluently?

Framed in her doorway, he saw, not without a faint inner disturbance, the still handsome, still regal figure of Amanda Lightfoot. Fifty-eight, if a day, but marvellously preserved, with the bright blue eyes, the rich colour, the foamlike hair of a woman who had consecrated her resources to a losing battle with time. He wondered why she did not darken her hair, and acknowledged the next instant that he respected her more for disdaining the subterfuge. Most women and a few men professed to admire grey hair when it crowned so youthful a face as

Amanda's; but he had always disliked it, and now, with the
essence of spring filtering into his mind, the vision of his first
love aroused the obscure despondency with which he stood apart
and surveyed the passage of years. In his early youth, the youth
of another century, he had adored Amanda Lightfoot to the edge
of delirium. At that picturesque period, she had been what he
and other gallants of his day were fond of calling his ideal; and
though ideals had changed perceptibly since the eighteen eighties,
he realized, with a vague sense of reproach, that Amanda had
retained the earlier pattern unaltered. In outline, she was to-day
precisely what she had been when he loved her; but it was the
outline, he felt, of a pressed leaf that has grown faded and brittle.
Yet he could not banish completely the feeling that he was, in
some inexplicable way, to blame for his own unfaithfulness to
his ideal as well as for the embalmed perfection of his Amanda.

Thirty-seven years ago, for a few blissful months, he had been
engaged to her. His ecstasy was as antiquated now as her curving
waist. There was to-day even a tinge of irony in his thoughts, as
if he were ashamed of having been so hopelessly in love with a
woman who was now no longer young. But in his youth, before
and even after his marriage, he had been consumed by the white
fire of his passion. She was then, and she remained for twenty
years afterwards, the crowned belle and beauty of Queenborough. In a city famed for beautiful women, no later belle had
approached her in loveliness. Three blissful months, and then
suddenly, without warning, they had quarrelled. After thirty-
seven years, he was obliged to search his memory before he could
recall the occasion. Had they actually quarrelled because
Amanda—the middle-aged lady he had just observed holding her
Prayer-book—had danced too often with a young man of attractive appearance but undesirable progenitors? The episode was a
comedy when he rehearsed it now in his mind; but thirty-seven
years ago it had been tragic enough. Immediately after the
quarrel, Amanda, who was a mettlesome beauty, had broken her
engagement and had fled to Europe, when the Atlantic Ocean
was wider and Europe farther away than they appear to the far-

sighted vision of the twentieth century. Had her flight been merely a coquettish gesture, he had since wondered, and had she expected him to follow in pursuit by the next boat that sailed? Well, whatever she had expected, he had intended to follow her. It was on shipboard some months later, in the very act of pursuing Amanda, that the versatile emotions of man had entangled him in an affair with Cordelia; and almost automatically, it appeared when he looked back, he had found himself engaged to her. He had been happy with Cordelia, as a man may be happy in a marriage with any agreeable woman when he stops thinking about it; and yet his happiness had not extinguished his desire for Amanda. For a year or two, before his first child was born, there was a period of madness which, with his natural aptitude for evading unpleasant truths, he had dismissed from his memory. This morning, however, for the first time in years, as if the resurrection of spring had summoned it from the grave, he recalled the April night when he had rushed to Amanda and implored her to go away with him.

Only her steadfast virtue (though this was the easiest part for him to forget), only her unswerving devotion to duty, had saved them both from disaster. To-day, in sudden poignant longing, he lived over again the old torment of his passion. Well, he was still in love with Amanda; he would be always in love with her; but it was with an ageless Amanda of the mind, not with the well-preserved lady of the tarnishing years.

Afterwards, even when his children had grown up and married, his knowledge of her hopeless love for him had run like a scarlet thread through his life. That she had remained unmarried for his sake was at first a hope, then a belief, and at last, as her hair began to whiten, a source of tender regret. Only recently, since his wife's death, had this regret become faintly flavoured with bitterness. He could not fail to perceive that, in the twelve months of his bereavement, public opinion had been firmly but delicately pushing them together; and the firmer the push toward Amanda, the more obstinately he thrust his will into the ground and refused to advance. It was true, as he reminded himself so often, that Amanda was his ideal. Patience, sweetness, serenity, all the Victorian virtues had flowered in her mind and heart. And that queenly pride, which, like most men, he admired more than any other attribute, had left him as free to follow his later fancies as if she had not been the one great love of his life. Never, he knew, would she make the slightest gesture of allurement. Never would she reveal by the faintest quiver of an eyelash that he had ruined her life. Yes, there was much to be said in favour of the womanly woman. At least men felt safe with her.

As he rolled past her gently expectant gaze, he found himself thinking impatiently that it was a pity she had never married. Some man had missed happiness, was the way the phrase shaped itself in his reverie. A wonderful woman, but, with her silver-grey hair and her fifty-eight years, she must have put the hope of love well out of her life. During the war she had become prominent, he was aware, in work for devastated France; and now, since distance robes even Armenians in an azure hue, she was gazing romantically at the Near East.

A few blocks away stood his house, of which he was inoffensively proud; a collection of brownstone deformities assembled, by some diligent architect of the early 'eighties, under the liberal patronage of Queen Anne. In front of the stone steps, as they flowed down from a baptismal font of a porch, he recognized the heavily built figure of his twin sister, who was engaged in a dramatic monologue for the benefit of two restless listeners.

"Bella Upchurch and her daughter Annabel," he thought before he passed, with fraternal lack of enthusiasm, to his sister. "This reminds me that I ought to have sent the girl a present at Easter. Bella must have a hard time managing on her small income, and she hasn't asked for help recently. What was it I heard about the child's unfortunate love affair? Wasn't she engaged to that scamp Angus Blount, who went abroad to study and married some French hussy? Well, whatever it was, it won't do her any good to see too much of Edmonia." It occurred to him, as he approached, that it couldn't be good for any one, including her twin brother, to see too much of Edmonia. The mystery to him was that Queenborough society, though it seldom closed its doors to a prodigal daughter when she returned bearing the fatted calf on her shoulders, should have opened its arms to so notorious a sinner. To be sure, her collection of husbands was as authentic as her fortune, while the unnumbered hosts of her lovers were merely apocryphal; but even then, he argued sternly, it was not only Edmonia's past, it was her point of view that was disreputable.

Large, raw-boned, with strong, plain features, where an expression of genuine humour frolicked with an artificial complexion, and a mountainous bosom, from which a cascade of crystal beads splashed and glistened, Mrs. Bredalbane billowed toward him, while he thought: "If only she would dress with the dignity suitable to her size and her mature years!"

But Edmonia, who had been born with the courage of her appetites, feared to be stout in age as little as she had feared to be scandalous in youth. A daring combination of American frankness and French epicurism, she was fond of succulent food and of wine, especially when it was red; and she had lived long enough abroad, he regretted, to acquire both the taste for gallantry and the horror of iced water. Her judgment, which had been weak in the beginning, had ripened, he admitted, in the sun of opportunity. Though she had little wisdom, she had had four husbands; and it is impossible to have had four husbands without learning something of the nature of man. In her later understanding of life, she excelled even Mrs. Upchurch, who had made a precarious though eminently respectable living by nursing the vanities of her own and her late husband's male relatives.

The Judge, however much he disapproved of his twin sister, heartily admired Mrs. Upchurch. Physically, she embodied to perfection that indirect influence which had been formed by, and had formed in turn, the men of his time. Brisk, plump, pretty, with a way of her own, a short fringe, which was very becoming to her dove's eyes, and an expression of resigned but playful archness, she had gained by strategy everything she had ever wanted from life except a rich and indulgent husband. Though she was below medium height, with waxen features and miniature hands and feet, she was endowed with an energy of soul which had worn down the opposition and the nerves of her parents, her husband, her lawyer, her family physician, and the numerous young persons who waited upon her in shops. While the Judge admired her as a woman and respected her as an irresistible force, he was never able in her presence to over-come a feeling of moral inadequacy; and for this reason, in spite of her pleasant face, his eyes left her quickly to linger upon the charming and intelligent features of Annabel.

At his first glance, for he had known her too well when she was a child to be impressed by her sudden flowering, it did not occur to him that she was more than attractive. His preference was for a queenly presence rather than a fragile figure; yet, though he admired curves more than hollows, he was not im-pervious to the subtle fascination—was it only glorified sex-magnetism?—which the girl diffused like a fragrance. She was one of those rare women (he felt this with the dreaminess of the spring) whose charm is more potent than beauty. Was it merely her vital radiance, her indestructible belief in love, that brushed her soft eyes and smile with a wistful glamour, as if, he found himself thinking sentimentally, she had walked straight out of allegory? Or was it simply that he had heard her pitiable story, and that her solitary passion in an age of varied inclina-tions had tinged the dull complexion of his thoughts with romance?

"I wonder what became of the fellow," was his next ques-tion. "Well, this is what we must expect, I suppose, when we try to build up the morals and the reputation of Europe."

Notwithstanding his many summers abroad, he had never lost the distinction between an international attitude of mind and a foreign bent in morality. French morals (they were free to call them that if they pleased) had not only corrupted Edmonia, who was as wax, of course, to any sinister influence, but they were not derived, he felt, from a true reverence for pure womanhood.

"Anyhow, she is getting over it, poor girl," he decided at last, after his look at Annabel's small heart-shaped face, with its faint golden freckles and geranium mouth. The dress she wore, a short, scant frock of green and brown stripes, clothed her in an odd effect of fields and streams, as if she were standing in the midst of tall wind-blown grasses. Where her nut-brown hair was combed back from her forehead and twisted into two clusters of curls over her ears, it reflected the coppery glow of November leaves in the sunshine; and he felt that this glimmering brightness was interfused like magic with her fresh young voice, which held the sparkle of rippling water. He wondered what the colour of her eyes could be, and decided that they were grey-green as an April mist. Her thick black lashes curved upward; and everything about her repeated this flying rhythm and sprang upward with her winged eyebrows; her hair, her smile, her few swift gestures, the corners of her red lips, and even her small fragile body. As light as a swallow, he thought, with poetic imagery, as light and graceful as a swallow in the air.

"Annabel was just telling Mrs. Bredalbane that she hopes you are coming to her party," cooed Mrs. Upchurch, who had a small mind but knew it thoroughly. "It was the first thing we thought of."

"What party?" He had not heard it mentioned before, and he liked to be definite.

"The one Cousin Amanda Lightfoot is giving for her. Tuesday is Annabel's birthday. She will be twenty-three."

Twenty-three? Well, she looked younger; she looked, indeed, scarcely more than a child. Yes, he remembered now. The invitation had come, and he had laid it aside in his desk and forgotten to acknowledge it. Cordelia had given up parties in her later years, when she found that dinners of rich food brought on a return of his dyspepsia; and after her death he had spent most of his evenings at home with a book. Occasionally, he strolled into the club for a game of chess or bridge; but even these harmless diversions had palled on him, since the fatal chill of prohibition had infected his club, and he preferred, on the whole, the drowsy hours by his fireside.

"I'm afraid I'd be a kill-joy at a birthday party, Annabel," he said gently, for he hated to disappoint her if she had really expected him; and, like most men, he found it agreeable not to question Mrs. Upchurch's veracity.

"It would do you a world of good to go out a little," Annabel's mother urged when her daughter was silent. "I'm sure dear Cousin Cordelia would wish you to keep up your spirits; and how can you keep up your spirits if you shut yourself away with your grief? Don't you agree with me, Mrs. Bredalbane?" she inquired suddenly, turning to the startled Edmonia, who had already wondered what Bella Upchurch could be trying to get out of Gamaliel.

"Well, if you ask me, Bella, I believe in taking all the pleasure you can find," Mrs. Bredalbane replied. "There isn't any sense in the world in Gamaliel's not going out as much as he wants to."

"And it would please Annabel." Mrs. Upchurch was gazing like a pretty pigeon into Judge Honeywell's face. "She was saying this morning that it would please her so much if you would come."

Annabel's defiant laugh fluted gaily above the cooing murmur of her mother's voice. "Oh, no, Mother, you've forgotten. I was talking about a new dress," she said.

"Annabel!" Mrs. Upchurch exclaimed, and the edge of her tone had sharpened to a prickly sweetness.

Was the girl merely teasing him, or was she deliberately rude? Her grey-green eyes turned to gold when the sun shone into them, and her adorable mouth, which reminded him of a crushed strawberry, curved and dimpled into merriment. He looked at her as if they were alone in the street, and while he looked a strange, an almost miraculous thing happened. Suddenly, so suddenly that the vision came and went before he had seized it, the playful wind blew Annabel's striped green-and-brown frock like shreds of mist from her body, and he saw her white limbs dancing against a background of fields and streams. An instant only! Then the enchantment vanished in a golden haze, as all enchantment must vanish sooner or later, and he realized that he was trembling.

"Well, you know I was talking about a new dress, Mother." The girl's voice was so thin and faint in his ears that it seemed to drift, like the far-off music of a flute, across the young green of the meadows.

"Why shouldn't you have a new dress, Annabel?" he heard himself asking with a lump in his throat.

"Why, indeed?"

Yes, he knew now that she was mocking him; but, through some natural perversity of the emotions, the knowledge served only to quicken his interest. "I ought to have remembered your birthday," he said, after a brief hesitation. "Your Cousin Cordelia never forgot anniversaries. If it slipped my mind, you must forgive me."

It was true that he had intended to look after Cordelia's poor relations; and of them all, numerous as they were, there was no doubt in his mind that Annabel was her favourite. Not that she had approved of Annabel, for Cordelia had had little patience with the follies of the rising generation; but, though she disapproved, the Judge remembered now that she was fond of the girl. For Cordelia's sake, if for no other reason, it was clear to him that he must look after Annabel. Encouraged by the sense of duty, he continued almost gaily: "You must have that dress, Annabel. I'll send a cheque to your mother the first thing in the morning."

"Perhaps Mrs. Bredalbane will help us select it," Mrs. Upchurch suggested, with artful diplomacy. For she had seen and heard enough of life even in Queenborough to conclude that women who combine such frailties with such figures are often of generous disposition.

"Well, I'm glad he is opening his purse," croaked Mrs. Bredalbane, with the vulgarity of speech which, as Mrs. Upchurch frequently had cause to regret, was not a stranger to several of the best families. "I believe in taking everything that's offered you as long as you're young enough to enjoy it. You don't live but once, and you'd better get all you can out of your single opportunity. I was telling Gamaliel that yesterday. There's no need for him to shut himself up and mourn like a widow, when nobody expects it of him."

At this Mrs. Upchurch's artificial brightness was faintly overcast. She felt that Mrs. Bredalbane, even for a twin sister, was going too far.

"Of course, we understand and sympathize with the dear Judge's feelings," she murmured vaguely.

"I am afraid I have let my own trouble absorb me too much," Judge Honeywell began, in what for him was a hurried manner. "It is my duty to think of Cordelia's relatives, in whom she took a motherly interest. It is my duty," he repeated earnestly.

"I think you are an old dear, Judge Honeywell," Annabel said, with careless sweetness. Though her voice soothed his ear, he wondered what had brought the worried look to her brow, as if she were annoyed by a stinging thought that she could not dislodge. "But you must not let Mother vamp you," she added, while her lower lip curved mutinously. "When she wants anything she can charm the birds from the trees."

"Annabel!" Mrs. Upchurch exclaimed for the second time, but whether in reproach or interrogation, the Judge could not decide. In either case, he told himself, Mrs. Upchurch's conversation would become monotonous if you were thrown too much in her company. Strange, as he had already remarked, how often women become either monotonous or ejaculatory when they reach middle age. Though it seemed foolish to acknowledge it, for Mrs. Upchurch was many years his junior, he felt nearer to Annabel's generation.

"Oh, you're both charming enough," he retorted gallantly, with all the sensations of a young blade.

These sensations, which were as strange to him now as they were enjoyable, quickened his deliberate gait into a springy step while he followed Mrs. Bredalbane's grotesque figure into the house.

CHAPTER 3

✿ ✿ ✿ ✿ ✿ ✿ ✿T OUR age, Gamaliel," began the formidable
✿   ✿ Edmonia, removing the most startling of Pari-
✿   ✿ sian toques from the ambiguous brown of her
✿   A   ✿ hair, "at our age, it is a mistake to sit down and
✿   ✿ brood over the past."
✿ ✿ ✿ ✿ ✿ ✿ ✿ Turning his dignified head, Judge Honeywell
studied her for a moment in silence. It appeared to him incredible
that even his twin sister should associate their ages in her mind.
He felt, and he was confident that he looked, at least twenty
years younger than Edmonia.

"As far as my age goes, Edmonia," he rejoined stiffly, after
giving her time to become subdued by his manner, "you may set
your mind entirely at rest. I never felt better in my life, and my
game of golf is as good as it was at thirty-five."

"Oh, I feel well enough, too," Mrs. Bredalbane retorted, "but,
after all, we are neither of us chickens, and there's no use pretending that we are a match for Annabel, or even for Bella,
though poor Bella has been too busy flattering other people to
spare any of her activity to keeping young. I believe in enjoying
life as, Heaven knows, I've tried to do, but there are some
luxuries that are fit only for young arteries, and nursing grief
is one of them."

"There are subjects, Edmonia, that I allow no one to discuss
with me."

"I know that, Gamaliel, but when I see you going downhill
as you are doing, I can't help wanting to hold you back."

"You are giving yourself needless anxiety. As a matter of fact,
I consider that I am still in the prime of life. You must remember
that a man remains young longer than a woman of the same
age."

She had brought this rebuke upon herself, and he could but feel that she had richly deserved it.

Mrs. Bredalbane, who was settling herself in the softest chair in the room, laughed with the genial insolence which, it seemed to him, Nature had reserved for twin sisters.

"I wonder what lascivious old male first invented that theory?" she inquired, with amiable coarseness. "But you can't pretend, Gamaliel, that you have preserved your youth as well as I have mine? Why, I was just wondering what had made your hair so white."

The Judge stared mildly. "And I, Edmonia, was wondering what had made yours so brown. But I was not speaking of artificial aids, of which I do not approve."

"Oh, I'm not speaking of them, either, though I do approve of them, or I shouldn't spend so much of my time trying to find out which is best. I don't imagine for a minute that they ever fool anybody, and to tell the truth, the only person I try to deceive is myself. If I keep my hair brown, it is because I hate the sight of white hair in the looking-glass."

"Well, you must remember that you were always a—shall I say a remarkable woman, Edmonia?"

"No, not remarkable, Gamaliel, merely honest. I dare say I'm the only truthful woman you ever knew, which isn't surprising, when you consider how few there are in the world."

"Well, I am glad you have been able to preserve your good opinion of yourself," he rejoined stiffly, resisting an impulse to be more sarcastic. "I suppose most of us, as we grow old, cling to some last straw of illusion; but I should not have imagined that veracity was the trait you held hardest by. Now, Mrs. Upchurch impresses me as a rather silly but sincere little woman."

"Bella Upchurch!" Mrs. Bredalbane exclaimed; and she continued with one of those ill-natured stabs which, her brother reflected disapprovingly, women are so fond of inflicting. "Yes, she's gone to a good deal of trouble to impress men that way, and I suppose it has been worth her while."

"One of the last things a man ever understands about women," resumed the Judge, who was beginning to feel exasperated, "is their inability to perceive fine qualities in one of their own sex. You will tell me next, perhaps, that the little girl is a dissembler also."

"Oh, no, Gamaliel, I sha'nt tell you that. The trouble with Annabel is that she hasn't pride enough to dissemble. Of course that affair with Angus Blount would have gone hard with any-body, and I hope she got rid of some of the bad effects by talk-ing about them. She is an intense little thing, and instead of keep-ing her suffering to herself, she worked it off by telling every-body, even the woman who comes to wash her hair whenever she can afford to have her."

"What became of the scamp? Went to France, didn't he, and became involved in—in——"

"In the French manner," concluded Mrs. Bredalbane, who was always ready and occasionally accurate.

"Yes, in the French manner," the Judge repeated, grateful for any convenient euphemism.

"I hear she has taken it very hard."

"On the contrary, her mother assured me the other day that all romantic feeling is dead between them."

"Romantic feelings," Mrs. Bredalbane breathed from the abyss of complete knowledge, "never die until they are under-ground."

A dull flush stained the Judge's aristocratic features and van-ished into his silver beard. "I'd like to horsewhip the scoundrel! To think of any man being such a blackguard as to trifle with the feelings of an innocent little thing like that!"

Mrs. Bredalbane sighed as a lover but assented as a philosopher; for her encounter with the fluent nature of emotion had made her charitable to all infirmities of character that resembled her own. "I suppose you are right to be indignant," she answered, "but I scarcely call Annabel, or any other girl of the rising gen-eration, innocent. No one would ever have called me innocent, except by moonlight, and I'm sure Annabel knows more to-day than I ever dreamed of when I was young."

On the Judge's face the flush of chivalry paled to the threatening frown of justice. "You must admit that you were an exception to every rule, my dear sister."

"Yes, I may have been," Edmonia conceded, with a satirical twinkle in her hazel eyes, which had grown lighter, or so it seemed to the Judge, as she grew older, "but I could never understand why ignorance is supposed to suffer so much more than knowledge. Annabel is a bright little thing, with a refreshing charm, and in this age a wisp of a girl is considered attractive. Everything that she does has a kind of fascination. It's a great gift, but I dare say moralists would call it a dangerous one." She sighed, without knowing why she sighed, and gazed earnestly toward the door in the hope that a julep—or, if the mint were not yet high enough, a cocktail well fortified with brandy—might appear before lunch. Surely, even if Gamaliel lacked the proper consideration, Constable, whose punch she had once christened *pasticcio*, would not insult her digestion by the spectacle of iced water?

But the Judge's mind was far from drink at the moment. "I'd like to help the little thing," he said gently. "Cordelia was fond of her."

"Well, you've promised her a dress, and if you feel like doing more, you might start her in business." Mrs. Bredalbane was too amply provided for in her own right to cherish any qualms about the generous impulses of another person, even of her closest relative; but the diminishing hope of a julep, or—since the mint was not high enough, she had decided after a glance through the window—any adequate substitute, deepened the masculine gravity of her voice. "I think that is what Bella has been hinting for all along. If people only knew how much time they waste in tactful approaches! So far as I can make out in Bella's maze of diplomacy, the child has a fancy for landscape gardening, or it may be funeral designs, which would be more original. Anyhow, I know it has something to do with flowers, and I had intended to help her myself," she added, for Edmonia's hand was as open as her heart, and what more, asked the Judge silently, could be said of her?

While he pondered the question, Mrs. Bredalbane's satirical eyes rested upon his silken grey head, where she could just see the thinning place on the top. Not unattractive, she thought, in spite of his dryness, and probably as little tiresome as a man of his age could be. But her opinions were less emphatic than usual. Though she had a generous disposition and a catholic mind, her interest in elderly persons had never extended beyond herself.

"The child must feel the need of an occupation," the Judge conjectured, as the result of his long meditation. "That shows character, I admit, and should be encouraged. About this party, now," he proceeded with attention, "don't you think it might be well for us to drop in for at least half an hour?"

"Oh, I never dreamed of not going," his sister replied, "but I'll be sure to stay the whole evening. I never leave until after the music, and then I remain for ham and eggs if I'm invited, though I dare say that admirable custom has not been adopted in Queenborough."

Judge Honeywell, who had imagined that such sunrise parties were confined to college commencements and dissolute New Yorkers on the first day of the year, was uncertain whether it was expedient to laugh or to frown.

"Would a man of my age, in—in the circumstances, be expected to take part in the dancing?"

"Of course, Gamaliel!" The twinkles were spinning in Edmonia's eyes. "You must not fail to dance once with Amanda Lightfoot. Considering she has waited thirty-seven years for you, a dance at the end is as little as she could expect."

Her brother's face, which had looked refreshingly cheerful, became overcast with solemnity. It was astonishing—it was positively amazing to him that Edmonia should have lived to her present age without acquiring the good taste which, like dyspepsia, was hereditary in the Honeywell family.

"I do not understand what you mean by 'waited thirty-seven years,' " he rejoined haughtily.

"Why, Gamaliel! Are you pretending that you don't know Amanda has stayed single all these years on your account?"

Gamaliel, who knew it very well and wished that he didn't, looked depressed but obstinate, while it seemed to him that he could feel the claws of his will fasten into the solid structure of resistance. If Edmonia and the rest of Queenborough society were trying to push him in the direction of Amanda, he was becoming more determined every minute (it was surprising how this determination had hardened within the hour) that he would refuse to be pushed.

"I can only reply that your assumption is unwarranted," he returned in judicial accents.

"My dear brother, she was over head and ears in love with you, and she has been always. Do you imagine for a moment that, with her money and good looks, she couldn't have married anybody she had wanted in all these years? Why, she has been mobbed with proposals. Mobbed—that is the very word Dr. Buchanan used when he was talking about her."

However flattering to his vanity (and what elderly man could fail to be flattered when he heard himself described as a Lothario in his youth?), the dominant emotion in the Judge's mind was one of dismay. It distressed his benevolent heart, which wished well to every one, and particularly wished well to the women whose lives he had inadvertently blighted. Yes, Amanda Lightfoot was still his romantic ideal, he assured himself again, as far, at least, as it was possible for a grey-haired lady (this was how he had begun to think of her) to be a romantic ideal. He sighed while he dwelt sympathetically though ponderously upon her frustrated womanhood. It was, he felt, pathetic, it was even tragic, that she had never known the complete joy of belonging to some good man. So deeply moved was he by this reflection that he would have made a sacrifice in order to unite her to any good man in the world except himself. For his own part, as he now confided to Edmonia, there was room for no woman in his life after Cordelia.

"I shall remain faithful to Cordelia as long as I live," was the dramatic way in which he expressed his resolve.

"Well, I've heard that before, Gamaliel," Mrs. Bredalbane commented, with her usual levity, "but you can't deny, all the same, that Amanda has been faithful to you."

"Our engagement was broken thirty-seven years ago by her express wish." He spoke with difficulty, for he was opposed to stirring the dead embers of sentiment.

"You know perfectly well that she never expected you to take her at her word. It was a lovers' quarrel, and she thought you would follow her on the next boat." What a disastrous gift a long memory was! That was why so many women led disappointed lives, he supposed: they insisted upon dwelling within the damp shadow—for surely such sepulchres were damp—of buried happiness.

"I did——" he began, but checked himself before he had lost either dignity or sincerity. For he had recalled suddenly that it was in pursuit of Amanda that he had fallen—by accident, it seemed to him afterwards—into the willing arms of Cordelia.

"You can't blame her for not knowing that you would meet Cordelia on the way," Mrs. Bredalbane resumed. "And you can't blame her because, after thirty-seven years of waiting, she is beginning to show the strain, though I must say that she has picked up wonderfully in the last two or three months. But the trouble with women who have never married is that you don't realize how little there is in it until you've tried it at least once or twice. It is human nature to overestimate the thing you've never had. Why, I remember, during my first honeymoon, I was saying to myself every minute, 'After all the fuss that has been made about marriage, isn't there something more in it than this?' "

She had gone far, though her soft, deep voice, which made the

Judge feel as if he were swathed in purple plush, muffled the cutting edge of her words.

"I can only say that your remarks are both uncalled for and vulgar," he replied with severity. "I——"

His sentence was never finished, and even Edmonia, who could jump at any conclusion within her range of vision, had not the faintest idea what it was that he intended to say. For, at the crucial instant, Constable appeared, though without fortifying cocktails, in the doorway.

T HE next afternoon, as soon as she had received the generous cheque and visited the best shops with her daughter, Mrs. Upchurch called upon Judge Honeywell and expressed her gratitude with even more than her customary effusion. Without Annabel, who was trying on a dance frock of blue gauze at the moment, her mother was more completely herself, if any woman can be completely herself who has been obliged to rely, through an unhappy marriage and a disappointing widowhood, upon the adroitness with which she has managed the men who controlled her affairs. Being a cheerful and pretty widow, with a cooing tongue, she had little difficulty after the loss of her husband; though, in common with other mortal states, the period of widowhood had fallen short of her sanguine expectations.

Plump, flattering, pink-cheeked, she sat now before Judge Honeywell, with her small black velvet hat resting like a benediction on her fluffy grey fringe, and her satin dress lifted, with a coquettish though antiquated modesty, from her prettily turned ankles. Through her veil of spotted illusion, her merry grey eyes gazed up at him with an agreeable deference.

"But for you, the Lord only knows what would have become of us," she began in melting tones. "I must have said that to Annabel no less than a hundred times. If it wasn't for Judge Honeywell, the Lord only knows what would have become of us! Oh, if you could only realize how my little girl admires you! You'll never hear it from her, she is such a shy little thing; but there isn't any other man in the world that she respects and admires as she does you. When she was scarcely more than a baby and Cousin Cordelia was so kind to her, she used to say to me, 'Mother, I hope I'll marry a man like Judge Honeywell.' "

With all his legal learning and his heroic virtues, which were numerous, Judge Honeywell was afflicted with the common infirmity of a sensitive ear, and the oil of adulation was as soothing to him as it is to most men in his established position. "A great lawyer but a perfect fool," was the way Mrs. Bredalbane would have described him with the smallest encouragement.

Annabel was a pretty little thing, and it pleased him beyond measure to hear that such a pretty little thing admired him. She was, also, a badly treated little thing; and since he was the pattern of chivalry, it incensed him that any man in the world should have been capable of such conduct to a woman who combined the merits of being both little and pretty. He felt as if she were his daughter, and yet in some profound sense, which he prudently refrained from analyzing, as if she were not his daughter.

"Cordelia was very fond of her," he said good-humouredly, for Mrs. Upchurch always made him feel on better terms with the universe. "For her sake, if for no other reason, I should like to help the child to some fresh interest. What about this flower-shop Edmonia was speaking of?"

Mrs. Upchurch smiled beamingly. "Not exactly a flower-shop. She has studied landscape gardening, you know, and she would like to open a small place where she could work out her designs and take orders for gardens. I encourage it," she continued discreetly, "because the poor child has had such a trying experience. If she were not a brave little thing, it would have gone very hard with her."

"I hope she is not wasting any sentiment upon that scamp," said the Judge, and the flush of indignation in his face was very becoming. A remarkably youthful man for his age, thought Mrs. Upchurch, and one that almost any woman who knew the world might find attractive, if he were sufficiently generous. With a fortune like that (for he was probably the richest man in Queenborough) one could so easily make allowances. "I could grow really attached to him in time," she reflected, though, with her usual sagacity, she did not nurse extravagant hopes for herself. Younger than the Judge in years, she was not less than a century older in worldly wisdom; and she knew that to a wealthy man, provided he is not committed to a parsimonious habit of mind, nothing is unattainable in the matter of age.

But the idea of marriage, which has brooded through the centuries over the narrow field of woman's prospect, had not risen above the horizon of Judge Honeywell's consciousness. If Mrs. Upchurch ever entered his thoughts, which she did but seldom, it was, in company with Amanda Lightfoot, as an agreeable grey-haired lady, whose character was above reproach, but whose love life was well over. And this classification was so intuitive in its processes, was so entirely a product of the chivalrous interpretation of biology, that no one would have been more astonished than Judge Honeywell had it been brought to his judicial attention.

"Oh, no, I'm sure she never thinks of him," Mrs. Upchurch replied eagerly, almost too eagerly, she told herself the instant afterwards. "But an experience like that ages a girl and makes her too mature for the frivolous pleasures of her own circle."

Her dove's eyes were shining with tenderness, and had the Judge been endowed with that illuminating vision which is confined to the reversed views of life, he would have recognized all the happiness that might have been his in later years gazing up at him through the veil of spotted illusion. But, with the sad propensity of human appetite to the unwholesome, the prohibited, and the immoral, he looked, without even knowing that he looked, straight over the possible joys toward some imaginary adventure.

"Well, we must help her to get over it," he said at last, while the glow faded slowly from the clouds at which he was gazing. "She is a brave child, and she deserves all we can do for her."

"She says herself that all romantic feeling is dead in her," Mrs. Upchurch resumed, after a moment of hard thinking. "She isn't in the least like other girls of her age. I mean, you know, that the kind of things they enjoy seem silly to her. You wouldn't suspect this if you were talking to her because, as I have said, she is so shy, but she has determined that she will make something of her life now that romance is all over. That is why she has taken up landscape gardening. I think it is splendid of her, don't you?"

"Admirable, admirable. We must see what we can do. Tell her, if she needs help, to come to me."

"Indeed, I shall. She will be delighted to have your advice. There isn't anybody else, I know, that she would turn to so quickly in time of trouble. I sometimes tell her"—a little laugh, as soft as a pigeon's note, rippled from her lips—"that Judge Honeywell is the only man she believes in."

That odd palpitation had started again in Judge Honeywell's breast. Just as in the cemetery, before the marble angel, he felt that downy wings were fluttering within his heart, imprisoned and trying to break free. "She's a dear little thing," he said warmly. "At her age, you must remember, hurts are not mortal."

"Oh, I tell her that so often." With an air of victory, Mrs. Upchurch had risen to her feet and was holding out her small, soft hand. "Then we may expect you at the birthday party? I want you to see Annabel in the dress you gave her."

The Judge laughed with the embarrassment of a boy. "Oh, I'll be there. Tell her I'll be there, even if I have to take dancing lessons."

Mrs. Upchurch caught airily at the suggestion. "Well, why not? So many men who are no longer boys are doing it now. They say it is the best exercise in the world."

She left triumphantly, and sinking back into his easiest chair, Judge Honeywell stared thoughtfully over the window-boxes, where black and purple pansies were blooming. Outside, in the flushed evening light, sparrows flitted over the grass; the magical scent of lilacs drifted in from the walled garden; and the vague sounds from the street, where dusk dropped like a blue shawl, were caught up into some mysterious, impalpable zone of the spirit.

While he rested there against the soft old leather cushions, impressions rather than thoughts swam into his mind, and these impressions were as faint and tremulous as the shadows of leaves on running water.

The last year had been hard on him. He felt the loss of Cordelia. His health was not so good as he had a right to expect. Perhaps he had, as Edmonia told him, been brooding too much. There was something in what she said about not having time to live in the past when you were beginning to get on in years. Though he felt like a man of thirty-five, and his golf was as good as ever, he must remember that he was not so young as he used to be. New interests. Regular exercise. What was it Mrs. Upchurch, a sensible woman, had suggested? Dancing? Ah, yes, it might not be a bad idea to take a few lessons in dancing. The fox-trot? Was that what they called it now? Well, of course, for the exercise. A great many men of his age were doing it. There was Colonel Brockenborough, and Frederick Cavendish—why, Cavendish must be nearer seventy-five than seventy, and yet he went to every cotillion last winter. . . . Hearing the clink of ice in glasses, he said, from habit: "Just a thimbleful of old Bumgardner, Constable." . . .

In the last few weeks he had been vaguely troubled in mind. It might be a good plan to have a doctor go over him. Buchanan would probably tell him there was nothing the matter. Yet there were things that you could not confess even to a physician. Things too trivial to mention; indefinite symptoms; suspicions rather than certainties. He had been disturbed by the ignoble character of his vagrant thoughts, and now his dreams, over which, of course, he had no control, were distressing him. The slightest contradiction sharpened the edge of his temper. He had been always a man of an equable habit of mind; not easily put out; on good terms with his world; difficult to make into an enemy; ready to hold out a helping hand when one was required. But in the last year, since the shock of Cordelia's death, he had felt that his disposition was changing; that he was, in fine, becoming irascible. Nerves, he supposed, were at the bottom of it. Everything was reduced to a question of nerves in this generation. Yet his father, a robust and bellicose old gentleman, in spite of hereditary dyspepsia, had begotten seven sons and five daughters, and lived to be upward of ninety, without discovering that he had a nerve in his body. Healthy children, too, not like the delicate girl and temperamental youth who had sprung so perilously from his union with Cordelia, and were now struggling with dubious marriages in distant parts of the world. Yes, times had changed, there was no doubt of it. Dancing, perhaps, would be the best way to glide over the slippery transitional period. . . .

It was absurd, for example, the way that incident of two or three weeks ago haunted his mind. Most men would never have thought of it twice. But he was of different clay. Useless to deny that he had been troubled, trivial as the occurrence had been. He wouldn't have believed that he was capable of such an impulse. If you had told him before it happened, he would not have believed it. And, after all, what did it amount to? Nothing. Absolutely nothing. He had gone unexpectedly into his room one morning, where Alberta, a bright mulatto girl who had taken old Martha's place while she was indisposed, was engaged in making his bed. She was a fine, strong girl, just budding into womanhood, with skin like yellow satin; and her large bronze arms, as round as columns, were beating one of the big feather pillows. At first he had simply glanced at her; then suddenly, swift as a blow, he had been seized by an imperative desire to touch her arms. Merely to touch her arms and discover if they were as hard as they looked.

"Alberta!" he had said sharply; and his voice had surprised him by springing from his lips like that, unprompted, undisciplined by the ruling principle of his will.

She had turned quickly and stared at him; and with her look, the look of a servant who is awaiting an order, reason was enthroned again in his mind.

"Alberta, have you seen my glasses?" he had asked, and had turned and gone out before she could search for them, before she could even reply to his question.

A trifle; nothing to disturb his equilibrium, only he had never been, even in his full vigour, that kind of man. The next day he had given orders that his room should not be attended to until he had left the house. "It interferes with me," he had said irritably to the housekeeper, who had followed Cordelia. "It interferes with my comfort." Well, he couldn't help it if he were getting irascible. Perhaps, after all, it would be prudent to see Buchanan. There might be some obscure physical cause. There was, he had read somewhere, a physical cause for every nervous disorder.

Turning on the lamp, he picked up a legal brief from the desk, and bent his mind on the case. Application had been his peculiar gift as a student, and after years of renown in his profession, mental concentration had become an inflexible habit. He read the brief carefully, and not until he had mastered the finer points of the argument did he permit himself to withdraw his attention and glance at the clock. Well, he would have time for a nap, after his thimbleful of old Bumgardner, before he went upstairs to change.

With a sigh of satisfaction, he drank the whiskey and stretched himself on the broad sofa, which was upholstered, like his chairs, in soft ruby leather. There was ample time for a rest, he reflected, while he drew over his knees the dark red robe Cordelia had knitted for his nap in the library. Yes, he was tired; he was depressed by the spring weather. After a little doze, he would wake up refreshed and ready for his game of chess at the club. He closed his eyes, and no sooner had he closed them than an iridescent mist floated into his mind. He was lost beneath greenish skies, amid low-spreading boughs and tall windblown grasses, while over the April meadows there drifted toward him, as in a dream that is more vivid than dreams, the glimmering ivory shapes of nymphs, who danced on rose-white feet to the music of running water. In spirals and wreaths and garlands, faintly coloured like the earliest spring petals, they spun round him, whirling, drifting, flying, in the wind that raced among the low boughs and the high, blown grasses. Between them and himself there was only the green and gold brocade of the spring landscape. Clusters of women, scarcely women even, they were so young and slender. Clusters of girls, curving, swaying, bending, advancing, retreating, and always smiling as they retreated, into the iridescent mist of April. . . .

Starting up, he flung the robe aside and sprang to his feet. For an instant, his dismay was so intense that it brushed the edge of a deeper emotion. Terror? Anger? No, it could not be terror. It could scarcely be anger. Had he been asleep or awake? After all, perhaps it was only a dream that had startled him, and he was not responsible for his dreams. He had had them before. Not like this one, not so vivid, not so persistent; but dreams had disturbed him long ago, when he was just growing to manhood. It was incredible that these early visions should return now as he was settling down into the tranquil brightness of his later years. Visions of the glimmering ivory beauty of girls that was changing into the smooth marble beauty of women. Strange, too, strange and incredible, that his emotional nature increased while his vitality diminished. And it was not as if he had been an intemperate man, or an immoral one. All his life, he had obeyed every mental and physical law. He had done no harm. He had never betrayed a woman. He had, indeed, respected women even when they had ceased to deserve it. . . .

"Edmonia was right," he thought, "I have brooded too much since Cordelia left me." Ah, how he had loved Cordelia! How he had depended upon her! And it occurred to him that he had never, except in the very beginning, told Cordelia he loved her. He had lived with her for thirty-six years, and they had grown to know each other so completely that they had stopped talking. What was the use of words when your wife knew everything you thought before you had spoken it? But he had loved her, even though he had stopped telling her so. Somehow, it wasn't easy to utter things like that in marriage. It would have been easier for him to have said, "I love you!" suddenly like that, to a perfect stranger than to have said it to Cordelia, with whom he had lived day and night for thirty-six years.

Yes, he had brooded too much over the past. He needed a fresh interest in life; he needed some healthful exercise like dancing; he needed (this was clear to him) to see more of people. What had become, he wondered, of the circle of sweet girls who used to visit Cordelia? Even if they had scattered, he might make an effort to bring them together again. For he felt remarkably young for his years, and after all—he had all tradition behind him in this opinion—a man is only as old as his instincts.

DJUSTING his white tie before the mirror, Judge Honeywell regretted that society in Queenborough remained still in the infantile stage. Social rites, though numerous and brilliant, were restricted, by the value of tradition and the unanimous verdict of parents—the only members of the community who could afford lavish entertainments—to a dance of adulation before the consecrated idol of the Young Girl. While he dressed, the years burdened his heart; but encouraged by a second thimbleful of old Bumgardner, he meditated upon his distinctions and felt that his self-esteem was restored.

Even before he entered Amanda's house, while he was passing under the striped awning on the pavement, the dance music, gay and defiant, floated out and captured his spirit. In the long drawing-room, with the palm-wreathed walls and shining floors, he was submerged in waves of brightness, colour, and sound. The lights, the music, the spinning airy skirts, like so many hollyhocks, the rose and ivory of the young girls, fragrant, blossomlike, ardent, enchanting—all these wonders transported him, as if they streamed from an inexhaustible fountain of youth. Distinguished, impressive, still handsome for his time of life, with a silken gloss on his hair and beard and the glow of a boy in his dark eyes, he made his way through the variegated throng to the place where his old love was receiving her guests.

A voice croaked in his ear: "There isn't a girl here who can hold a candle to Amanda Lightfoot in an evening gown. Where are the reigning beauties in this generation?"

It was Edmonia. Of course it could be nobody but Edmonia who said that.

"Quite so, quite so," he assented formally to a face that reminded him of a cheerful raven. From her brown locks, which were piled high over a diamond bandeau, to her aching feet (they must be aching feet, he decided) in the most eccentric of French slippers, she was grotesque, if any one so overflowing with the pleasure of life could be really grotesque. After all, perhaps that was the true art of living, to take what you pleased, when you pleased, as you pleased, and to hold yourself superior to comment and criticism.

"That white and silver dress suits her perfectly," continued his sister, who, with the recollection of four husbands, even though three of them had proved inadequate, could afford to be generous. "I never saw her more brilliant."

For the first time since he had entered the room, Judge Honeywell looked at Amanda with his undivided attention. Though he had been slowly moving in her direction, the better part of his interest had been fastened on the rich profusion of girls among whom he was threading his way. Yes, Edmonia was right. One of the most exasperating things about her, considering how wrong she was in principle, was her incurable habit of being right in fact. Amanda, tall, regal, willowy, in her white and silver brocade, with her crown of foamlike hair, her bright blue eyes, her high colour, and her royal manner, was as beautiful, he found himself thinking pensively, as the evening star. She looked, as Edmonia had observed, brilliant to-night; and even the Judge, whose mind refused to be hurried into opinions, could not fail to perceive that some inner flame of happiness illumined her features.

"Yes, she wears her years wonderfully," he remarked in a tone which he tried in vain to make ardent.

"It is the first time you have been anywhere, and she feels your coming," Edmonia whispered.

Frowning slightly, the Judge was silent because he could think of nothing to say. Any woman who talked as incessantly of things that were unmentionable among delicate-minded persons, would be, he concluded, as unanswerable as Edmonia.

"I am glad to pay her the compliment," he brought out at

last, after a long pause; for this, in view of the circumstances past and present, was the least, it seemed to him, that he could do.

"I am sure, if you were to search the world over, Gamaliel, you couldn't find another woman who understands you so well."

This, also, was true, though the crudeness of Edmonia's methods shocked his refined sensibilities. It was natural, no doubt, that she should rely upon her powers of matchmaking, since they had been so successful in her own unenviable career; but he surmised, with a shudder, that the men she had pursued must have been already hardened to marriage. As for Amanda, he was perfectly willing to confess again, as he had done so often before, that whatever his ideal may have been thirty-seven years ago, she had embodied it. She had been a beautiful woman; she was still beautiful for her age; but (though he was not yet prepared to acknowledge this even to himself) beautiful women who were no longer young had ceased to interest him. Though he respected Amanda as deeply as he respected the memory of his mother or the Ten Commandments, he could not dismiss the thought that neither the memory of his mother nor the Ten Commandments insisted upon being romanced about as well as respected. And, ready and willing as he was to revere his old love abundantly, he vaguely resented the expectation that he should be romantic about a belle and beauty of another period. He vaguely resented, too, without knowing that he resented it, the burden of her long constancy, of her long and hopeless waiting.

So he threaded his way carefully in and out of the dancers, trying to escape Edmonia, who would not be eluded, and followed, like a tawdry destiny, upon his heels.

"You will lead the first march with Amanda, won't you?" she asked now in his ear.

He turned courteously but stiffly. "If she will honour me." Revolt, if it must come to revolt at last, was gathering within his peaceable soul.

Notwithstanding his profound respect for Amanda, an object of respect, he was beginning to perceive, was far from being the partner with whom you would prefer to dance. Quite shamelessly, he longed to dance with those images of fire and snow, without corsets and without conversation, who melted to wisps of tulle over soft little bones and wisps of gold or brown hair over soft little minds. Not deliberately, for he was a man of conscience and of rectitude, would he have harboured such impulses; but, secret, strong, and brooding, this wish, which was more an instinct than a desire, welled up from the deep below the deep in his consciousness. And while it welled up, it seemed to him that the delicious aroma of youth was penetrating his spirit.

As he approached Amanda, he felt her happiness reaching out to him. Soft as the glimmer of the evening star in the dusk, her silvery light enveloped him in its beams. But for Edmonia, he might have been less constrained, he might have been more fervent in his greeting; but it was useless to deny that Edmonia had poisoned his mind. That was Edmonia's way, he recalled; she spent her life poisoning people's minds; and though she maintained it was from the best motives, the working of the poison was as fatal to peace as if she had been inspired by malevolence. It was Edmonia who had instilled fear into his thoughts; fear of his old love; fear of her constancy, of her tenderness, of her statuesque beauty; fear lest in some way he should be held responsible for the unchanging ideal she embodied; fear, above all, lest he should be expected to be faithful to that ideal.

She looked at him with a luminous but impenetrable gaze, and he bowed over her hand, which was still the most beautiful hand, though of this he was unaware, that he had ever held in his own. From Amanda herself, grave, stately, self-possessed, confirmed in queenliness, wrapped in her Victorian reserve as in a veil of mystery, he knew that he should have nothing to fear. The women of her generation had known how to suffer in silence. What an inestimable blessing was this knowledge, especially when it had passed into tradition! What suavity, what harmony, it infused into human relations! What protection, what safety, it afforded the chivalrous impulses!

"I am so glad you could come," she said softly, and not a tremor in her voice, not a quiver of her eyelashes, betrayed her. Only that: *I am so glad you could come.*

Standing there before her impenetrable eyes, knowing that he was safe with her, that the ideal he had evolved would protect him, he remembered against his will how passionately he had loved her. Nothing had been like that. Not his love for Cordelia; not his marriage; nothing. Precious it had been, infinitely precious, and terrible as an army with banners. And now it was over. It was over, and never could it return. No matter what happened to him in the future, never could he feel again the burning rapture of his old passion.

She had still what they used to call a perfect figure. Perfect! That was the reason, perhaps, that she had remained subdued to the queenly Victorian curves, though she was so slender that she might have worn one of those straight modern frocks like Annabel's without looking ridiculous. Her mysterious eyes, softened by happiness, and silver-blue to-night as the evening sky, shone on him serenely. Beside her majestic height, the thin slips of girls revolving about her appeared as trivial as painted dolls. The women of her age were taller, he found himself thinking, and more mysterious. Yes, the traditional feminine virtues—patience, gentleness, moderation, reserve, especially reserve—were excellent things in woman. Though he saw that they were excellent things, he saw also, with the waywardness which rules our destiny, that they were not the things that he wanted. He no longer desired the statuesque virtues of the eighteen eighties; he no longer desired even to be understood as the eighteen eighties had understood him. He desired (how clearly he saw this now!) the very things that were not good for him: the excitement of novelty, the ringing challenge of youth.

"It is delightful to be with you," he answered, smiling into her eyes, which were so mysterious and yet so safe.

"It is a pleasure to watch young people," she said presently, for, besides being charming and kind, her ideas were so correct that it was sometimes difficult for her to make conversation. Talking must be easier and topics more plentiful, she imagined, when one is slightly unsound either in one's mind or in one's opinions. There were occasions, indeed, like the present, when she was so uncertain what the safest and soundest opinion would be that she discreetly said nothing more original than, "Young girls are so lovely."

"Quite so." Taking her at her word, and turning his gaze away from her, he watched the dancers.

"It seems to me that they grow prettier every year." Her voice, as smooth and soft and as expressionless as liquid honey, flowed over him.

"There isn't one among them," he could make this declaration with sincerity, "as Edmonia has just pointed out to me, who could hold a candle to what you were at that age. There were queens in those days."

Had he looked at her and not at the dancers, he would have seen that silvery radiance suffuse her features. For an instant, she was silent, breathing tremulously with happiness, though she would be fifty-nine in a few months, and must, in the Judge's opinion, have put the hope of love well out of her life. Then she murmured in the musical tone of her girlhood: "I am so glad you remember me like that." It was the nearest that she could come to losing her self-possession after the stern discipline which she had endured in the last thirty-six years. For ideals are difficult models to imitate, particularly when they are the ideals of and for the opposite sex.

"It is the only way I could ever remember you," he rejoined gallantly, with his eyes on the wisps of delight that were drifting before him. Not since he was a boy, not for thirty years or more, had he responded so ardently to the allurement of women, of young girls just blooming into womanhood. Strange that all those placid years with Cordelia should have kept such possibilities of renewal, of resurrection, he might almost call it, within his heart! The spirit of youth rushed through him like a tinted flood, like a river at sunrise. "I feel as young as I ever felt," he thought triumphantly, while the music throbbed in his pulses, and he sipped from the sparkling glass some one had handed him.

And it seemed to him unfair, it seemed to him a vicious sport of the years, that, while he still felt like a boy, or at least like a very young man, he should be assigned by the people about him to an elderly woman, to a spinster, too (though handsome and well preserved), with grey hair which she made no attempt to conceal.

"You must be sure to dance with Annabel," a voice cooed at his side. "She will be disappointed if you neglect her."

On his right, in a group of ladies, who wore the black satin and jet of rapidly diminishing bereavement, Mrs. Upchurch fluttered like a pigeon before it settles for crumbs. Struggling to break away from her grasp and reach the younger generation, he recognized the pompous figure and empurpled features of old Colonel Bletheram, an octogenarian Don Juan, who, having arrived too soon at the restful age, was still pursuing, with brittle bones but unimpaired ardour, the bright eyes of danger.

"Ah, there she is! I was just looking for her," the Judge replied, as Annabel was blown by as lightly as a spring cloud in a high wind. She was, as usual, wearing the shortest and thinnest of frocks, something that reminded him of the colour of love-in-a-mist. In an instant she had flashed by. Her vivid face, so small, so sparkling, so pathetic, and yet so defiant in its pathos, drooped toward him before it was lost among the other faces in the dance, which all seemed, in some strange fashion, to resemble her. Even that glimpse of her quickened his pulses. Yes, she was a good little thing, a brave little thing. He was glad that she would be disappointed if he neglected her, and not for the world, he told himself, would he disappoint her deliberately. Though his reason reminded him, with the prudence which makes reason so much less popular than impulse, that Mrs. Upchurch, who earned her living precariously, trusted more to fancy than to fact for inspiration, he dismissed the warning as a sting implanted by one of the poisoned darts of Edmonia. He had no idea of doing anything so absurd as falling in love with a girl of Annabel's age. What he felt, while her face drifted away from him, was the yearning to be kind and warm and benevolent, to give happiness to all the soft little things whose lives had been ruined, or at least saddened, by unprincipled scamps. And this yearning to be kind, to give happiness, to fondle gently, included not only all the soft little things in the room, but the whole world as well, with the possible exception of handsome spinsters who had kept—by Heaven knows what sacrifices!—their late-Victorian figures. To confer happiness! Surely this was the highest privilege that money could bring! The power to give happiness to others, to restore wounded spirits, especially young and innocent spirits—what could be nobler than this? And interfused with his yearning, as starlight interfuses a mist, there was the agreeable recollection that some women, very young women in particular, who have been disillusioned by a tragic experience, prefer older men who have learned to be kind without being exacting. He had heard (it was Mrs. Upchurch who had told him this) that many women approve of grey hair and consider eyeglasses—rimless ones of course—distinguished on a man of fine presence.

But, while he stood there, drawing his tall figure very erect, dignified, inscrutable, and impressive, looking, as indeed he was, a man of prudent habits and indestructible integrity, no one would have suspected that such flighty and roving fancies had been liberated by the punch and the jazz rhythms, and were flitting through his narrow head beneath the deceptive gloss on his hair. Nor, for that matter, would even the most curious have surmised that Amanda Lightfoot (standing close at his side, though separated from him by two dangerous ages) was thinking swiftly, like the flash of lightning in a clear sky: "Oh, how happy I am! I am so happy to-night that I feel as if I were a girl again!" For she was holding lilies-of-the-valley, that symbolic flower of the Victorian influence, which he had sent to her. . . .

THE noise stopped after the abrupt habit of jazz, and Annabel stood beside him, flushed, glowing, and so pretty, he decided, with his infirm but still nimble masculine logic, that she was obliged to be good. Her pale brown hair, loosened by the dance, curled enchantingly over her ears; her April eyes were starry and mocking; the colour that came and went in her cheeks reminded him of the flush of sunrise on ivory—or was it, he asked himself with an inward tremor, on apple blossoms?

There are a few women so vital that their very presence awakens everything around them to an intenser life; and this was the miracle that Annabel, breaking off in her wild dance and looking up into Judge Honeywell's face, worked upon the petrified forms in his mind. While he gazed down on her, he felt that his inarticulate longing to protect, to be generous, to give presents, to fondle gently, was swelling from a river to an ocean within his breast. She was holding the gardenias he had sent her (just as Amanda, only more firmly, was holding her lilies-of-the-valley) and he recognized the extremity of his emotion, when the thought shot through his frugal mind, "I wish I had sent twice as many!"

"Annabel, Judge Honeywell wishes to speak to you," Mrs. Upchurch began, with maternal ineptitude. "I've been telling him that he must not neglect you."

With a laugh, Annabel held out the bunch of gardenias, while an expression of gay derision flickered beneath the black edge of her eyelashes. "I hope you don't believe all that Mother tells you, Judge Honeywell." She laughed again and continued mockingly: "I wonder why all good women are deceitful?"

Though the Judge was shocked, so far had he fallen from judicious rectitude that the shock, instead of being painful, was pleasantly stimulating to his new-born vitality. The sensation, he felt, was instinct with audacity, and audacity is of all qualities the most youthful.

"Well, it was the way of her generation, I suppose," he tossed back daringly, almost recklessly.

Annabel frowned, and even her frown was charming, as if her dark winged eyebrows fluttered down over her unfathomable gaze.

"Oh, you were all like that, I know," she replied, embracing him flatteringly in her mother's generation. "You were all so busy trying to pretend things were what you wanted them to be that you hadn't any time to spare for looking facts in the face. If you were a woman and a man broke your heart," she added scornfully, "you pretended that you enjoyed it."

Mrs. Upchurch looked distressed and annoyed, which had become almost her usual expression since Annabel's unhappy affair, and Amanda looked distressed and pleasant in the way she had practised when she was having affairs of her own. There had been so many occasions in Amanda's past when the social moment, the very surface of manners, had depended upon the facility with which she could look both pained and pleasant at the same instant, that she had learned to achieve this unnatural union with the utmost dexterity. It was a matter of regret to these good women that Annabel should be so deficient in proper reserve; but then, as Mrs. Upchurch had taken pains to point out, proper reserve was not missed nowadays as much as it would have been in former years.

"It was so kind of you to select our favourite flowers," Amanda said crisply, and her eyes added fluently, "You have never forgotten that the lily-of-the-valley is mine!" For when she was a belle and a beauty, all the deepest sentiments were uttered, not with the lips, but with the eyes; and this language, for one whose eyes are more eloquent than her lips, has its advantages.

"Oh, I forgot to thank you. It was perfectly dear of you!"

Annabel exclaimed, while he saw, for the first time, that her face wore a restless and tormented expression, as if she were driven by some inner pang and could not be still. In her eyes, too, there was this look of fear and disaster.

"Is it possible," the Judge inquired of the invisible Powers, "that she is still grieving for that cad who deserted her?" Edmonia had called her an intense little thing, but it was inconceivable to him that any little thing should carry intensity to an extreme so regrettable.

"What she needs is to have her mind taken off that fellow," he continued earnestly to himself. "If landscape gardening, or even funeral designs, will help to do this, we must see if we cannot provide the opportunity."

"They are going to play an old-fashioned waltz," Annabel said, in her enchanting voice, with its mingled gaiety and sadness. "Why don't you dance with Cousin Amanda just as you used to do? Every one would think it romantic."

The Judge frowned, and Mrs. Upchurch, who responded automatically to changes in other people's faces, protested brightly: "You mustn't be deceived by Annabel's manner. She tries to pretend that she is pert and flippant, but the truth is that her heart is too big for her body. Why, what did she do this morning when Mary Preston lent her her car but take out an old lady from the Confederate Home. You'd never imagine to hear her that she spends half her life doing good."

"Oh, these mothers, these mothers!" the Judge exclaimed mutely, while Annabel broke out, "Why does Mother always make me ridiculous?" A thunderstorm had gathered over her sea-green eyes (strange, mused the Judge, how the colour of her eyes altered when she was angry!), and she added in a flash of temper: "Why are parents so impossible?"

"Well, you really have a kind heart, Annabel," Amanda said, with gentle rebuke. "I don't see why you should be more ashamed of your good qualities than of your bad ones."

"It isn't that my heart is kind," Annabel rejoined indignantly, "but nothing cheers me so much as to see people who are worse off than I am. Mother knows that, because, whenever I am dreadfully depressed, I always beg her to tell me about some perfect wrecks of women she has seen recently. As for the poor—well, she ought to understand by this time that I can't abide them. Now, I am waiting for Judge Honeywell and Cousin Amanda to waltz."

The Judge turned deferentially to Amanda. "May I have the honour?" he asked in the grand manner of the eighteen eighties.

Amanda's large blue eyes, which had been always deep but empty behind her impenetrable reserve, rested upon him with a kind, though not too kind, expression. "Not until all the guests have come," she answered, for she was a hostess even before she was a woman. "Why don't you dance this with Annabel?"

He looked at Annabel, hesitating but solicitous, and she smiled back at him carelessly, for her impertinence increased with her mother's politeness.

"Oh, I don't mind," she replied, and the melting charm of her voice softened the rudeness of her reply, as she yielded herself to his arms.

The deep but frustrated instinct of fatherhood, that immemorial need to protect and defend something, which had never found its natural outlet in his own children, enfolded yearningly the girl's fragile body; for it seemed to him that her spirit must be as helpless and clinging as the web of tender flesh and bones that enveloped it. And this instinct of fatherhood, which, bursting suddenly from a seed of sympathy, had shot up like the fairy beanstalk in his mind—this prodigious instinct absorbed all that was tender, as well as all that was sublime, in his nature.

They waltzed correctly though stiffly to the other end of the room, where Annabel stopped and looked at him over an immense blue feather fan, which was attached, he saw, to her arm.

"Too bad that Cousin Amanda couldn't dance with you," she said.

He smiled down on her, as he might have smiled down on his daughter if she had not inherited the moral fibre of her mother.

"I hope she will later," he answered, "but this is our waltz, Annabel."

For an instant the feather fan waved between them. Then she furled it slowly and spoke with an impetuous rush of words. "You mustn't let them fool you about me, Judge Honeywell."

"I think I know you, Annabel, as well as they do," he answered, and he really thought that he did.

"I haven't many virtues," the girl said slowly, "but I hate shams. That is why it makes me want to scream when Mother goes on as she does. I am not a bit the kind of girl she pretends I am, though, poor thing, she has pretended so long that I suppose she believes it. But I despise the poor and I cannot endure the sight of the sick. All I really care for is beauty—well, and perhaps joy, if you could ever find it."

"There is nothing wrong in that. You were made for joy."

"Do you really believe there is any of it left in the world? Didn't the war kill it?" Her voice was subdued to a plaintive melody.

"It can never die while youth is left," he replied. "It can never die while the longing for youth remains in the heart."

She sighed. "But youth isn't happy. Youth is sadder than age."

"For itself, not for others. You are joy for others, even if you have missed it yourself."

She looked down. "Yes, I've missed it," she said, and her lip quivered.

"Well, you must find it, my dear. We must find it for you," he answered, while it seemed to him that bands of iron were fastened over his swelling heart. Pious memories culled from his happy though reverential childhood were imprisoned there beneath those bands of iron; and mingled with these were his sentiments as a vestryman on Sunday mornings and his emotions as a bereaved husband beside the grave of Cordelia. "You must let me help you to find it," he added in an earnest voice.

"Oh, I'm not looking for joy." One of her startling changes passed over her, and she lifted her small bright head with a defiant gesture. "But I'd like, if it isn't asking too much, to have a shop in its place."

"A flower-shop? Of course you shall have it. You shall have anything that is in my power to give you."

Her eyes laughed. "You're a good sport, Judge Honeywell, and you make all those silly boys look so common. I'd rather have money than anything in the world!" she exclaimed, and for the first time she spoke with genuine passion. An ignoble passion! Yet penetrating the heart in the wistful charm of her voice. What magic in the girl was linked with an ecstasy he had dreamed of, but never known in reality? Was there some imperishable essence in life, some bouquet more intoxicating than any he had ever discovered?

"If you were in need, Annabel, why didn't you come to me?" he asked, shocked by the thought that she had suffered from poverty. This was the kind of shock, he felt without understanding it, that any sordid fact associated with a woman produced in the sheltered life of his mind; for he was by temperament, as well as by training, an idealist in matters of sex, and his desires, even his dreams, had been sublimated into illusions.

She laughed. "Well, I wasn't starving. That is, I wasn't starving for bread. But what is the use of living if you can never see beautiful places?" Then, since she was both by temperament and by the thorough training of adversity a realist, she laughed again more derisively. With the sound of her laugh, a subtle thrill, a deep pulsation of joy, quivered through him to the secret labyrinth of his spirit. Something was there beyond, something that he had missed and that he must capture at last before it escaped him. He had again the strange feeling of freshness, almost of surprise, as if he were about to begin anew the next instant, as if he were plunging into a virgin wilderness of experience.

"You aren't unhappy now, are you, Annabel?" he asked in a whisper.

"Unhappy?" she raised her luminous eyes. "No, I'm not really unhappy. Only, when I see beauty, I feel that, if I cannot have love, I shall die."

He hesitated, and then spoke more clearly. "I hope, my dear child, that you are not grieving for that scoundrel."

"Grieving?" Her voice was as sharp as a blade. "Who told you that? Not Mother? She wouldn't be such a fool. Of course I'm not grieving. I hate him. I've always hated him." While the loud music drowned her words, that bladelike voice reached him with the shrillness of a scream that is miles away in the cloudy distance. "Why, I hate him so that I wish he were dead." Closing her eyes, she opened them suddenly and stared at him.

Though the Judge listened to her in distress, for his was a civilized mind, it was an unfamiliar distress which was permeated with thrills of relief. He felt responsible, not only for the violence that his indiscreet question had provoked, but for the undisciplined behaviour of Angus Blount and the whole pitiable tragedy. So heavy was this sense of responsibility, that he began to wonder what he could do to mend the poor child's broken faith.

"My dear little girl," he said, and his fine eyes were humid with sympathy, "we must see what we can do."

When he went home at two o'clock, he assured himself that he was more cheerful than he had been since Cordelia's death. A little healthful diversion was, no doubt, what he needed. Not only did he feel more cheerful, but he felt younger, more vigorous, and certainly more active in body than he had felt for years. While he undressed, he reminded himself that at sixty-five he was too young to renounce the innocent pleasures of life; that he must mingle more with young people; that he was indeed, thanks to his frugal habits, at least twenty years younger than most men of his age. The image of old Colonel Bletheram in perpetual pursuit swam unsteadily before his mental eye; but this shade was scarcely an auspicious one, since the Colonel, still active in his eighties, had seldom pursued temperance.

Lying back on the large feather pillows, where Cordelia's initials were intertwined with a device of garlands and doves, he settled himself between the lavender-scented sheets, and turned out the night-lamp by his bed. But no sooner had he closed his eyes than the iridescent mist floated into his mind, and he saw the glimmer of ivory forms, which fluttered down upon him, advancing and retreating, like a scattered flock of amorous furies.

Flashing on the light again, he reached out his hand for the nearest book, which chanced to be Cordelia's Bible, and read himself into a dreamless sleep.

I N T H E morning, he awoke with a dull headache, which passed away after he had had his bath and his coffee. While he waited for his second cup, he looked at the bar of sunshine slanting over the pot of yellow tulips on the breakfast table, and felt that the freshness of the day expanded his heart. Everything ahead of him, his work, the men he should meet, the dry business of the law, the game of golf in the afternoon, the game of chess in the evening—all these ordinary details of living were irradiated by the beams of sunlight.

As he took his seat and unfolded the Queenborough *Post* by his plate, he made a facetious remark to his housekeeper, a withered and incorruptible woman, who had lost everything but virtue and clung firmly to that.

"What we need, Mrs. Spearman, is more brightness in the house."

Over the coffee-pot Mrs. Spearman lifted her opaque glance to his face. There was, as she frequently told Judge Honeywell, nothing wrong with her sense of humour, only the things other people laughed at seldom seemed amusing to her.

"I am sure I try to make it as pleasant as I can," she replied in a crushed voice; for she was as suspicious of men as any heroine in early-Victorian fiction, and she knew what to expect when gentlemen who had lost their wives began to be fussy about their clothes. Struggling, that was what he had been doing in the last few months. She had seen it with her own eyes, and since there was, in her opinion, but one end to such struggles, she was speculating, while she watched him furtively, upon her chance of securing another position. Something permanent, she hoped, next time. A bachelor, perhaps, not a widower, for anything less permanent than widowers she had never encountered.

"You have done very well, Mrs. Spearman. I am not complaining. I only meant that we might find the house less depressing if we were to have a few young people here now and then."

"Maybe your grandchildren will be coming soon to pay you a visit."

"In the summer possibly, unless I should go abroad." The idea of going abroad had just occurred to him, and it seemed to be an excellent one.

"I hope you are satisfied with the way I've looked after you, sir. I am sure the house has never been depressing to me," remarked Mrs. Spearman, who was humble but had her feelings.

"Don't give yourself a moment's worry, Mrs. Spearman. You have done a great deal to lighten my loneliness."

Mrs. Spearman stared bleakly over the silver service. "I hope you slept well after your party. I saw you had your light on until late."

"Fairly—fairly." The Judge frowned and turned back to his paper, for the question had recalled to his mind the fluttering visitations of the darkness. Yes, it might be as well to have Buchanan look him over in the next two or three days. Though he felt so vigorous, it was possible that there was something wrong with either his nerves or his digestion. He sighed heavily over his paper; and Mrs. Spearman, hearing the sigh, concluded that the battle was lost, and resigned herself to the prospect of a bachelor, or at least of a gentleman (this was her secret ambition) whose life was hopelessly deranged but harmless. "Fairly, sir?" she repeated, and choked over the echo.

Judge Honeywell, who respected print and had done his duty by contemporary literature, could not have escaped the knowledge that women suffer from strange delusions and are often the victims of their sacrificial virtues. There had been occasions when he had looked earnestly at Mrs. Spearman's emaciated frame and wondered where she found room to hold her suppressed desires. He would have been grieved rather than astonished if sex had gained the victory over her one day, and she had become suddenly temperamental with a knife or a gun. But it had never entered his head that a mere trifle, a mothlike instinct and a discredited one as well, could invade the provinces of a seasoned intellect, of a renowned authority upon jurisprudence, of an international attitude of mind. Surely in these impregnable defences, if anywhere, there was security.

"I've tried to do my best, sir," Mrs. Spearman confided to her black-bordered handkerchief.

"And a very good best it has been, Mrs. Spearman," the Judge responded, as he rose from his chair, and proceeded to the serious business of life, which did not, he was sure, embrace withered and incorruptible women.

On his way to his office, for he had retired from the bench into the less private practice of law, he stopped long enough to send orchids, or, if orchids were over, gardenias to Annabel. If a little thing like that could give the child pleasure, he ought not to neglect it; and then, since his mood was benevolent, he noticed lilies-of-the-valley blooming modestly behind a glass case, and ordered a bunch of moderate size for Amanda. Not until he had stepped into his car did he remember that Wednesday was his day for taking flowers to Cordelia's grave; and turning back, he entered the shop again and added this order to the others.

"Could you," he inquired, with embarrassment, "arrange to have these flowers sent out to Rose Hill this afternoon?" And when the florist replied that it would be possible, the Judge gave directions (which were unnecessary since the florist knew his world) for reaching Cordelia's grave. It was the first time that he had broken his habit of visiting the cemetery; but, overlooking the day, he had made an engagement for golf in the afternoon, and he assured himself, as he drove on, that Cordelia would have been the last woman in the world to wish him to sacrifice his health on her account. She would have been, also, the last woman in the world to encourage unnecessary brooding, or, for the matter of that, anything that was unnecessary. Nursing grief was what she had called it, and he had heard her frequently condemn such useless rebellion against an Act of God. For Cordelia had been endowed with that safe point of view which refuses to be impressed by any rebellion until it has assumed the dimensions of a revolution. Acts of God, like amendments to the Constitution, were respected by her as long as they were enforced. There was, she had often reminded him, as little nonsense about her as there was meretricious appeal. She was before all else—and he had been grateful for this in his tranquil moments —a good woman. Sober, intelligent, an enemy to vehemence and self-indulgence in any form, the only defect he had ever found in her was her failure to be amused by his jokes. A deficiency that was easily overlooked amid so many perfections; yet, in spite of (it could not be because of) her moral excellence, the idea had crossed his mind that the worst of all possible worlds would be one invented by good women.

Yes, he had been completely in letter, if incompletely in spirit, a faithful husband. Faithful, except for those days in the spring (he could not deny them now) when he had felt a mysterious vibration at the sight of a strange face in the crowd; at the whisper of the April wind in his ears; or at a gesture that was ended before it had fulfilled an imagined curve of perfection. He had had his moments when he was young. And now at the suave touch of spring, from some cause so obscure that it had not ripened into a definite longing, he suffered again from an inappeasable restlessness of the heart.

That afternoon, when civilization had triumphantly defeated nature in his mind, he found that his game of golf was even better than usual. He played with younger men, and, as he told Mrs. Bredalbane with pride upon his return, he had "polished them off nicely." His face was still shining with pleasure when she captured him in the hall; and though he looked, as she said to herself, spindle-shanked in his stockings of Scotch plaid, his appearance, since he was unaware that it could strike anybody as ridiculous, failed to dampen his enthusiasm.

"You have a great many compensations, Gamaliel," she remarked.

This he admitted almost too promptly for a widower. Life, he pursued cheerfully, was full of compensations, if you took the trouble to look for them. "You must accept things as you find them," he concluded, with the seasoned wisdom of platitude.

"Well, you look much better since you've taken that view of life," she returned briskly.

"You're right, Edmonia. I am convinced that you are right."

"I just stopped as I was passing to ask how you are. I know you are dying to get under a shower. By the way," she added, moving in the direction of the door, "I saw Amanda at luncheon wearing more lilies-of-the-valley. They made her look fifteen years younger than her age. It is wonderful what lilies-of-the-valley will do for grey hair."

Hearing this, the Judge tried in vain to think of a reply that would be gallant and yet casual. "For her years she is a remarkably young-looking woman," he said at last, and felt that Edmonia would consider the remark superfluous, provided, of course, she could recognize superfluity when she saw it.

Mrs. Bredalbane stopped to calculate, which she did on her fingers but accurately. "She is seven years younger than we are," she said presently. "That would make her just fifty-eight."

Just fifty-eight! He frowned while he followed his sister's immense hips to the door. Not only did he dislike an unprofitable comparison of ages, but he disliked even more the cheerful inaccuracy with which Edmonia assumed that he was as old as she because they had been born twins. It was on the tip of his tongue to try again to correct this impression; but, being a peace-loving man and disinclined to wound the feelings of any woman, he waited until the opportunity was lost in Mrs. Bredalbane's ensuing offence.

"What do you do with yourself in the evenings, Gamaliel?"

He looked at her thoughtfully, surmising the end of her catechism, yet hesitating from habit before leaping to a conclusion.

"I spend my evenings very quietly, Edmonia, as you may imagine. Occasionally, I drop into the club for a few minutes."

"Don't you find yourself getting lonely?"

"One must expect loneliness in my situation."

"Why don't you go to see Amanda Lightfoot?"

For an instant, the audacity of her challenge shocked him speechless; then he replied with all the rebuke that his tone could carry: "I feel no inclination to pay visits."

"Well, I'm sure it is time that you did. Conventions have changed, and nobody would think any the worse of you if you began going there every evening. Especially as everybody knows how faithful Amanda has been to you all these years."

Even he, with his painful knowledge that Edmonia was capable of stopping at nothing behind his back, had hardly expected her to go so far as this in his presence. "I think, Edmonia," he responded gently, because he was judicially weighing his words, "that, at your time of life, you might find something better to do than interfere with the private affairs of other people."

Mrs. Bredalbane laughed without offence. The trait that made her invulnerable to criticism, he perceived now, was her complete immunity from offence. It is difficult to deal successfully, he decided, with a woman whose feelings cannot be hurt. He wondered drily how her husbands had dealt with her, and remembered that three were in their graves while the fourth one was a stubborn fugitive from monogamy.

"At our time of life, Gamaliel, there isn't much else that we can do," she rejoined in her hearty manner.

"I should have supposed you could find a better way to employ yourself than in meddling and idle gossip. There are surely opportunities to improve your mind and character."

Mrs. Bredalbane gasped a little, though good-naturedly. "Why, what in the world is the matter with my mind and character?" she inquired. "I had mind enough to catch four husbands, and I've had my character restored four times, which is more than most women, even in Queenborough, can boast of. The trouble with you, Gamaliel," she added, patting the sleeve of his leather coat, "is that you did not have enough sense of humour to stand the strain of being a Judge and an old Virginia gentleman combined. We started equal, I dare say, but while my observations of the world have cultivated my humour, it has taken every particle of yours to bear up under the dullness of your life."

"Dullness?" the Judge repeated, while a dark flush stained his pallid skin. Did Edmonia imagine that his life, either in the seat of justice or beside Cordelia, had been dull? "Your observations we will not discuss," he said indignantly, "but I can assure you that a respectable life is not necessarily a dull one."

Again Mrs. Bredalbane patted his arm, and he felt resentfully, through his sleeve, that the pat was maternal and protective. "Well, I'm glad you haven't found it so," she answered. "All I can wish for you, my dear, is that you should have enjoyed your life as much as I have mine."

A melancholy frown clouded his face. How times had changed indeed, and how standards had fallen! Was this stout and disreputable dowager, this excessive, this quadruple matron, the frail, lost sister of his early manhood, the wayward daughter for whom the lamp had burned and forgiveness waited in vain? Where was the remorse of the sinner? Where, he demanded, almost passionately, were the wages of sin?

"I have had the satisfaction, Edmonia, of feeling that I have tried to do my duty."

She had passed out on the porch, and her hand was on the iron railing of the steps, while one large and determined foot hung suspended in the air. "You are welcome to all the satisfaction you can get out of duty," she responded, "and I may say that you look to me as if you had lived on it. That is the trouble with all of you in Queenborough, especially the women. You look as if you had lived on duty and it hadn't agreed with you."

With the solid substance of her person in front of him, it was impossible to deny her accusation. She was immoderate; she was indecorous; she was reprehensible; yet she was again, he felt, in some absurd and even sinister way, unanswerable. According to the inflexible logic of consequences; according to all civilized rules of conduct and everlasting principles of morality; according to the profuse testimony of literature;—according to this menacing cloud of witnesses, she should have returned unhappy, penitent, and partly, if not entirely, impoverished. In this extremity, which was the moral as well as the conventional end to her career (and what were conventions, after all, but organized morals?) he could have opened his heart to her with the fraternal compassion an erring sister deserves. But her attitude was abandoned, he told himself, and the extremity a preposterous one. Her sinful past, for her many marriages had merely whitewashed it, had not saddened her, had not sobered her, had not even, he concluded, with his stern but just gaze on her broad and lumpy back, diminished her size. She had not only thriven, she had fattened on iniquity. At sixty-five, a time of life surely when bad women turn to remorse, and even good women find little to turn to but duty, she flaunted (there was no other word for it) she actually flaunted her brazen past. "It is the war that has made such conduct possible," he pondered gloomily. "Before the war no woman could have been so bold with impunity."

"I hope you are more careful in your conversation than you have been in your conduct," he said presently.

For, extraordinary as it appeared, the rising generation in Queenborough not only accepted, but gave every evidence to the legal mind of enjoying Edmonia. While elderly ladies of vacant memories and unblemished reputations nodded by lonely firesides, Edmonia was eagerly sought after by the inquisitive youth of the period. They clustered about her, he had heard with disapproval, in candid pursuit of some esoteric wisdom of sex; and he had observed, at Amanda's dance, that they treated her scarlet letter less as the badge of shame than as some foreign decoration for distinguished service.

Mrs. Bredalbane's heavy foot descended; but before it reached the step, she glanced back over her shoulder. The attitude was not graceful, and he recalled that, as a girl, Edmonia had had too thick a neck and a figure which, though vaunting a waist like a wasp's, promised to be corpulent with increasing years and dissipation.

"You know I never pretended to have an orderly mind, Gamaliel," she said. "All I ask is to be interesting. So long as the young people flock to me, I feel that I am a success."

"That is exactly what I object to, Edmonia. If it did not sound harsh, I should say that I do not consider you a proper example for the young."

This appeared to amuse Mrs. Bredalbane, which was the last thing he had anticipated. Her deep, thick laugh gushed out. "Oh, they aren't waiting for an example," she replied. "Or a warning either, for that matter. You take my advice, Gamaliel," she tossed back encouragingly over her shoulder, "and don't let the grass grow under your feet. If I were you, I'd go to see Amanda Lightfoot this very evening. You won't gain anything by waiting, not after thirty-seven years." By this time she had reached the pavement; but instead of proceeding on her way, she turned squarely and looked up at him. "I forgot to tell you how glad I am that you are going to help Annabel. People here don't understand that child, because they have no feeling for temperament. There is a great deal more in her than anybody suspects."

His face flushed, and since she had grown far-sighted, his sudden change of colour did not escape her. Yet he was merely thinking that he must warn Mrs. Upchurch, with the utmost discretion, of course, against permitting an intimacy between Annabel and Edmonia. Twenty years ago, even ten years ago, such advice would have been superfluous; but it appeared that even the influence of fast women was no longer circumscribed. He remembered Edmonia in the 'eighties, dark, flashing, "mannish," as her mother had wailed, in spite of her elaborate chignon, her deep feminine curves, and the hump that she wore below her waist in the back. The vision, surveyed through the haze of time, was starched to the point of rigidity. As stiff as whalebone, he said to himself, remembering the inaccessibility of Cordelia in her wedding-dress of white satin. How, he wondered, had sex attraction survived the perils of the Victorian age? Yet Edmonia in those rigid styles, with that ridiculous hump, which was the last word in fashion, had been one of the reigning belles, though deplorably fast, of her day.

"I am glad that she has a serious interest," he returned. "If more girls would take up some kind of ladylike employment, their parents would sleep easier."

"Yes, it's a good thing," Edmonia assented. "Anything that occupies your time and gives you something to think about is obliged to be wholesome. Annabel seems to be the kind of girl that would make a success of whatever she undertakes, and that is why I can't understand her losing Angus if she wanted him, though, of course, being in love puts you at a disadvantage in a love affair."

"I hope her suffering has not embittered her," he said sadly.

"Well, that depends. Some women enjoy suffering, and some do not." She was still gazing up at him, and arrested by a fleeting light in his face, she added crisply: "Never forget, Gamaliel, that the wisest man has only the wisdom of a fool when he tries to understand a woman."

"You are not in a position, Edmonia, to give me advice."

"It isn't advice, Gamaliel; it is a warning. We can't remind ourselves, and we can't remind each other, too often that there is no fool like an old fool."

She moved away, walking painfully on her French heels, while he looked after her (he was forced to emphasize this precept) more in pity than in censure. There was no doubt that she was showing her age. She had become rambling in her remarks, and she had fallen into the deplorable habit of repeating what she had told him the day before. It was, perhaps, advisable for her to remind herself that there is no fool like an old fool.

The flushed air was so soft that he lingered a moment before going indoors; and it was just as he was turning away that he caught a glimpse of Annabel through the web of sunlight and shadow under the elm boughs. Swiftly, mockingly, she came toward him, like some vision that is woven of desire and illusion;

like some vision, he felt, that is as transparent as sunlight and as unattainable as ideal beauty. And while he watched her, it seemed to him that youth itself was approaching; youth as fugitive, as radiant, as hauntingly sad, and as immortally lovely as the dreams of age. In his eyes was the vision, and in his ears was that April whisper of an ecstasy which he had never known in the past, and which, since he was old, he could never hope to know in the future.

I WANT to make something of my life," Annabel said, perching on the arm of one of his leather chairs, with her slim legs in flesh-coloured stockings swinging beneath her. "I don't want just to fritter my time away."

This was commendable; Cordelia would have approved of it. There was something in the girl's character and in the curve of her chin that reminded him of Cordelia in her early years, when she had been more interesting than admirable.

"You are making a wise decision, my dear child," he answered, "and you may count upon my help and sympathy."

Her smile quivered like an edge of light on her lips. What was it, he asked himself, that endowed her with this poignant appeal to his protection, with this quality so touching and so poetic? In the end, he decided, it was her look of helpless yet trusting confidence. He had always cherished a sentimental fondness for things that were young and small; children just beginning to walk; puppies not old enough to train; birds when they were learning to fly; and the sentiment Annabel aroused in him was merely a stronger response to this noble infirmity. Never, indeed, had he felt more elevated in purpose, more generous and disinterested in mind and heart. Leaning back in his easy chair, he folded his strong and slender hands on the knees of his tweed knickerbockers, and fixed his brown eyes, with their expression of bright benevolence, on her face.

"We must find a nice little place for you," he continued. "A house with a garden attached where you can experiment with your designs."

"Why, I never dreamed of that! That would be wonderful!"

"It can be arranged." He appeared to advantage, and this was not lost upon him, when he was arranging things. "We'll begin looking for the house to-morrow. There is a small white house in Littlejohn Street, with a square of garden at the back. I remember it because one of my needy relatives used to live there, and last year she died. I dare say the place can be bought reasonably. It will need some repairs, but there is a charm about it, and a fine old willow tree near the back porch."

Annabel's face bloomed like a flower when the sunlight touches it. How responsive the girl was, and how swift and lovely were the changes in her eyes! She had never, she hastened to assure him, imagined anything so delightful as a house —a real house with a garden, and white too! Did he say white?

"You are an angel, Judge Honeywell! How can I ever repay you?" she asked, and the more grateful she felt, the prettier (or so it appeared to him) she became.

"By being happy, Annabel. By letting me see that you are happy."

"But you must be happy too," she responded in her rippling voice.

He smiled down on her, for she had slipped from the arm to the low cushions of the chair.

"My happiness will come from seeing yours," he replied. Then, as a shadow crossed her vivid face, he looked at her searchingly, and added, with the merest hint of severity in his words: "But you must promise me to be happy. You must let nothing interfere with your happiness."

At the change in his manner, the light faded from her face. "Oh, I am happy. I am perfectly happy," she rejoined carelessly, and he was distressed by the tinge of bitterness in her laugh.

"Not like that, Annabel. That isn't the right tone."

"What is wrong with my tone?"

"It isn't a happy tone."

"Well, I can't help it. How can I help it? Nobody would choose to be unhappy."

"No, but you can nurse disappointment." Strange, how infallible he sounded whenever he used a formula of Cordelia's!

"You can fight against the tendency to look on the dark side of life. After all, you must remember that your troubles are light compared to those of other people. You must refuse to allow yourself to be depressed."

"How can I help it?" Annabel asked in a voice that had lost all its sparkling music.

"You can always help it if you are in earnest. It is nothing more than the triumph of your moral sense over imaginary trouble."

For an instant, Annabel stared at him mutinously. Then her soft mouth grew tremulous with feeling. "I haven't any moral sense, but I have a heart," she said, and burst into tears.

"There, there," he began pleadingly; but realizing, after a moment, that protest was useless, he leaned back in his chair, and watched her with a shocked and miserable expression. Had she been an older woman, her tears would have irritated him (he had detested tears in his youth, even from Amanda), but it was impossible to be irritated by a girl who cried as naturally as a baby, without apology and without subterfuge. So he waited in silence, hoping that the flow of grief would grow lighter and finally cease; and at last it was Annabel who relieved the strain by holding out a frivolous bag of green and red beads and asking him to look for her handkerchief.

"I—I can't see," she sobbed, and wept again more passionately.

"Try to control yourself, my dear child," he urged gently, attempting to bring her to reason, and feeling as helplessly adrift as a man of sense always feels with a person who refuses obstinately to be brought anywhere. "You must really try to control yourself." As he finished he plunged his fingers into the beaded bag, which seemed to shrink to a scrap in his grasp.

"I am trying. Can't you see I am trying?" she threw back at him defiantly.

"But what is the cause of it? I said nothing, I hope, to hurt you."

"Oh, it wasn't you," Annabel sighed, with weary impatience.

"Then what was it? Do you mean that you are still letting your mind dwell upon that—that old disappointment?"

"If you knew all, you would understand," she answered, and he realized, with a shiver, that she was struggling against an impulse to confide in him. Obviously, she had had many such struggles, and from what Edmonia had let fall, he inferred that the impulse had invariably won the battle. He disliked confidences of any kind, being subject to them, though only from corporations, in his profession, and particularly he disliked confidences of an emotional character. Notwithstanding forty years of the law and thirty-six years of marriage, he had never lost a proper regard for reticence and a moral shrinking from what he felt to be an indecent exposure of the emotions. Nakedness of mind or body was abhorrent to him, and mortifying episodes had taught him that when a woman begins to reveal her soul, she is seldom satisfied until she has stripped it bare.

"Try not to think of it, my dear little girl. Try to forget it," he urged.

"I feel that I shall have to tell you," Annabel began tremulously, and turned away and wept, convulsed by a memory.

Gripping his thin knees in his locked hands, on which the veins started out like cords, he prepared himself to listen, with more patience than sympathy, while she plunged incoherently into her confession. Sadly, he reflected that the recital must be as unpalatable to her as it was to him; but in this he was mistaken, for Annabel, who frequently confused her dramatic instinct with her emotion, derived not a little pleasure from making a scene.

"He belonged to me. No one else had a right to him," she began, with a violence that sounded to the Judge like primitive fury, though he was willing to admit that he had only a superficial acquaintance with the primitive, and an even slighter one with fury.

"But that is nonsense, pure nonsense," he commented in a sanity which was wasted upon her.

"No, it isn't nonsense. We fell in love at first sight—the very first instant. There had never been anybody else for either of us. Of course we'd had fancies, but they didn't mean anything." She dismissed them impatiently. "We knew from the first minute we looked at each other that there wasn't any one else—that we belonged to each other, that we were in love for good and all——"

"But——"

"Of course we had our quarrels. That's a sign of being really in love. We quarrelled incessantly——"

"But, my dear——"

"Oh, quarrelling is one of the nicest parts when you are really in love. It is so thrilling. And then the making up afterwards! If you have ever been madly in love, you know that making up is the best part."

He didn't know, and he had never, he inferred now, been madly in love. Cordelia and he had never quarrelled (Cordelia was too sensible not to be satisfied with having her own way about everything), and upon the solitary occasion when he had fallen out with Amanda, they had never made up again—at least, not while they were lovers.

"When he was here, it didn't make so much difference," Annabel resumed, after a sobbing pause, "because we could always make up quicker than we fell out. But after he went abroad, things were worse. Then we began to quarrel by letter and cable, and it is very expensive to quarrel by cable. You have to pay for it, word by word, and if you try to economize— Mother never wanted me to send cables—if you try to save words, you are sure to make things worse instead of better." She stopped to wipe her eyes, and continued despairingly, "He was always writing to me of some French girl, and you know how they are about men." With a shuddering sigh, she rushed on, as if she were eager to gain the precipitous peak of her tragedy. "I showed him from the first that I suspected her of not being nice and warned him against her in every way that I could. Then, when I felt that I couldn't stand it any longer, I cabled him that I never wanted to see him again and he had better marry her. It cost frightfully to do it, but Mother thought I needed some new slippers—I did, too, dreadfully—so she gave me the money, and I spent it every bit on cables. Of course he ought to have known I didn't really mean that, but the very next day he cabled back: '*Taken your advice and married Yvette.*' It was all just to spite me, and I hate him so that it feels exactly as if I had a knife in my breast." With this she began to weep again, and her tears flowed so plentifully that in a minute her wisp of handkerchief had melted like a ball of wet tissue paper.

"Can't you see, my dear little girl, how foolish it is?" asked the Judge wearily, for he was feeling the strain. In this mood, he was able to rejoice because he had been married to a superior woman. Temperament possessed its allurement; but for daily companionship there was nothing that could take the place of a normal point of view. His interest in Annabel was entirely paternal, and since it was paternal, he allowed himself to hope that she would work this dangerous nonsense out of her system and become as sensible as her mother.

"I know it is foolish," she assented, "but that doesn't help."

"That Angus Blount is a cad—an unprincipled cad. Though you must have been trying," he said judicially, "and it is never safe to try a man with an ocean between you."

"It is having to sit still and bear it that I can't stand!" she wailed. "I could get over it so much quicker if I could only hurt him as much as he hurt me." And more in the same morbid vein, which was deplorably human, and remote from all the best traditions of true womanliness. Lovable, no doubt, but insufficiently civilized.

"There's no use my trying to help you unless you will promise to put him out of your thoughts," he insisted. For his mind was firmly made up on this one point; he would receive no more confidences upon the unpalatable subject of Angus Blount.

"I'll try as hard as I can," she answered submissively, rising to her feet and looking up at him with a smile which shone as softly as the moon through a cloud. The tone of authority, he perceived with satisfaction, was the acceptable one. Her submissiveness was so touching, so softly feminine in its appeal, that the disappointing prelude was obliterated from his thoughts. After all, women, particularly young and attractive women, admired the assertion of authority in a man who was masculine.

"Then, that's a promise and an agreement," he said, holding out his hand. "We won't think of him again, and we'll start tomorrow in the matter of the house."

The decorous surface of his mind was still regarding her with paternal anxiety; but beneath this well-governed province, in some lawless region of sensation, he felt suddenly a blind and vagrant groping toward her softened beauty. His fingers, which had been loosely fumbling for the bag she held, fastened on the edge of her short sleeve, and after a moment's hesitation, he began stroking the satin texture of her arm between elbow and wrist. As she only looked at him with indifferent and miserable eyes, making no effort to draw away, his hands slipped to her shoulders, and turning her face toward him, he stooped and kissed the rich curve of her lips. While a shiver of delight ran through his nerves, and his mouth, which had felt old and dry, became warm and moist with youth, the voice of his inexorable conscience demanded: "Is my conduct in keeping with my reputation, and with her respect for me?" At the warning whisper, his arms dropped to his side, and he waited in silence while she turned away to open her vanity case and powder her nose.

"When may I see it?" she inquired, ignoring what had been to him an emotional crisis.

"As soon as I can arrange it. Perhaps the day after tomorrow."

Having returned the vanity case to her bag, she lifted her restored features to the window. "I know I look a perfect fright," she said, "and I think you are much kinder to me than I deserve."

He laughed like a boy, while all the delicious warmth flooded his heart again. "Well, I rather think so myself!" he exclaimed.

A little later, he opened the front door for her, and she descended the steps and passed into the dying flare of the sunset.

With dazed eyes, he looked after her until her slender, trailing shadow vanished, as an illusion vanishes, in the silken obscurity of the distance. For a long time after he had lost her, he stood there and watched; but the fleeting pretence of youth had recoiled into sombreness and depression.

If only he could settle down for the end! If only he could be content to grow old! His judgment whispered that there remained the serene and ample pleasures of the closing years; yet he felt passionately, while he winced under the admonition, that he could find no relish in the compensations of age. "This will pass with the rest," he told himself presently, though he knew in his soul that he did not wish the flickering flame to die down to ashes.

Up the long, straight street, the burnished light was enmeshed in the pale green of the branches. Faint, provocative scents of earth and flowers drifted toward him, now approaching, now roving away, as the wind stirred the fragrance. Warm, palpitating, amorous, all his thwarted hunger for life was enveloped there in the quivering breath of the twilight. The wistful sadness of spring, so different from the hopeless melancholy of autumn, brushed his mood with the taint, not of decay, but of desire. He felt again that he had missed the secret of life, the supreme gift of experience, that he had lost beyond recovery something indescribably fresh and satisfying. Was it merely his own irrevocable loss, he asked himself, or was it the universal tragedy of our mortal lot that the power of loving and the need of love should remain for ever unequal? Was it an ironic law of our nature that as the one diminished the other increased for a season?

Turning away, he went slowly indoors, and it seemed to him that he carried the inescapable burden of the April twilight within his heart.

✽ ✽ ✽ ✽ ✽ ✽EFORE the little white house with the garden was ready for its occupant, Annabel was securely enthroned in Judge Honeywell's heart, though less securely in his purpose. He was still able to throw a manner of paternal solicitude over his tenderness; but in his own mind he had definitely abandoned both verbal subterfuge and moral evasion. If there was ecstasy, there was terror also in the violence of his longing; for with the passion of adolescence he combined presently the tormenting suspicions of age. Cautious by temperament, he became morbidly careful lest he should startle her innocence by one of his sudden though brief gusts of feeling. For even he, who was almost as innocent as Annabel, was amazed less by the strength than by the brevity of his emotions; and he asked himself relentlessly if she would demand of love or life a fulfilment which he had lost the power to bestow.

For the first few weeks there was sufficient pleasure in the exercise of his generous instincts; and, though he enjoyed as little as other men the feeling that he was giving something for nothing, he found an agreeable, if inadequate, reward in her girlish delight over his gifts. Once only, when she kissed him gratefully, he flinched away from her with a low murmur of pain.

"Oh, I am so sorry. Did I say anything wrong?" she asked.

"N—no. You couldn't say anything wrong. I was thinking."

"Of course." Her eager little face softened to sympathy. "It was about Cousin Cordelia, wasn't it? I know it is terrible the way you miss her. I can understand," she continued, with a depth of insight that amazed him, though it had so widely missed its mark, "because I have those flashes of remembrance too.

Isn't it strange the way it all comes back to you? You may have forgotten all about it for weeks, and then suddenly, without warning, it will start up again like the nerve in a tooth that is dying."

"Do you really suffer as much as that, Annabel?"

She answered with a little strangled moan that cut into his heart. Though he bitterly regretted the backward flight of her thoughts, he could see no hope now of avoiding the rush of her confidence. The only way to save her was by patience and tenderness, especially by tenderness, until her imaginary passion (monomania was his name for it) wore itself out. Such things, he had heard or read, did wear themselves out if you gave them time; yet at sixty-five he felt less disposed than at any other period of his life to deal interminably either with an unbalanced mind or with the hovering wraith of Angus Blount. By this time, considering his unlimited patience and almost unlimited presents, it seemed to him that Annabel might have at least begun to show signs of recovery. Though his heart ached with tenderness for her, he could not dismiss the feeling that he deserved some return for his generosity. It was absurd to maintain that you could not, by a well-directed effort of mind and a determined refusal to dwell upon the errors of the past, triumph over a mistaken affection.

While he looked at her now, he found that he was not only resenting the way Angus obtruded himself—or his memory—into their association, but that he was growing a little irritated with Annabel. Yet, through some perversity of the human heart, this very irritation, smothered as it was in tenderness, inflamed rather than extinguished his passion to comfort. So ardent had this passion become that it devoured every fugitive impulse, and he was at last unable to govern properly what he had thought of, for thirty-six years of marriage, as the peaceful territory of his own mind. Instead of his usual equable temper, he had indulged recently in acrimonious complaints to the superlative widow who arranged his creature comforts, after sleepless nights, with infinite worry. Worse than this, there was often a sluggish sensation upon awaking, and a dull headache after the most frugal evening with Annabel and her mother.

"You are not keeping your promise, Annabel," he said sternly.

She laughed. "I didn't promise you that I'd stop hating him."

"But as long as you hate him so passionately, you will never find peace. What you ought to cultivate," he added wearily, in Cordelia's dignified style, "is indifference."

"I don't want peace. There is time enough for that when I am too old for anything else. Peace, like God, will be always there."

He winced. "Do you mind my being so much older, Annabel?" he asked, for he could not bring himself to say just "old."

"Oh, you're not old. You don't look old and you don't act old," she replied, with encouraging alacrity, "and, besides, I despise young men!"

Well, this at least was consoling. Poor child, she had lost too early the romantic illusions of youth. The pity of it moved him to the bewildered tenderness she had awakened in his rejuvenated heart. The disaster in her look, in her voice, in her smile, would have been tragic, he felt, if youth could ever appear genuinely tragic to age. It occurred to him now, as it had occurred several times within the last few weeks, that Annabel needed him almost as desperately as he needed her. Not only did she need his help in material ways (for she must find their meagre income increasingly irksome), but she needed him also to heal the throbbing wound in her soul. Hadn't she just confessed to him that she no longer liked young men, that she preferred mature minds? This confession had thrilled him while she made it, for it had sounded reassuring; and he had reached the thin-blooded years when impulses are perishable, and one grasps eagerly whatever is warm and comforting in human intercourse. Gradually, for, even if he had lost his head, he was still holding fast to his prudence, the indecision of the spring had begun to fade from his thoughts. With it there vanished the fear lest he should be unfair to Annabel, and this, to do him justice, had been his gravest anxiety. But it wasn't, he caught himself insisting while he gazed at her, as if she had had no experience of romance and might reproach him in the future for spoiling her life. On the contrary, she had had her adventure, and had been completely disenchanted with love. She could never accuse him of thwarting her, of snatching the cup of joy from her lips, when all he asked was the sad privilege of sheltering her in her profound disillusionment. She needed gentleness, poor child; she craved consideration; and, with God's help, he would be gentle, he would be considerate. There were women, young women (for in his present mood all women who were not young were either negligible or useful) who chose the forbearing caresses of an elderly husband, provided, of course, he was indulgent in other ways, rather than submit themselves to the imperative demands of youthful ardour. No doubt these were rare women of delicate natures—and it was impossible to look at this little thing and not realize that she was as sensitive as a mimosa flower—who were made to be worshipped instead of devoured. The mere idea of that fragile body in rough hands was intolerable to his imagination.

"My one desire is to see you happy again, Annabel," he said, after a long silence.

She looked at him with startled wonder, and he watched the glow of surprise stain her cheek. "Oh, but I can never be happy, Judge Honeywell."

"Never is a long word. When you are older, you won't use it." He was smiling down on her with an overwhelming desire to give her everything that she wanted, and, for the first time in his successful career, he endured the secret humiliation of the rich man who discovers that, though pleasure may be purchasable, happiness cannot be bought for a price.

The colour flowed away from her face as suddenly as it had come. "You forget that he is married."

So here it was again, he thought bitterly. Here it was again, this deplorable moonstruck folly! For a moment, while he had weighed the moral and material advantages for her in a prudent marriage, Angus had been far from his thoughts. Now, simply by looking at him with her disconsolate eyes, she had summoned that ill-starred adventurer from the shades of the past.

"I wasn't thinking of that," he answered in a tone of exasperation, for he could not suppress the feeling that she was not only
childish, but ungrateful as well.

"Weren't you? Well, what were you thinking of?" She turned
away with a dazed look, as if he had plucked her back from a
dream.

"I was thinking of what you promised me."

"I know, but I can't help it." Her voice was humble, with a
humility that was lost to everything but one tremendous resentment.

"Have you no pride?" he demanded sternly.

She shook her head. "Not when it hurts so. When it hurts so,
you can't think of anything else."

"That's weakness, Annabel."

At this she nodded, determined, he saw, to be amiable since
she couldn't be amusing. "I know," she responded in a meek
whisper. How lovely, how endearing to the heart was meekness
in a woman—in any woman except, perhaps, Mrs. Spearman!

"I am disappointed in you," he said slowly, for he wished to
prolong a surrender that was so feminine and so gratifying to his
sense of superiority. "After telling me that you would do your
best to get over that—that infatuation."

"I have done my best."

"Then why can't you stop talking about it? Why do you in-
sist upon dragging it in at every opening?"

"I don't drag it in," Annabel protested, too unhappy to take
offence. "I have tried as hard as I could to forget it. There are
whole days and weeks," she continued passionately, "when he
never enters my mind, and even Mother thinks I am cured. Then,
all of a sudden, just as it happens with you and Cousin Cordelia,
it starts up again and begins aching. The worst part of it is that I
never know when this is going to happen. It may come, with a
stabbing pain, at a party, or while I am having my hair washed,
and then all I can do is stop and walk about until I am tired. Or
it may start in the middle of the night after I've been asleep——"

"If only you would try not to talk about it. Don't you realize that, as long as you allow your mind to dwell upon it, you are retarding your recovery?"

He was observing her intently over his spectacles, which he had put on to glance at a note on his desk and forgotten to remove, while his rimless eye-glasses dangled by a black silk cord from his coat. Had Annabel been less deeply immersed in her own misery, she might have noticed that his hair and beard were trimmed more closely than usual, especially on the temples and about the mouth, where the patches of white were conspicuous, and that the dark blue clothes he was wearing for the first time, after many visits to his tailor and an immoderate amount of fussiness over the details, made him look fresh and spruce for his years.

"I do try," she answered, and then asked, with a plaintive note in her lovely voice, "Hating him isn't so bad as loving him, is it?"

"Oh, no, it isn't so bad as that," he conceded, and felt as if he were condoning a breach of ethics—or was it merely of etiquette?

"It's just because I can't forgive him for making me suffer. I want to hurt him. I want dreadfully to hurt him. And I shouldn't want to hurt him if I still cared, should I?" she demanded triumphantly.

"No, I suppose not. I cannot imagine a true woman wishing to hurt the man she loved." Though he was shaken in his emotion, he was still securely rooted in the inherited principles of behaviour.

"Then that settles it!" Annabel exclaimed, with a spirited gesture. "Only I sometimes wonder," she resumed after a pause, "if I am really a true woman. True women don't seem to be a bit human."

"My dear!" There were times when she shocked him, but there was never a time when the shock was anything but delicious.

"Well, how could they keep alive with things like this bottled up inside them? If they never talked of them, and Mother says they would have died first, they must have let themselves be eaten away in secret."

"I fancy, Annabel, they did not have such feelings."

Conventional to the core, he found, with surprise, that he was already asking himself whether the mistake dwelt in Annabel's intuitions or in his own ideals of her sex? And even while he suffered the recoil of sentiment, he felt, in some primitive fibre, that only by stripping away conventionality could he release the imprisoned ardour of his spirit.

"Then what has happened to us to-day?" Annabel's voice had grown resentful. "Nobody could possibly want to suffer. We didn't ask to be different. It isn't fair to us to make us like this."

She possessed, he had discovered with pleasure, a commendable idea of fairness. This was the only moral trait he had been able to detect in her, and, while he classified it, he felt that it compensated, in a measure at least, for graver deficiencies.

"Does it ever occur to you that it is your own fault?" he inquired mildly, for this was the kind of thing that had been said to him in the 'seventies, when he was young.

"It isn't my fault," she retorted bitterly. "I don't believe anything is anybody's fault."

This doctrine, which he recognized as one that was dangerous in theory and fatal in practice, could not, he told himself, be passed over in silence.

"If my affection means anything to you——" he began, and broke off because he saw that she was not listening.

As he stopped, she turned toward him, and he said over again very slowly: "If my affection means anything to you——"

She interrupted him with a smile. "It means everything to me. I don't know how I could live without you." After a tremulous breath, she added in a tone so low that it melted to air before it penetrated his thoughts, "You are the only one who understands me."

"If that is true," he could scarcely keep his voice from vibrating with happiness, "won't you try to be brave and not nurse this unwholesome fancy?"

"I don't want to be ungrateful after all you've done for me," she returned submissively. "I do try to please you."

"It isn't only to please me. I shouldn't like you to think that you are under an obligation. I am begging you, for your own good, not to spoil your life by brooding over what can't be helped. All I have done for you, I've done freely without thinking of gratitude. I wish to help you for two reasons: one is that you need someone to protect you and the other——"

He hesitated, and she raised her luminous eyes to his face. "I know what the other reason is," she said in a caressing voice.

"You know?" He had not dreamed that he had let his secret escape him.

"Yes, I know it is because of Cousin Cordelia. You are trying to do what you think Cousin Cordelia would wish."

The blow was so unexpected that, for a few breathless moments, he was unable to collect his faculties. He felt a violent revolt from the false attitude in which Annabel's artless interpretation of his motives had placed him. And in his logical mind he was not convinced that Cordelia, who had been penny wise though far from pound foolish, would have approved of his munificence.

"Of course I cannot forget that your Cousin Cordelia was fond of you," he returned, since there was nothing to do but agree with her. "But I am fond of you, too, Annabel."

"You've been an angel to me," she said, and he could see that she meant it. "There isn't anybody in the world like you."

She lifted her face, as she used to do when Cordelia was living, and he stooped and kissed her with outward restraint but inward confusion. At the touch of her fresh, firm lips, it seemed to him that his inelastic arteries, as well as his dried and withered soul, were charged with the vital distillation of youth. It was all madness, he told himself; it was all dangerous madness, for he should probably awake with a headache and an injudicious temper in the morning. But he knew that he had lost the power to resist it, that he had lost even the wish to be saved from disaster. Forty years of the law had prepared him inadequately, he found, for close contact with life.

"Wait," he called after her, as she descended the steps. "Let me see you safely home, dear." For he felt that he could not bear to lose sight of her while this enchanting softness was in her eyes and voice.

HEN he left Annabel at her door and turned back into the drifting gold of the sunset, it seemed to him that he had found a luminous centre of joy in the vast melancholy of existence. For the hour, he had risen superior to doubts and fears; he had risen superior even to the vacillation of human destiny. Happiness, after all, was a matter not of age but of circumstances, he reflected consolingly; for the exhilaration of his emotions had not subsided and his retributive headache had not begun.

Inextricably woven into his thoughts, like a bright thread twisting through dark brocade, ran the inspiring words: *"I don't know how I could live without you."* This single sentence brought home to him, as nothing else in their association had done, the idea that he might, after all, be more than a friend to her. And his eager mind worked with this bright thread over and over again, until it had embroidered all the sombre screen of the future. It was not, he assured himself, as if he were falling intemperately into one of the selfish passions that he had seen afflict other men. He was thinking more of Annabel than of himself. She was so obviously in need of all he could give her, and he could give, thank God, in abundance. He could give her everything in life, except the one thing she had had and no longer valued, the wild flare of youth. Love, sympathy, tenderness, protection, and wealth. Though it was characteristic of him to include wealth as the least of the cardinal benefits, it was equally characteristic of him to assign it to its modest but honourable position.

As he approached the end of the block, he saw Amanda Lightfoot leaving the house of old Mrs. Burwell, who had been ill for months; and stopping in the middle of the pavement, with a curious feeling that he was lingering in the road to ruin, he waited for the perpetual beauty to sweep with her imperial gait down the steps. How fashions in belles had altered, he thought critically, as if she were a generation removed from him. Forty years ago there wasn't a woman in Queenborough, as Edmonia had reminded him, who could hold a candle to her. While she descended toward him, in her handsome grey satin, worn longer than the fashion, with a chiffon parasol held over her stately head and her large, round eyes, which were as blue as lapis lazuli in the golden light, he was obliged to acknowledge that she was the living embodiment of what he admired most in the world. Everything was there, everything but the fleeting breath of desire. The curving bosom, the rounded hips, the regal carriage, the calm and flowing walk,—all these feminine perfections, once so potent to awaken the longing of man, had lost now, even for the elderly, their ancient allurement.

She turned on him the waxen smile with which her beauty had triumphed over the years, while he was enveloped in a funereal gloom that issued from the source of his memory. A meeting with her always depressed him, and, for this reason alone, he tried, whenever it was compatible with politeness, to avoid her society. She depressed him, not only in the natural way, because she was no longer so young as she used to be, but, even more, because his judgment warned him that both the everlasting purpose and public opinion had selected her as his suitable mate. That she was endowed with every affirmative attribute made no difference to him, since he no longer even desired to desire her. Yet he still felt for her the reluctant tenderness that a man never loses for a woman who has been faithful to him without restricting in the slightest degree his liberty to be unfaithful to her.

"I've just been to inquire after poor Mrs. Burwell," she murmured in her level, and, it occurred to him for the first time, monotonous voice. "She has only a few days to live, her cousin told me."

"Very sad, very sad."

He turned, and with an ease that surprised him, fell, after a few nervous steps, into the measure of her flowing pace.

"I'm afraid I am taking you out of your way," she said, gently demurring.

"It is a great pleasure to me," he rejoined. How different girls were now, he thought, and could not decide whether he approved of the change.

"Her death will be a great loss to poor Mrs. Morland," Amanda resumed, for she was still clinging to the safe sorrow of old Mrs. Burwell. "She lost her only son in the war, you know."

"Yes, yes." The mention of the war jerked him up sharply, too sharply. He remembered it as seldom as possible, for the recollection brought with it a creepy sensation, as if he were taking some unfair advantage of all the young men who had given their lives in France. Just by living in their place, and reaping the harvests they had missed, he felt, unreasonably of course, that he was taking an advantage of them.

"I never come up this street that I don't regret the old gardens." Warned by her admirable intuitions that something was wrong, she was making, he could see, a noble effort to find a subject as innocuous as the Christian end of old Mrs. Burwell.

"Yes, we do miss them," he answered, and gazed at her thoughtfully. Though she still carried herself with her royal air, he had surprised a stricken look in her eyes. "Yes, we do miss them," he repeated.

Walking there at her side, outwardly as prim and dry as one would expect a renowned jurist of sixty-five years and innumerable honours to appear, he felt within his soul that he had become a victim of all the conflicts and cruelties of life. The last thing he wished to do was to hurt her—was, he amended precisely, to hurt any woman. He had never been able even to hurt Cordelia without suffering pangs of remorse. "She must have given up all those hopes years ago," he thought, and shivered because he saw the eyes of Mrs. Upchurch upon him as they went by her windows.

"I hope dear Cordelia's flowers are still living," Amanda said in her tenderest voice, while she lifted her melting glance to his face.

"Yes, they are doing well, especially the roses. I have had them looked after."

"And her canary birds? I think so often of her fondness for birds."

He sighed. Even Cordelia, for all her robust common sense, had displayed this feminine predilection for dwelling upon the past.

"We lost two of her best songsters last winter," he replied gravely. "They got a chill, I imagine. Canaries are delicate creatures. I have not yet bought any to replace them. Perhaps next year——" His voice dropped into silence, and he thought vaguely of Annabel.

"You might like one of mine. I have so many, and I should love to give you one. My first canary was a gift from dear Cordelia."

Though he accepted the bird gratefully (what else was there for him to do?), his antiquated sense of honour began immediately to trouble him. Was it chivalrous of him to take this canary from her when she was, he feared, offering it under the misapprehension that he might relapse into some sentimental survival? Though he tried his best to become modern and devoid of the sense of responsibility, the traditions in which he had been brought up were always ready to strangle his efforts.

After the future of the canary had been happily settled, he could not fail to observe that her composure became more natural.

"Will you come in and choose it?" she asked, as they reached her door, "or shall I pick out one for you?"

He shook his head, with a murmur, which he felt, desperately, she might interpret in any way that she pleased. He would always admire her deeply—far more deeply because he was protected by her invincible breeding—yet this very security placed, as it were, a debt of honour upon him, and he preferred, when all was said, to admire her at a distance. So he told her in his softest tone that he would send the empty cage in the morning, and after a few discreet amenities, he saw the door close behind her, and turned away to the pavement. "A little walk will set me up," he thought briskly. "There is nothing like a little walk and a thimbleful of old Bumgardner before dinner."

Wheeling about, he started down the street with a swinging stride; but, however rapid his walk, he found that the universal melancholy would not let him escape. Saturated with the languor and the subtle agitations of the May evening, this melancholy floated toward him on waves of twilight, until, suddenly, in the midst of his reverie, the image of Annabel darted, like an evocation of youth, into his mind, as if a solitary nymph had detached herself from his visions. Though he was prepared for these rosy temptations before he slept, they had never until this instant pursued him in a public street.

"It is because I have been a moral man," he thought, embittered by the monstrous injustice. "If I had been a rake, this would never have happened."

All the women whom he had respected instead of enjoying, all the women whom he had resisted, and (more intolerable still) all the women who might not have resisted him—these hopeless phantoms fluttered back to him from the purgatory of thwarted desires. He thought irrelevantly of the frivolous French maid his wife had brought over and then sent home again because she had turned out to be "not a serious person."

"I need exercise," he said sternly. "I must arrange to play regularly. The game yesterday made me sleep better." Glancing up, he saw that he was approaching Dr. Buchanan's office, and his mind added automatically: "It would be well, perhaps, to have Buchanan go over me."

Ascending the steps, he rang the bell and waited, in the hope that, since it was not his usual hour, the great specialist might refuse to receive him; but a minute had barely passed when the door opened, and the physician himself appeared and dismissed a patient.

"So it's you, Gamaliel," he began heartily, for they were great friends and played both golf and chess together. "I was thinking this morning that I should tell you to come round and be thumped. You deserve a thumping after the way you finished me off yesterday."

The Judge flushed with pleasure. "My golf, at least, is as good as it ever was."

"Well, keep it up. Don't be afraid to feel young."

It was impossible, reflected the Judge, for any one to have a more encouraging manner than Dr. Buchanan's. Many people came to him, especially elderly people who wanted to feel young again; for he was modern and skilful and very expensive, and he had a diet list for every taste, as well as for almost every tendency.

"I thought I'd let you go over me a bit," Judge Honeywell replied, a trifle nervously. Why had he come? he asked himself. Was there a purpose? Or wasn't there a purpose? Well, whichever way it was, it made little difference. "Not that there is anything wrong with me," he hastened to add, "the only thing I can complain of is an occasional headache in the morning when I first wake up. At my time of life, I suppose, I may expect this?"

"Been overdoing it a bit, eh?"

"On the contrary. The fact is, I've missed my golf, as you know, several times in the last two weeks."

"That may be what's wrong. Take off your coat and shirt, and we'll see in a minute."

"I was wondering if you'd advise me to change any of my habits?" the Judge inquired, watching the plump professional hands wind a band about his arm. Was there a purpose in his visit? Or wasn't there? Well, no matter.

"Not unless they are bad habits." This was so neat a retort that both men chuckled over it. Dr. Buchanan, who was an authority upon behaviour as well as upon diet, knew that the Judge's habits, supervised by Cordelia, had been impeccable for thirty-six years. He knew also, though his patient was ignorant of this, that a powerful but stealthy motive was now fermenting in the Judge's mind.

"Then you would not advise me to give up drinking or smoking? I take only an occasional whiskey and soda."

"I advise but one thing, my dear friend, and that is moderation. Moderation is the first law of health, and you yourself are a splendid example of that. Digestion, heart, lungs, liver, all as sound as a dollar. Your blood pressure is better than a man of your age deserves. Does anything else trouble you?" After his thumping and listening, the doctor looked up.

Did anything else trouble him? A little dazed by the physician's assurances, Judge Honeywell stared back at him with innocent and slightly blinking eyes. No, nothing troubled him. Nothing troubled him, but, perhaps—yes, but this shifting sensation—this indefinite feeling that he was losing control of his faculties. Nothing but these—well, these spells of loose thinking. Ah, that was the weakness that he disliked and condemned in the present age; for his own mental state resembled, at its best, a reservoir of opinions rather than a babbling stream of consciousness. Loose thinking. Lack of discipline, lack of precision, lack of proper coördination. These absurd and vagrant fantasies now—what else could he call them? Yet even calling them by their right name did not make them exactly the kind of troubles he could confide to a physician. Certainly not to a physician with whom he played golf three times a week and chess every Saturday night.

"No, nothing that is worth bothering you with," he answered at last.

"Well, keep up your pleasures, and don't be afraid to feel young. If you've noticed any unsteadiness in your nerves, it is probably the need of a fresh interest. Seclusion is bad for anybody, and as a general law there is nothing better than: Trust in God and keep your diet light." The doctor's immense laugh boomed out. "With religion and a light diet, you may live to be a hundred."

The words and, even more than the words, that commanding voice, summoned order out of chaos in Judge Honeywell's mind. What had been merely a stealthy motive when he entered the office, became a dominant purpose as he descended the steps.

"I sha'n't hesitate any longer," he decided, with an inspiring sense of mastery over life. "After all, it may be for the best. After all, who knows but I may make her happier than a younger man could have done?"

CHAPTER 11

F COURSE, I am fond of him," Annabel said artlessly. "He gives me such nice presents."

"You must remember," Mrs. Upchurch admonished, with the sprightly cynicism she reserved for difficult situations, "that only elderly men give so many presents. Young men are not generous, my dear." And she sighed presently, "They don't have to be."

Her words or her sigh had put a new thought into Annabel's mind, and in her flighty way, for her sagacity, unlike her mother's, was entirely natural and unpremeditated, she pursued it daringly into the open. "If only he wanted to marry you, Mother, it would be so much more suitable. Why, he is ever so much older than you are."

"Widowers of his age, my dear, seldom marry middle-aged widows."

"But they are the very ones they ought to marry. It is so suitable."

Again Mrs. Upchurch sighed and reflected. "They usually want young women, Annabel, and when you have had more experience, you will understand that it is not easy to curb the nature of man."

For an instant Annabel stared at her in silence. Then she rejoined with a mocking laugh, "I can see why men should hold that opinion, but what I can't understand is the way the Judge has passed over a woman who wouldn't curb him for a woman who would. Now, you would make exactly the right wife for a man who has never been curbed in his nature."

For the third time Mrs. Upchurch sighed, after she had ceased to reflect. Annabel, as she was fond of complaining, was altogether too much for her; and though she was only forty-eight, and very pretty still, she had cheerfully relinquished her prospects of marriage to her daughter. It is true that she would not have refused any promising offer; but, after her maiden effort, she had failed to bring genuine enthusiasm to the pursuit of men, and since her interest had flagged, she found it less exhausting to struggle for her daughter's provision than for her own. Marriage, as she remembered it, was a wearing experience; and though she still besought Providence for a rich and indulgent husband for herself and father for her child, her prayers had become simply another monotonous ritual.

"Of course, every woman would prefer to marry for love," she said, and qualified her assertion with, "at least for the first time. Love fills the lives of most women, especially the lives of women who have never had it. All girls ought to have the experience once, if only to find out how much it has been exaggerated."

"I wish I could never hear the word love again!" Annabel exclaimed, with smothered violence, which brought a flush to her cheeks and made her look indescribably lovely. "And I've told you a hundred times that I despise young men!"

"In that case," Mrs. Upchurch rejoined crisply, "there is less reason why you should not marry an elderly one. After all, every woman has to choose, if she only knew it, between a young husband who is seldom there when you want him and an elderly one who is always there when you don't want him. I don't mean, of course," she hastened to explain, "that Judge Honeywell is really old. Only that he is a great deal too old for you."

"So long as he is old," Annabel declared, "I don't care how old he is. It is this horrible poverty that I can't bear," she continued passionately. "It's bad enough to be poor when you're happy, but to be poor when you're unhappy is too much to endure."

"I was just thinking that, Annabel. Of course I wouldn't for the world advise you to do anything you might one day regret;

but it had occurred to me that, since you feel that you can never be happy again, it might help you a good deal to be comfortable. Now that this last cotton mill has closed down, and every room we can spare has been let to a lodger, I really don't see what we are going to do. And the Judge's wanting to marry you has in a way complicated the situation. When he gives so many useless presents, it makes it all the harder to ask him for absolute necessities."

"Oh, these lodgers!" Annabel gasped. "When I wake up in the night and want to scream, I feel that they are suffocating me."

She glanced about the shabby bedroom, and then at the door, which they kept tightly closed, even in hot weather, because of the inquisitiveness of lodgers. Beyond the door, her imagination passed into the narrow hall, with its dingy staircase, where the perpetual odours of food hung suspended.

"Is this what you call genteel poverty, Mother?" she inquired in accents of desperation.

"I suppose it is, dear," Mrs. Upchurch admitted, and she added presently: "If beggars only realized their advantages!"

"Even if I make anything from my landscape gardening, it won't be enough for us to live on. Not for years anyhow."

"And we can't very well go on taking help from Judge Honeywell after you have refused him."

"We can't!" Annabel retorted in surprise. "Why can't we?"

Mrs. Upchurch shook her head. "Because men aren't made that way, Annabel."

"But he has always helped us."

"Not to the same extent. Very sparingly, indeed, since Cousin Cordelia died. In the case of most rich men," she concluded briskly, "generosity requires the spur of some other impulse."

"Well, if I married him, would he give you a home—a comfortable house, without lodgers, and with servants in clean aprons?"

In rare moments, and this was one of them, Mrs. Upchurch

felt that Annabel's charm brought a lump to her throat. There was a quality in the girl's loveliness, a romantic appeal, that, she told herself, no man could resist. Yet the passion of men, she knew, is as uncertain as their liberality, and in marriage, however disappointing, the law did make provision.

"You must not think of me, darling," she answered, with a strangled sob. "I have but one desire on earth, and that is to see you happily settled before I die."

"You aren't thinking of dying, Mother."

"One can never tell, my child. Women of my time of life often develop some fatal malady. In any case, all I ask is to see you safely settled."

For a few moments, Annabel pondered the complications of living, and then, since there were evidently complications here also, of dying. At last she said, in a small precise voice, "I don't know that I should mind it so very much."

"Mind what?"

"Mind marrying him. I'd do almost anything not to have to worry about money. Do you suppose he'd pay all our bills?"

Mrs. Upchurch answered this question with a prompt retort: "You don't know what marriage means."

Annabel, who was young enough to dislike being told there was anything she did not know, and who had read all the forbidden books she could borrow, as well as many others, responded in a tone of careless confidence, "I know more than you think."

"Do you? Well, you didn't learn it from me," Mrs. Upchurch breathed from the depths of her heart. "That comes, I suppose, of so much reading, and even if reading improves the mind, I'm sure nobody could pretend that, in these days, it benefits the morals."

Though she had retained few moral prejudices, and those few were of the major variety, which does little harm, she was still shocked by the levity with which the youth of the present picked its dangerous way over the bare rocks of vital statistics. Amid the decent conventions in which she had been educated, people dealt only in private, and even then evasively, with the facts of life; and she could not divest herself of an impression that the facts of life were not of a character to bear public exposure. Surely there were some things that God knew best about.

"I would not for the world have you do anything that you might regret," she repeated nervously. "But, of course, if you are sure that you have got over all romantic feeling——"

Instead of completing her sentence, for, unlike Annabel, she felt that there were some things you simply could not put into words, she leaned forward and fastened her anxious gaze upon her daughter.

"The funny part is," Annabel said resolutely, "that I used to think he belonged to Cousin Amanda. Is there anything between him and Cousin Amanda? I wouldn't take a man away from another woman," she added, "if he were as rich as Crœsus."

Mrs. Upchurch hesitated for an instant, and in that hesitation she was stung by the prick of her conscience. She knew Amanda's history as well as any one, perhaps better, for her penetration was keen in such matters; yet she could not, in her own mind, decide where to place the blame for the unhappy end of that old engagement. Such faithfulness was magnificent, of course, but it was not human. She was sincerely sorry for Amanda, and she regretted that her own reduced circumstances compelled her to encourage Judge Honeywell's attentions to her daughter; but, after all, didn't the whole unfortunate affair only go to prove how little spinsters really know about life? To spend more than thirty years preserving an ideal merely to discover that the old ideal has been discarded for a new one, was, she admitted, sufficient to destroy the hardiest perennial among illusions. But what married woman, above all what widow who had been left unprovided for, would have shown so little understanding of the true nature of man?

"All that happened long ago," she said vaguely.

"Then it did happen?"

"Then what happened?" Mrs. Upchurch echoed, playing

gallantly for time. In her adroit handling of human frailty, all that she had ever asked of Providence was a little time.

"Whatever was between them?" Annabel persisted.

"Well, they were engaged. But that was before he met Cordelia."

"Did Judge Honeywell treat her badly?"

"Oh, no." Mrs. Upchurch breathed more freely. "No one ever intimated that. Amanda broke the engagement."

"She must have seen that he wanted it."

"But he didn't want it. He was almost distracted. Of course I was a child when it happened, but I remember hearing afterwards that there was a quarrel. It seems so strange, because Amanda has always had the sweetest disposition on earth, and never quarrelled with anybody else in her life. But there's something in love, especially when it is very intense, that seems to upset the temper. Anyhow she made the mistake of going abroad, and he couldn't follow her immediately because he was a young lawyer with several important cases. When at last he was able to go after her, he met Cordelia on the boat and——"

"You mean she caught him on the rebound?"

"Well, that isn't a nice way to put it. But he was wrought up and emotions are queer things. The most opposite ones like love and anger seem to plunge straight into each other without warning. It was the time, chiefly, and Cordelia happened to be present. When you know men a little better, my child, you will understand that it isn't so much the person as the time with a number of them. Even beauty or charm isn't so important as being right on the spot."

"Did it go hard with Cousin Amanda?"

"That is what no one ever heard from her lips. The nice women of her generation never talked of their feeling for men. For a year she stayed abroad with a nervous breakdown, and they were not nearly so common then as they have become since the war. But when she finally came home, she was as lovely as ever. She turned down every eligible man in Queenborough, and I think, poor dear, that she got some silly idea into her head that she had been to blame and that she would make reparation by being faithful to the past as long as she lived. Of course she never mentioned this to me. She has far too much delicacy to confess that she had been disappointed in love; but we could see that she has just gone on trying harder and harder to be what he had always admired. She has even gone on, year in and year out, wearing her hair the way he preferred, no matter what the fashion was at the time, and she has never worn any colours but blue and lavender because they used to be his favourites."

"He likes red and green now."

"I know, but, you see, she never took into consideration the way tastes change. She simply made a fetish of faithfulness."

"Do you think she has got over it?"

"Oh, she must have. Why, she can't be far from sixty to-day."

"Well, he's over sixty-five," Annabel rejoined. "I wish he would fall back in love with her. It would be so romantic."

"He wouldn't think so, my dear. Men aren't made like that, and they have their own peculiar ideas of romance—even the elderly ones. If you refuse him, he won't turn back to Amanda, but toward one of the buds of next season. Of course, it is disgusting, but, after all, that's the way they're made, and when an elderly man has once got the maggot of youth in his head, it takes him a long time to get over it. If he had never thought of you, or of any other young girl in that way, he might have married Amanda, but you never can tell. You must remember," she concluded, with a refrain which was less irrelevant than it sounded, "that he has a great deal of money. Some young girl will always be ready to marry him."

"I could never do it," Annabel said resolutely.

The front door downstairs opened suddenly, and the marching tramp of feet ascended the staircase. A few minutes later, the odour of a cheap cigar floated in from the bedroom across the hall.

"You mustn't raise your voice," Mrs. Upchurch whispered warningly. "The lodgers are coming in. Now, about this matter of the cotton mill. Do you think it would be a lack of delicacy to consult Judge Honeywell?"

Annabel sprang up from the couch where she had been lounging, and shook down her hair with a spirited gesture. What lovely hair it was, Mrs. Upchurch thought while she watched her. Just enough coppery lights in the brown to enhance the creamy tones in her skin. And those grey-green eyes exactly the colour of dawn on the sea! How foolish she had been to regret that her baby had not inherited the obvious blue of her father's eyes!

"Are you going out, dear?" she inquired, still watching Annabel divide the short, thick waves of hair and twist the shining clusters into two soft rolls behind her pretty ears. "Remember to hold up your head. The curve of your profile is lovely with your head held up, and, besides, it's a good habit and wards off a double chin."

After powdering her nose and touching her lips with a red pencil, Annabel turned away from the mirror. "Yes, I'm going out," she replied in the repressed tones they had both used since they had heard the lodgers enter. "Isn't it simply hell to be poor, Mother?"

Mrs. Upchurch nodded. "It is not easy, my child."

Annabel, who had dipped into the closet, emerged with a cloche of brown felt, which she pulled firmly down over her hair and one eyebrow. Standing there, in the band of sunlight that streamed through the window over a whitewashed wall, she seemed to her mother, as she had seemed to the Judge, the youngest thing in the world. Not that she was really so young, pursued Mrs. Upchurch, who was nothing if not accurate in her calculations. Twenty-three, even in these days, was a good marriageable age; but there was an elemental freshness in the girl's nature that kept her childlike in spite of her misadventure in love. And she could never be too thankful, Mrs. Upchurch reflected, that there was nothing of the flapper in Annabel. She did not drink or smoke; and she had never, even before she fell in love with Angus, indulged in wild escapades. She was an earnest little thing, for all her mocking defiance; and there were moments when her strength of character was almost a shock to her mother, who liked to feel that she could twist men and women alike through her capable fingers. It was just as if in gardening her trowel had suddenly struck against a rock beneath the fragile bloom of a flowerbed. Yes, an earnest little thing, and generous, too generous for her own happiness, Mrs. Upchurch mused; for she had not failed to observe that generosity, though meritorious in principle, is not a virtue that advances you in the affairs of the world. Especially in love. Yes, especially in love, she proceeded, arrested, after the curious habit of women, by the high-sounding word. Though she was chaste by instinct and cheerful from necessity, she had had her dreams, and it seemed to her regrettable that the hearts of men, like professional beggars, should thrive better upon a dole a day than upon a bountiful feast.

Still sighing, she asked in her clear voice, which cooed only when she wanted something, "Are you going out, dear?"

Annabel turned and looked at her with one of those flashes of independent judgment to which Mrs. Upchurch had never become reconciled. "I am going to ask Cousin Amanda if she still cares for Judge Honeywell," she answered, calmly adjusting on her slender wrist a gold-mesh bag the Judge had given her.

Mrs. Upchurch opened her merry grey eyes still wider. "Oh, Annabel, you can't ask her anything like that! Haven't you a particle of delicacy? Besides, she wouldn't dream of telling you."

Annabel shook her head impatiently. "Why shouldn't she? How can you expect people to know things if you don't tell them?"

"But she doesn't want you to know. Even if she still cared—and no woman who is upward of fifty-five would nourish any such feeling—she would pretend that she didn't."

"I know you used to be that way," Annabel said scornfully, "but I don't see what good you got out of it."

"My dear child," Mrs. Upchurch murmured feebly. "Even in my day, and I am ever so much younger than your Cousin

Amanda, self-control was still considered a virtue in women."

"But what was the sense of making a corner in virtue, and leaving none for men to exercise their character upon? If men have become morally flabby, women like you and Cousin Amanda are to blame."

"Annabel!" For this was more than Mrs. Upchurch could hear without protest.

"I am sorry, Mother, but you know how I hate shams. Even if we aren't any better to-day, we are certainly more real, and that's something to be said for us. Anyhow," she added gaily, as she opened the door, "I am going to ask Cousin Amanda. It isn't my fault that you are all such unconscionable liars!"

"Hush, Annabel. Remember the lodgers," Mrs. Upchurch whispered nervously.

"I am remembering them, and Judge Honeywell too. That's why I'm going. Liver again, and fried!" she called back from the head of the steps. "Why, I wonder, does the frying of the poor smell so much more opulent than the frying of the rich?"

On the front pavement, in the very act of turning into the gate, she encountered Mrs. Bredalbane, who was obliged to finish her panting before she could begin to articulate.

"I am trying to get up an appetite for dinner," Edmonia explained, "so I walked up from the hotel. If your mother isn't at home, I'll have to rest a bit, anyway."

Her voice was hoarse from dryness, and there was a string of beads on the black down that bordered her upper lip. Musty with age, Annabel thought, positively musty, though interesting because of her unusual opportunities.

"Oh, Mother is there, and she will be glad to see you."

Still heaving in distress, Mrs. Bredalbane planted her feet in the path. She had evidently no intention of moving until she had recovered her breath, and the sound that issued from beneath her handsome black lace mantle did not encourage the hope that her recovery would be a rapid one.

"I've just come from Gamaliel," she gasped presently. "He told me he'd started you in business."

"Yes, he was a perfect dear about it."

"Why didn't you wait until you'd married and been left a widow?"

"I mightn't have been left a widow. Some people aren't."

"You will be, if you marry Gamaliel. But you will pay a high price for the perquisite. Not that I am running down the condition of widowhood, but no woman ought to marry for the first time a man old enough to be her father or grandfather. I thought," she panted moodily after a pause, "that Gamaliel was going to marry Amanda. Heaven intended him to marry Amanda."

"Then I wish he'd go and do it," Annabel replied with spirit. "Heaven doesn't wish it a bit more than I do. Perhaps she won't marry him. I am going now to ask her how she feels about it."

Mrs. Bredalbane strangled a husky laugh. "And you expect her to tell you?"

"Why shouldn't she? I told her about Angus. I told everybody about Angus. What is there so moral or delicate in lying?"

"Oh, you moderns!" Mrs. Bredalbane exclaimed heartily. "It's safer to be modern now than it was when I grew up and had to leave Queenborough. But the truth is, I suppose, that Gamaliel thinks he is too young for her. He thinks he is too young for me, though we were born twins. I must say the delusion agrees with him. I never saw him look better."

Annabel nodded. "Yes, he is a very distinguished-looking old gentleman."

" 'Old gentleman,' you minx! Haven't I just told you that Gamaliel and I are twins? As long as I can keep an appetite and am not afraid of food, I shall think twice before I admit that I am an old lady."

"Well, I don't care whether he is old or not. I don't like young men."

"You won't say that twenty years from now, nor forty, either, for that matter. That's the worst thing about growing old. Old age always wants to pick the wrong associates. Now, Gamaliel has got the notion that it makes him appear young to gad about with what he calls his sweet girls, but, if he only had sense enough to see it, he'd stay young twice as long with Amanda. With Amanda, he is a middle-aged man, but with you he looks what you've just called him—a distinguished old gentleman."

"I don't see why he doesn't want to marry Cousin Amanda. It would be so suitable."

"That's probably the reason. The suitable is the last thing we ever want."

"Anyhow, I'm going to ask her."

"Well, run on. It will be improper, but thank the Lord that you live in an age when you can be improper without having to go abroad. In my day, you couldn't be, though that's all changed now, and Amanda can't do any worse than pretend to you, which is the only thing she has done since she became Gamaliel's ideal."

She waddled resolutely up the path on her way to advise Mrs. Upchurch, who found nothing more depressing than advice, since she knew her own mind but needed money, which even the best advice seldom brought.

I N HER dull drawing-room, Amanda sat looking thoughtfully, though as usual she was not thinking, at her gilded bird-cages. Serene, unselfish, with the reminiscence of a vanished day in her face and figure, she belonged to that fortunate generation of women who had no need to think, since everything was decided for them by the feelings of a lady and the Episcopal Church. Even this matter of unrequited affection, this very urgent and painful matter of a broken heart, was eased of confusion, if not of soreness, by the infallible instinct that impelled her to pretend it away. She was wearing a dress of lavender crêpe, with a modified late-Victorian waistline, and her abundant hair, like powdered twilight, was arranged à la Pompadour. Neither time nor her blighted romance had been able entirely to destroy a complexion that, as Mrs. Bredalbane had remarked almost forty years before, was the only perfect substitute for intelligence.

"Why, Annabel," she said, rising gracefully and bending to kiss the girl's cheek. "It is so good of you to come. This is what dear Mother used to call her lonely hour."

"Oh, I like to come," Annabel responded, sitting down on the edge of a hard sofa that was upholstered in plush. "I am fond of you, and I am fond of the birds."

"They are darlings," Amanda assented, in so musical a voice that the canaries began to pipe in their luxurious cages.

"Cousin Amanda," Annabel began courageously, "are you happy?"

"Why, yes, dear." Amanda's tone was tinged with astonishment. "I should be very ungrateful if I were not happy, with all my blessings."

"But blessings don't make us happy," Annabel returned, and she thought, "She is so noble that she creaks. I wonder if they were all like that, except Mrs. Bredalbane, who is disreputable?"

"They do, if we attune our minds to them."

"Yet so often they aren't what we really want, but what God or other people think best for us."

"Well, my dear, who should know better than God?"

"That's what Mother says, and I suppose it's a comfort if you can feel like that, though I don't see how you ever bring yourself to it. Now, I know the things that I want even better than God does, and I'd like to be consulted before I am blessed—permanently, anyhow. Nobody can make me believe," she finished passionately, "that it is good for my soul to live on fried liver and scrambled eggs."

Amanda's faith, though sufficient for an ample income, had never been called upon to contend with the sordid problems of poverty. Smiling as sweetly as ever, for only a surgical operation could have altered the prim sweetness of her smile, she murmured gently that God had been very good to her, and that even her dear father had been spared to her until he was ninety.

"I wish you and your mother could come to dinner often," she added generously, for as much mind as she had was practical, and she honestly wished to help the needy. "It is a great pleasure to have you. Mother used to say that Bella's sunny temper was worth a fortune."

Annabel laughed. "I wish somebody would buy it." For an instant, she hesitated and then resumed her intimate questions. "You never get lonely, do you, Cousin Amanda?"

Amanda lifted her calm eyes, which reminded the girl of blue enamel, to the portrait of a lady in an immense chignon and miniature bonnet. "I miss my dear mother and father, but I have the kindest nephews and nieces in the world, and they leave me so little time to myself. This house is filled with young people all day long. They refuse to let me grow old."

"And you don't miss anything else? Honestly, now, Cousin Amanda?"

A shadow as swift as the flight of a bird darkened the stainless enamel. Yes, Mother is right, Annabel thought, Cousin Amanda is a perfect lady, and the only trouble with perfect ladies is that they lie as perfectly as they behave.

"Oh, I haven't time to think of anything else. I am kept too busy making people happy about me," Amanda responded. "Every morning, as soon as I wake, I ask God to direct me to the greatest good I can do that day. Then, almost always, my prayer is answered before I've finished breakfast. I am sure to hear of some one who is ill, or one of the children runs in to have a hurt bandaged. Or there is a distressing case among my poor that must be attended to immediately. The days pass so quickly when you are doing things for others. Dear little Annabel"—the level tones rose suddenly in supplication—"God doesn't let you be unhappy while you are doing His will."

Didn't He? Well, what was His will, and how did you know it? demanded Annabel, who was sure that she shouldn't have been made happy by the will she had seen manifested to her mother and Cousin Amanda. Nor did Cousin Amanda appear to be so happy as she said she was—not when you were close enough to see the circles under her eyes. She looked quiet, but she looked also, in some inexplicable way, hurt, as if God's will with her had been firm rather than gentle, and had given her a moment, at least, of unpleasant surprise. Oh, if only people would be direct instead of painfully subtle!

"Then you never, never regret that you didn't marry?" she asked abruptly. "I am not just impertinent, Cousin Amanda. I have my reason, a very urgent reason, for wishing to know."

Amanda started, for questions like this, even with urgent reason, were never asked an unmarried woman when she was young.

"Why, no, dear," she replied with an edge of frost to her tone.

"You weren't sorry that you broke your engagement to Judge Honeywell?"

"Why, no, dear. You must remember that happened more than thirty years ago." If her face ached from smiling, there was no sign of pain in her manner.

"Mother said he was almost distracted. But you never regretted it?"

"Why, no, dear." Amanda hesitated, and then spoke in a frozen voice. "I broke my engagement just before I sailed for Europe with my dear mother, who died while I was over there. I felt that I could not be separated from my mother and father as long as they lived. That was why," she added unflinchingly, "I never married."

"You wouldn't marry him now, would you?"

At this impertinent question, Amanda lowered her gaze for the first time, while a burning flush stained her features. For an instant her throat quivered convulsively beneath the narrow band of black velvet.

"Why, no, dear," she repeated mechanically, and added with a touch of asperity, "At my time of life, one no longer thinks of marriage."

"But he might. Men do, don't they?"

"Well, men are different." It was the proverbial reply to such a question; yet hearing the classic precept for the hundredth time, Annabel asked herself if life had been less confusing to people who lived by a simple formula instead of by intricate reason. A law of nature might sound less final than an Act of God, but it was certainly more authoritative, as well as more consoling to religious minds, than a mere infirmity of man.

"Oh, Cousin Amanda, please marry him!" she cried out suddenly, with one of her dangerous impulses.

After all, she was obliged to make an effort to find out the truth, even if her questions did slide over the brightly lacquered surface of Amanda's manner. There were moments, and this was one of them, when it seemed to Annabel that the whole world and all people everywhere, except herself and Angus, whom she hated, were only half animate. Was there a sounder reality beneath this complicated system of living? Was it possible to make an impression upon that cool, inviolable texture of good taste? Good taste! thought the girl scornfully; for, as her mother so often reminded her, she had thrown not only good taste but decorum to the winds when she met disappointment. How could it matter, she thought passionately, whether you are unhappy in good taste or bad, so long as you are unhappy? Yet both her mother and Cousin Amanda put breeding before happiness even in tragedy, even at funerals, where the quality of the crêpe was more remarked than the quantity of the grief.

"Why, Annabel, are you out of your head?" A breeze of exasperation had at last ruffled the suavity of Amanda's voice. "Such an idea has never so much as crossed my mind. Judge Honeywell and I are the best of friends. The best of friends," she repeated, with firmness and without emotion, "but as to marrying him or anybody else, the idea has never crossed my mind. If you could see how full my life is, with the incessant demands of my nieces and nephews and all my charities, you would understand that I have no time to think of marriage. If I didn't marry when I was young and had so many opportunities, I should certainly not care to assume such responsibilities late in life. Indeed, I have always thought," she added with an earnestness which sounded sincere, "that it is a mistake for women to marry late in life."

Yes, it sounded sincere; but was it? Annabel didn't know, and she realized that she could never know, for the virtue of perfect behaviour lies, not in its rightness, but in its impenetrability. It might be, as her mother insisted, that all good women of the nineteenth century were passive in temperament, and were, therefore, more disposed to lean back upon the prerogatives of men—or the Acts of God, if they preferred to think in dignified terms.

Well, she couldn't help it, Annabel concluded, gazing with hurt and hungry eyes at Cousin Amanda, who was being noble in thought and attitude on a hard Victorian sofa.

"I wish you would talk freely to me, Cousin Amanda," the girl said, as she rose and turned her cheek for a kiss.

"Nice women don't talk about their private affairs, Annabel," Amanda answered, with recovered sweetness. "When you are older, you will know better. Nice women never, never ask each other such questions."

"I told you about Angus. I told everybody. If I hadn't, I should have died of the pain."

Amanda shook her head. "Not if you had governed your mind, my dear. You should study to control your temperament and govern your mind properly."

This was all. There wasn't any help in Cousin Amanda. She talked of temperament exactly as if she meant temper. Yet, in spite of her self-control and her governed mind and her reliance upon God's will, in spite even of her attentive nephews and nieces and her vocal canary birds, she did not look happy. Calm, perhaps; but was it, after all, merely the calmness of resignation? One thing, at least, Annabel told herself, she had discovered: there was little help to be found in perfect behaviour.

ELL, that was over, Annabel thought impatiently, as she descended the steps into the diffused violet dusk of the June evening.

Not only was she enveloped in this dusk, but it stole into her breast like a living thing, and ached there, struggling to break free, as if it were the vital spirit of summer. Why did she suffer so? What was there in beauty, and in the longing for beauty, that tormented her like a flame? Her mother and Cousin Amanda had not felt like this. But were they really happier? And what did anybody know about feeling? Why, for instance, did it die quite down, and then start up suddenly again from the dead embers? There were whole days, weeks even, when she did not think of Angus, or, if she thought of him, it was merely with the surface of her mind, where impressions skimmed like shadows, not with the deep places, not with the deep below the deep places in her soul. For weeks it would be like this. Then, without warning, in spring or summer nights, she would begin to ache again with the memory of Angus—or was it only with the longing for love? Was the memory of Angus inextricably woven with the thought of love in her mind, and would it be always like this?

"I can't bear it," she whispered, "I can't bear summer without love."

Why was it, she asked herself desperately, that love or hatred, or whatever the feeling was called from which you suffered, grew worse on hot nights, on summer nights, when the moonlight was alive and the scent of magnolia blossoms quivered in the motionless air, and there was a curious arrested excitement in your heart, an excitement that vibrated in circles but never flowed onward into space? And somewhere in France Angus was making love. Well, she did not care. She no longer loved him; but it was strange the way that hating a person could make you suffer so desperately. Even though she hated him, and wanted to escape from love as long as she lived, she still remembered the little things, the foolish little things, that made him different from every one else in the world. His smile, his eyes with the brown flecks in the grey, his queer frowning look when he was stirred . . . Oh, well, what did anything matter? . . .

Ahead of her, in the visionary passage between light and darkness, spreading elm boughs looked as diaphanous as mist against the greenish blue of the evening sky. Beyond the trees, where the shadows ended, a glaze of electric light fell over the pavement; and through this glaze, indistinct figures were swimming toward her. When they came nearer, she saw that one of these figures, and certainly the most impressive, was Judge Honeywell. As he recognized her, his grave Roman features were suffused with emotion, and he appeared surprisingly young for his years. Oh, what did age, what did anything matter when you were over with love?

"I've brought you a bangle I saw at Tiffany's the other day," he said. "It had just come in, and I thought of you as soon as I saw it."

"Oh, that was good of you. Of course, I adore presents!" (What was love, after all, and how did you bear it when it came and went like the pain in a nerve?)

They went up the walk together, and into the warm, gaslighted room, which had been, in the affluent days of an earlier generation, the front parlour. Remnants of the æsthetic taste of another century were still embalmed there in the changeless medium of straitened circumstances; and though Annabel had made half-hearted efforts to bring comfort out of nothing, the room had settled at last into the discouraging aspect of a place where only the things that nobody would buy were left.

Under the tarnished chandelier, the table was already laid for supper; but at the sound of a male visitor, Altrusa, the coloured cook, who was predestinarian in religion but had a firm hand with a crisis, had whisked away every reminder of the evening meal except its smell. Annabel, watching the hasty flutter of a soiled apron, and knowing that the liver waited, congealing in its grease, behind the door, thought quickly, as if it were a flash of pain instead of an idea: "Anyhow, I've played fair. I gave Cousin Amanda her chance. Perhaps she didn't want it. . . . Oh, well, what does anything matter?"

"It is very warm in here," the Judge remarked, which was true but superfluous.

While he commented upon the heat, he was slowly removing a small white box from his pocket, and after disengaging it from a shred of tissue paper and a bit of elastic, he held out a jewel case of crimson morocco. Having reached the time of life when even the best men, however securely rooted they may be as pillars of society, are obliged to depend largely upon presents in courtship, he was not unreasonably trying to make the most of the occasion.

"It is always hot here in summer," Annabel replied, and she added bitterly: "Another summer! I don't see how I can bear it in this house!"

At her wail of despair, Judge Honeywell opened the jewel case and disclosed a sapphire bracelet on a lining of white velvet. As he held it out, his admiring gaze travelled from the sapphires to Annabel's tragic face.

"My dear little girl," he said tenderly. "If only you would let me take you away! If only you would let me take you to beautiful places!"

Annabel was gazing up at him with famished, resentful eyes, with eyes which had not lost even for an instant the look of sudden despair that Angus had brought into them.

"Would it be a long way off?" she asked yearningly; for she cherished the general delusion that one can leave unhappiness at home, like a discarded garment, when one set out on one's travels.

"Anywhere. Round the world, if you wish it."

At this she drew a step nearer; and very gently, for Cordelia had severely discouraged the pleasures of love, he enfolded her in his arms.

"Do you know, I am really fond of you?" she said, smiling down on the bracelet.

Yet, with the words on her lips, she was thinking how different old arms were from young ones, how different Judge Honey-well's embrace was from the embrace of Angus, who was both impetuous and violent in his tenderness. Well, she was glad that they were different, that they were old arms, wooden arms, like branches of a dead tree, she found herself thinking, and there could be no reminder of last summer.

And while she was thanking the invisible Powers that he was not young and would not be too affectionate, Judge Honeywell, clasping her gently but ardently to his breast, was transfigured by a glow, a rapture, a vital flame. For, if his arms felt like the branches of a dead tree, his spirit was quickening with the deep pulsations of summer. Not only the cords of prudence about his heart, but the very crust of civilization, dissolved in the burning magic of that embrace. Forgetting his age, his dignity, his repu-tation, forgetting his secret fear of himself and of Annabel, he surrendered utterly to a youth which, since it lived only in dreams, was as inextinguishable as desire. And forgetting even the realistic tone of the period, he allowed his ecstasy to overflow in the grandiloquent pitch of the 'eighties.

"You little thing, you adorable little thing," he heard himself murmuring in a voice that was as faint and thin in his ears as the chiming of distant bells. "I know I am not worthy. I know I do not deserve such happiness. But I love you. I love you in a way I did not believe possible. For the first time in my life. For the first time in my life," he repeated, almost strangled by the fervour of his emotion, "I know what it is to love without one selfish desire. Your happiness—all I ask on earth is your happiness. If you will trust me, my darling—if only you will trust me. I promise you—I promise you, if only you will trust me——"

Upstairs, in her suffocating bedroom, where the gas sang as

it flared from the single jet that was lighted, Mrs. Upchurch was laboriously embroidering a frock of blue linen for Annabel, while she regretted, after her practical habit of mind, that machine stitching was held in disfavour. She had paused to wipe her flushed and perspiring brow, when she heard behind her the sepulchral whisper of Altrusa.

"Dat ar ole Jedge is down yonder agin wid Miss Annabel." Altrusa, who was old enough to have escaped the perils of public education, still yielded to the temptation of dialect in dramatic moments.

Mrs. Upchurch laid aside her handkerchief and picked up her needle. "Has he come back so soon?" she inquired, with interest. "Well, you'd better not wait, if it is time for your prayer-meeting. Just leave the things as they are, and I'll pretend we've had supper, and wash up after he has gone." Her ingenuity, as usual, was equal to the occasion. Nevertheless, she sighed as she ran her needle along the edge of the pattern; for necessity, which had reconciled her to pretending, had failed to overcome her deep-rooted objection to washing dishes.

"Whyn't you lemme ring de supper bell right close ter de do'?" Altrusa suggested.

"No, that would be rude, and we can't afford to be rude. Besides, nobody rings bells any longer. It's a funny thing," she mused, "that men never seem to realize that other people have hours."

"He's ole, an' hit's time he wuz gwine home," Altrusa persisted.

"He is a very distinguished gentleman, Altrusa, of great property," Mrs. Upchurch returned in an accent of rebuke. "But don't wait any longer. I'll go down in a little while and interrupt them. It can't do any harm."

After all, an interruption when things had gone so far made little difference. It wasn't as it used to be in her girlhood, when she had waited so patiently, and resorted to such ingenious manœuvres, in order to bring Jimmy Upchurch to the point of proposing. At this recollection she sighed again, and since there was no one near for whom she felt obliged to keep up an appearance, she drew out this sigh to its utmost dimension. Wasted time, she thought pensively. Wasted time; but then, of course, no woman knows that until she has tried it. "If I'd spent my girlhood learning some useful pursuit, how much better off we should be now," she reflected, with the calm judgment of complete disillusionment. "If I were Annabel, I'd think twice before I gave up landscape gardening for the richest man in the world. Whatever you earn honestly is money in your pocket, but in these days even rich men are not to be depended upon as providers."

Fifteen minutes later, with her sewing in her hand and her artificial smile on her lips, she tripped down into the drawing-room, where she was received, with open arms and a kiss of filial gratitude, by Judge Honeywell.

"A miracle has happened!" he exclaimed, with an emotion which seemed to her slightly exaggerated. "Annabel cares for me!"

Standing in the middle of the room, while she felt her brightness slowly escaping her, Mrs. Upchurch stared back at him, with an impulse to run away which was strangely like a sensation of panic. Whatever she had expected, this, she told herself in consternation, was too much. Yes, men were unaccountable. There was no use denying, she continued, with more compassion than ridicule, that men, even at the best, were unaccountable creatures. Could any woman on earth, could even the sanguine Mrs. Bredalbane, be so easily deluded? Well, since it had to come, she supposed this way was better than any other; but, even though she was prepared for anything, and most of all for excesses of masculine credulity, she repeated, with a dazed mind, that men were unaccountable creatures.

PART
TWO

B EYOND the railing of the deck there was a drift of apricot-coloured light over a sea of splintered sapphire. The day had been warm for the Atlantic, and the sun was going down in an illusion of tropical splendour.

Lying back in his deck chair, with a cap of Highland plaid shading his features, which looked dry and brittle above his pointed grey beard, and his long, thin legs stretched out beneath a peacock-blue rug, Judge Honeywell gazed placidly over the quiet sea to the mirage of sculptured clouds on the horizon. Though he was a little tired after the fortnight in which he had been an active companion to twenty-three summers, he felt, as he had reminded himself a hundred times since he had been on board, remarkably well. Why, this very morning, slapping his chest vigorously after his salt tub and his daily dozen, he had exclaimed with relish: "Not a day over thirty-five! Positively, I do not feel a day over thirty-five!"

Turning to the mirror, he had almost expected to see the firm flesh and enkindled blood of his youth; and, for an instant, so strong was the sensation of well-being, he had scarcely recognized the pale judicial countenance and the sallow skin, which had flushed to brownish purple after the strenuous rubbing. While he had looked at his reflection, an unutterable loneliness had oppressed him; but an hour afterwards, striding briskly up and down the deck in the keen salt air, he had found that the glow of exercise restored the damaged pride of his manhood.

Withdrawing his gaze from the sunset, he glanced down at the empty chair that Annabel occupied whenever she ceased her activities. Ever since they had sailed, she had appeared to him to live in an incessant whirl of agitation. A few minutes before, after a festive tea with a troop of college youths, she had flitted by to the games at the other end of the deck. Well, he was glad that she was enjoying the trip. He liked to see her amused; he liked to watch the tragic memory fade from her eyes and the light and laughter return. Moreover, he was ready (how ready, he hesitated to admit even to himself) for an occasional rest with his legs under the comfortable rug, which he pulled higher as the sun grew fainter and the evening breeze brought an edge of chill to the air.

"Your daughter left this book in the smoking-room," a voice said at his elbow, and turning, he met the fatuous expression of one of the college youths. How unintelligent were the young of to-day, he reflected, while he held out his hand for the book. Why should this immature mind have leaped to the conclusion that Annabel was his daughter? Why should it have overlooked the number of men who had married late in life women much younger than themselves? Indeed, since men retain their youth long and women lose theirs early, this was merely one of the many admirable provisions of nature. Besides, unquestionably, some women prefer older men. . . .

Picking up the book, he opened it where Annabel had left a small yellow handkerchief between the pages. Well, he supposed that women, even young and attractive women, who used to be shielded from contamination, read everything nowadays. It was not fair to judge people by what they read, since most of them, he inferred, read from curiosity the things that could be said only in print. But it was an inexhaustible surprise to him to discover the collection of rubbish, the varied odds and ends of misinformation that Annabel had tucked away in her shallow though obstinate mind. Vivacious, intelligent, the astonishing thing was that any one so soft in body could be so stubborn in purpose. Delicate as a flower on the surface, he lamented after the manner of Mrs. Upchurch, but with a vein of iron beneath. Undeveloped, that was the way she had impressed him in the last few weeks; undeveloped yet rich in the raw material of which character is composed. Useless to pretend that she was orderly, that she was disciplined in habits of mind or body. Mentally, indeed, he had assigned her to that prevalent class which our rude ancestors dismissed as scatter-brains, but which superior persons of to-day cherish as intelligentsia.

Now, for example, this book with her yellow handkerchief between the pages. Did this middle-aged young intellectual, who stalked through three hundred and fifty pages being solemn about sex—did he really imagine, Judge Honeywell speculated, bringing his legal opinion to bear on the question, did he really imagine that sex was more solemn than anything else in the universe? Than digestion, for instance, or even than dyspepsia? In any case, the Judge was far from convinced that the modern mind, with its mastery of vital problems, was an improvement upon the sentimental Victorian one, which, when all was said, had had its own way with sex.

Sitting there alone, with his eyes on the murmurous waves, he was plunged anew into that profound melancholy which differs from loneliness in being a more naked desolation of spirit. What he now endured was not the torment of an unequal passion, though this had left him only in a few brief moments of self-deception, but the dumb despair of a heart that has discovered its own emptiness. Though he loved Annabel, there were hours when it seemed to him that he was suffocated less by the flame than by the smoke of desire. He was glad to have her near him; when she was absent, he longed for the sight and touch of her fragrant youth, of her dewy freshness; yet he was never so distant from her in feeling as he was when she stood close at his side. Never so distant, except in those instants of poignant longing when he held her clasped to his heart and felt her fragile body harden within his arms. For the mild caresses he lavished upon her were too fleeting to ease the burden of his overcharged heart.

"What do you think of marriage, Annabel?" he had asked her once, yearning for reassurance, and she had answered with innocent candour, "It isn't so bad as I thought it would be." Cordelia, of course, would never have put it that way. No

woman, indeed, of his own generation would have responded so
tactlessly; but, then, as he admitted disconsolately, times had
changed, and not, so far as he could see, for the better.

And because everything, except the elderly like himself, was
different, he again picked up this extraordinary book, which
Cordelia would have called impure, and again laid it down, with
a sigh, in Annabel's empty chair. Well, they were, no doubt,
advanced, these dull and pompous romantics who found sex so
indigestible; but, after all, his legal mind, trained to exact obser-
vation, concluded precisely, they were advanced only to themselves and to those who were already behind them. To future
generations, their irreverent age would appear as backward in
perspective as other epochs.

Even now, he would have no quarrel with them, since his was
an unpolemical spirit, if they had not attempted to tarnish
with their impure fiction innocent natures like Annabel's. For,
in spite of his discovery that Annabel had devoured voraciously
and assimilated imperfectly more depravity in the form of books
than he knew even by name, he persisted in thinking of her as
both innocent and ignorant of evil. Training her tender mind
had been, from the beginning of his engagement, one of the delights to which he had looked forward with deep satisfaction.
During twenty, or even twenty-five years, if Providence spared
him (which, considering he had lived with prudence and sobri-
ety, Providence might very well be expected to do), he beheld
himself training Annabel's pliant reason in habits of wisdom,
temperance, and fortitude. Gently of course; for gentleness had
become the ruling principle of his marriage, gentleness and patience.

Gazing pensively at the last faint trail of opalescent light on
the sea, he told himself that unsound opinions make little difference in a true woman, since the beliefs of a wife are naturally
formed, or at least influenced, by her husband. His generation
of well-regulated minds had confirmed this view, and his dignified faculties would be the last to admit either that his own wife
was devoid of true womanliness, or that marriage with himself

would not cultivate in Annabel the admirable qualities it had never failed to develop in a true woman. What did ignorance, what did immaturity matter, when she enkindled in his sentimental heart the rainbow dreams of adolescence? A hard little thing underneath; yet with her moments, when she gazed on beauty, of an almost burning softness.

Rising from his chair, and disentangling his legs from the rug, he strolled slowly along the deck in search of the unfinished games. It was time, he decided, after a glance at his watch, to go inside and begin preparations for dinner, and he was longing, with a curious wistfulness, for the piquant moments in their cabin before they separated again. Nothing in his marriage had thrilled him more deliciously than the vision of Annabel dressing or undressing within the narrow space of the cabin. Though he was a man of precise habits, who would have died sooner than go to bed before he had folded and laid away each separate garment in its proper place, the charming disorder in which his young wife lived was suffused with romance. Coming suddenly into the room in the morning or afternoon, and finding her filmy clothes scattered over the bed and boxes, he would recapture for an instant the sensuous delight of his twenties. His was a benevolent heart, and he longed to confer rather than receive happiness; yet he asked himself, in these moments, if life were not a simpler matter for men of tough masculine fibre, who had learned to pluck the fruit of the world with ruthless decision.

At the end of the deck, Annabel was practising a new dance step with the fatuous but nimble youth. Glancing up as her husband appeared, she smiled brightly, and he observed, with a thrill of unselfish pleasure, that she was looking much happier.

"Go in. I'll come in a minute!" she called gaily. "I want to get this step right. We're going to dance this evening!"

"Then you'll be late for dinner."

"Oh, it won't take me ten minutes to dress, and even if we are late, it won't matter, will it?"

No, it would not matter, he assured her indulgently, though he was a punctual man, who had dined at exactly the same hour for thirty-six years, and who suffered from nervous dyspepsia when he was forced into irregular habits. Well, if tenderness, if consideration, if unselfish devotion——

For a few minutes, he stood watching her more with the solicitude of a father than the pride of a husband. Though he enjoyed her pleasure, he was never so keenly aware of the generations that divided them as he was when he watched her effervescent delight in exertions that bored or wearied him as mere human activities. For instance, those ridiculous steps! How could any sensible person, even a young and frivolous person who enjoyed exercise, find pleasure in making an absurd spectacle of her body? But so long as she did enjoy it, he would have patience. If she demanded nothing more than gentleness and patience in marriage, there need be little fear of disaster.

Turning away, while he waited for her lesson to end, he was engaged in conversation by several elderly ladies, who had kept to their chairs in a sheltered corner, under the impression, as they confided to him, that "a sitting posture is safest on shipboard." It was evident that they would have liked to indulge in a few reminiscences; but, after a moment of restless attention and a polite apology, he was able to slip away to the smoking-room. Estimable ladies, no doubt, but they were so obviously his appropriate companions that it was embarrassing to be seen in their company.

OR the next three months, which were pleasant but exhausting ones, he followed Annabel's temperament wherever it led her from England to the Continent. After a few weeks of unequal affection, he had realized that patience, that even gentleness, was not enough. Like a tantalizing dream of fulfilment, her loveliness was near and yet unattainable.

And following her vivacious temperament, he paused now and then, while she sped swiftly beyond him, to moralize over her disquieting difference from the sainted Cordelia. This second wedding journey bore as little resemblance to his first one as the swallowlike darts and curves of Annabel's delight bore to the methodical pilgrimage in which Cordelia had pursued culture over Europe. It was true, he reminded himself, that methods had deteriorated almost as flagrantly as manners. In the eighteen eighties a generous enthusiasm, even for the Old Masters, was discouraged by the best minds, and an attitude of suspicion toward works of art, however fine, distinguished the wealthy and cultivated classes in England and America. But, realizing all this, he was still impressed by the dissimilarity, even when the roads were the same, of the two journeys. Where Cordelia had been hemmed in by traditions, by exact rules of conduct and reticences of breeding, Annabel was not only untrammelled by these restraints, but appeared to find them ridiculous. From his superior eminence, which was that of the institutional mind, he looked down compassionately upon her aimless wandering through a labyrinth of blind impulses. She was without reverence, he admitted sorrowfully, for doctrine, sound or unsound. Indeed, it appeared to him at times that she was disposed to respect the unsound more than the sound, since she cherished the modern fallacy that whatever is false in theory offers a better prospect of becoming true in fact. It sobered him for a few days to stumble upon the knowledge that his wife, however young and pure, was destitute of the faculty known to Cordelia and himself, as well as to others of his age and civilization, as moral principle. Yet he was obliged to admit presently that, if she lacked principle, she was abundantly supplied with the quality of compassion. Her charity exceeded Cordelia ɔ, and he was constantly surprised by some manifestation of a crude, he had almost said of an inchoate, sense of justice. This bewildered him because she seemed to divorce justice from law, and he had always regarded them as one and indivisible in body. Her feeling for justice, moreover, was a spirit, he perceived, rather than a conviction. It scorned obligations that he recognized as imperative, and admitted claims that his judicial judgment would have denied. For instance, a sense of justice toward the animal creation! She treated animals with respect instead of mercy, as if they were within their universal rights and not dependent upon an ephemeral impulse of pity. The poor, too, and the afflicted received a different consideration from the sort Cordelia had visited upon objects of charity.

In Paris, where they spent three dazzling weeks, she blossomed overnight, or so it seemed to him, into an image of worldliness and fashion. Her features, which had been lovely but vague, were sharpened, by what arts he did not inquire, into the delicacy of a cameo. In long jade earrings, which dangled beneath lustrous waves of hair against the pearly texture of her neck, she had gained, he felt, in fascination what she had sacrificed in elusiveness. He was proud of her youth and beauty; yet there was, he had learned since his marriage, a ceaseless ache in his pride of possession. In his tenderest embraces, she might have been a vision painted on air, so light, so gay, so fugitive and insubstantial she felt in his arms.

But there were other moments when he assured himself complacently that his marriage, though imprudent, was not without its sweet, if perilous, recompense. In spite of the complications and costly discomfort in which Annabel preferred to travel, in spite of the uncertainty of ever catching a train or procuring a meal at the proper hour, he felt younger, at least until his attacks of nervous dyspepsia became frequent, than he remembered feeling since he had drifted into the stormy haven of middle age. This satisfaction might have lasted indefinitely; it would certainly have lasted, he thought, until their return to Queenborough, if it had not been shattered by the constitutional frailty that had given Cordelia so many anxious nights and cost her so much of the rich and highly flavoured food to which her healthy appetite had inclined. For thirty-six years, she had sacrificed her appetite to his digestion, and the immensity of her sacrifice he had never begun to appreciate until he had, from habit, left the ordering of their irregular meals to Annabel's perverted taste for eccentric dishes and dangerous French sauces. In the early months of their travels, before his dyspepsia had become chronic, and the distressing symptoms interfered with his activities by day and his comfort at night, he had tried to pretend that he enjoyed the food. But when the test came, his moral force was defeated by the infirmity of his stomach. After three days when he could eat no food whatever, and several more when he had lived upon soft-boiled eggs and very weak tea, they set out for Vichy, where he drank the water and was attended perseveringly but distantly by Annabel. It was, he felt, a discouraging incident, but he supported it with the fortitude of a generation that had been trained to accept adversity, even when it assumed the form of dyspepsia, as a dispensation of Providence. The immediate effect of this affliction, however, was a smothered regret that Cordelia could not have accompanied them upon his second honeymoon. Not, of course, in Annabel's place. No, certainly not in Annabel's place; rather in the capacity of a ministering angel than of a wife.

After this irksome interlude, when a severe diet and the healing waters of Vichy had brought relief, they proceeded to England and Scotland, where Annabel began immediately to buy gifts for the people at home. Trailing her pensively from shop to shop in Bond Street, he reflected, with the salt of philosophy, that he had never observed her character in action until she started to spend money. Before her marriage she had been curbed by the lack of money to spend; and her quick recoil from severe economy to wild extravagance would have chilled the generous ardour of a husband who was less well off in material blessings. But he had come to recognize too clearly that his generosity was his strongest hold upon her affection to risk the hazardous enterprise of a remonstrance. Once only he had ventured, with a mild and playful firmness, to remind her of the trouble she was preparing for them in the tedious business of the customs. "Couldn't you buy some of these gifts in New York, darling? They would never suspect the difference."

And Annabel, who had bought gifts, not only for her mother and Cousin Amanda and her girl and boy friends and Altrusa and the postman, but for a number of old ladies in the Church Home, and for the sewing-woman, who had neuralgia, and for the grocer in the market, who was so considerate in the matter of bills, and for the charwoman, who had lost her only real comfort through prohibition,—Annabel, having remembered all these with passionate selection, replied emphatically: "But it wouldn't be the same thing. It wouldn't be the same thing at all. They want presents from Europe. It means so much more having presents brought you from Europe. Can't you see?"

No, he couldn't see; but since she could, he endeavoured to supplement with wisdom her more inspirational vision. It was, he had learned, as useless as it was disagreeable to argue across the disparity of two (or was it nearer three?) generations. After all, he earnestly desired but one thing, and this was to make her happy in her marriage. If spending money was the surest way to achieve this felicity, then he could only rejoice because he was provided with a bountiful income.

"But these shawls, dear, for the old ladies. You can easily find them in Fifth Avenue."

"But they're from Scotland. Don't you see what a difference it will make to them to have shawls from Scotland? That plaid, too, for the postman. Why, he was of the Gordon clan, and he came from Scotland long ago when Mother was a girl. The thing that will please him most is that I got it for him in Aberdeenshire."

With a sigh he surrendered; for he was a careful as well as a kind-hearted man, and the women he had known intimately had been both careful and kind-hearted. He had no precedent to guide him in dealing with a wife who spent money, not after calculation, but in obedience to mere flashes of impulse. Impulse, he realized now, was a quality with which Cordelia and Amanda had been but moderately endowed. Well, even at sixty-six (for already another birthday had been celebrated), and upon a second wedding journey, he had still a good deal to learn about women. The first essential in marriage, he told himself, was to maintain an equilibrium and let nothing astonish you.

And so, very much in love and fortified against astonishment, he heard with relief Annabel's declaration that she had finished her shopping and was ready to go home to show her things.

"I've seen almost everything," she said. "Of course, I enjoyed the galleries most, but, after all, you can't take the pictures home with you."

Fortunately not. Fortunately, indeed, few of the works of art that she admired most fervently were for sale to Americans.

"You've had a happy summer, dear?"

"Oh, wonderful! Think of what it means to see Europe for the first time."

"Then you've had no regrets?"

"Oh, no."

He had hoped for an impassioned disavowal. She might, he felt, have kissed him of her own accord after his question; but it was not Annabel's way to be demonstrative. A cold little thing, notwithstanding her artistic temperament, which he had imagined, from the stress placed upon it in the lives of the poets, inclined one to affection.

"If you have enjoyed it, that is all I can ask," he replied, a trifle hurt in spite of his equilibrium.

"Of course, I've enjoyed it. Any one would, seeing Europe so luxuriously. Why, most of the girls I know had to pinch terribly to come, except the ones who had the time of their lives in the war, and even then they didn't have any money for clothes or presents."

When all was said, perhaps her temperament was less artistic than her mother had led him to expect. Perhaps, he mused cheerfully, fostering the perennial hope that sprouts at marriage in every husband's heart, he had won that paragon of wives, a perfectly normal woman.

The perfectly normal woman, he knew, since he had already been united to one, was neither temperamental nor demonstrative; and though these qualities were attractive in courtship, he suspected that even men who fell in love with temperament were seldom happy with that aspect of it which makes trouble in marriage. For marriage is above all things practical, he realized, and temperament, however impressive in opera, does not adjust itself easily to the true sphere of woman. From which it is evident that, though he had married in the post-war period, he still thought in the primitive terms of a world which, like the Garden of Eden, was unaware of its own innocence.

CHAPTER 3

ILL you be glad to get home, Annabel?"

"Oh, I suppose so. Won't you?"

How glad, he had not realized until this moment; for, after the cure at Vichy, his dyspepsia was troubling him again, and looking at famous places and pictures had made him feel very tired. With his increasing infatuation, which marriage had not appeased, he convinced himself that, if only he could have Annabel safely at home with him, everything would be different. The old, dimly lighted house in Queenborough, which Cordelia had furnished so solidly in the formidable taste of the nineteenth century, where every chair or sofa invited one to rest upon its firm, plump seat, and Cordelia herself, upholstered like the rosewood furniture in handsome brocade, hung over the ebony what-not in the front parlour,—the recurrent memory of this old-fashioned house was like the tranquil asylum of a happy marriage. And so tenacious were the intricate roots which bound him to each bed and chair, as well as to his consecrated habits of comfort, that it never occurred to him to regard their home-coming from Annabel's variable point of view. He had never doubted, indeed, that her impetuous youth would settle easily into the feathered nest of the past.

"Don't you think you'd better not put up those heavy lace curtains again?" she inquired carelessly when they were discussing next winter in Queenborough.

He started and gazed at her with a look that was sharpened by anxiety. "Those curtains? Why, we've always used them. They were made for us in Brussels almost thirty years ago. It would be impossible to duplicate them to-day."

Annabel laughed. "Well, fortunately nobody will want to. Lace curtains have gone the way of crinolines."

The way of crinolines! The phrase shocked him, and for an instant he brought his mind steadily to bear upon its significance. For almost thirty years he had been inordinately proud of those curtains, and of the handsome carpets, also woven in Brussels, after a floral pattern which some offensive wit (Edmonia it must have been, for it sounded like her) had compared to an august funeral design. When he had bought them, they had cost a prodigious sum. He remembered the exact figures, and he remembered as well that Cordelia had devoted that summer in Europe to a consideration of the relative values of curtains and carpets. No, he would not change them now. He could not, he knew, be happy in a house that had been robbed of familiar objects and tender associations. How could he feel at home in his library unless he could settle again into the comfortable shape of the old leather cushions? Yes, he would be gentle and patient, but he would be firm too. Though he craved youth, it was the friendly yet adventurous youth of the 'eighties, not the sharp, wild spirit that was abroad, like a March wind, in the world today. None the less, he said fondly, "The house will be bright enough with you in it."

"Oh, yes. We'll have dinner parties and play bridge. You're fond of bridge?"

Yes, he was fond of bridge; but while she spoke, his mood flattened out until it was like a balloon that has been pricked. He had had a vision of his home unchanged but for the sparkling glamour of youth which would soon brighten the old-fashioned rooms. Though he longed for his usual chair by the fire, he could not separate this yearning from the picture of Annabel buried in the deep arms of ruby leather on the opposite side of the hearth. No, what he desired was that each object should remain where Cordelia had placed it, in the precise spot, unaltered in feature yet illumined in aspect by Annabel's girlish charm. Strange that he had never realized how he valued his familiar surroundings until they were threatened! He was not, he assured himself, what Cordelia would have called set in his ways. On the contrary, he was inclined to the belief that when a man becomes too firmly fixed in a place or an opinion, he is beginning to petrify. But his very peace was bound up with these inanimate objects among which his comfortable life had been spent; and he felt that, if only Annabel would spare his home, while adorning it with her presence, he would give way to her destructive youth in everything else.

"If only I can make you happy, darling," he sighed tenderly, as he had sighed upon their wedding day and in every subsequent crisis.

They were on their return voyage, and while she leaned over the railing of the deck, she gazed out to sea with an expression that puzzled him. Was it wistfulness in her eyes, or merely the despondency of a bad sailor? Since he was never seasick (having acquired by long experience the technique of prevention) and she had been desperately ill, her suffering had made her dependent upon him in a way that he enjoyed even while he pitied her. The privilege of nursing instead of being nursed was worth all the deprivations and discomforts of shipboard.

"Oh, I know we'll have a nice time next winter," she responded carelessly; and turning swiftly, she smiled at him with her springtime glance. She was always sweet to him now, though her thoughtless affection was entirely different from the earnest solicitude he had learned to expect from women.

As she leaned over the railing, where the sea dipped and rose, her profile was cut with gemlike clearness against the translucent gold of the horizon. Seasickness had imparted a charming languor to her features, which had paled to the colour of ivory; and, while it lasted, her beauty was endowed with what he thought of as the enchantment of legend. From the collar of dark fur, her bright head sprang up, as sharp and delicate as a March flower from winter soil; beneath the sable toque, the soft waves of her hair flamed to copper in the sinking beams of the sun; her seagreen eyes, when she glanced round at him, were veiled in mystery. (After all, what did he know of her except that she was young and desirable? What did he wish to know of her except that her youth and her desirableness were his own?) There was the look in her face that he had surprised there once or twice since their marriage—a look which he would have called noble and earnest, if these fine words were not, he felt, inapplicable to Annabel's character.

With one of those piercing flashes of insight, which afflict even the best minds in moments of tragic intensity, he told himself that he had been abandoned by youth while his thirst for life was unsatisfied. His heart contracted in a spasm of yearning, and then shuddered back to its stoical melancholy. What he saw in Annabel, he realized, was more than her loveliness, was more even than her inaccessible spirit. What he saw in her was all the assembled beauty of the world, as a whole universe of sea and sky and sun is mirrored within the magic crystal of a ring. While he looked at her, he became aware of a multitude of forgotten influences thronging into his thoughts. These he knew he could never escape, for they flowed, like a distilled essence of the past, from his memory into his blood.

"Annabel," he asked suddenly, "have you any regrets?"

"Regrets?" Swiftly, as if his question had arrested the flight of her mind, she sparkled into derision. "What should I regret? Haven't we had a nice summer?" She looked down, stroking her fur, and her lips, which were paler than usual, curved into a smile.

"I was just wondering——" he began, and broke off with a sensation of helplessness, of disappointment. He could not tell for what he had longed, but he knew that it was for more than this; and, turning, he looked away from her with an illogical feeling that he had lost something he had never possessed. What was the meaning of it? Where was it leading him? Why should this will-o'-the-wisp have flamed in the long twilight of his heart, after he had left the sunshine of youth and passion so far behind him? Were they merely the inevitable processes of decay, this fire without heat, this greenness without roots, or had he alone been selected to suffer the torment of a fruitless regeneration?

And, after all, why was he not happy, when he held the radiant material of happiness within his grasp?

"Yes, we had a nice summer," he answered, and felt the surging of an inarticulate impulse against his lips. When all was said and thought about emotion, it remained, he told himself, merely a single province, a shifting and variegated province, of man's nature. Once at home again, with the restless pleasures of Europe behind him; once at home again, where he could eat bread and milk for dinner without feeling that he made a spectacle of himself before superior foreign waiters; once at home again, with Annabel settled in Cordelia's chair by the fire and on Cordelia's side of the bed;—once blissfully at home again, he would soon find that life had narrowed into a familiar and orderly pattern. His library, his club, his Archæological Society, his distinguished position in the community, and his church, of which he was a vestryman,—all these solid advantages were unaltered by the moral disturbances through which he had passed. Nevertheless, in his heart, he knew that, though these upheavals had been more painful than pleasant, he dreaded the moment when the effervescence would subside on the dull surface of life. Annabel, like youth itself, was a source of frustrated impulses and fruitless desires, but she was also the last thing on earth he would consent to relinquish. Illogical, absurd in the extreme, and unworthy of the judicial mind; yet wanting what was bad for one had been, he acknowledged, the private history of most minds, judicial or otherwise.

T THE end of the week, as Mrs. Upchurch sat at breakfast one morning, and reflected, while she poured her coffee, that her daughter's marriage must have been a success since the Judge was so generous in the matter of her own summer at White Sulphur Springs, there was a running step on the porch, and a minute later, a fashionable and sophisticated Annabel darted into the room.

"Oh, Mother, I ran over just to speak to you!"

"My dear child, my dear child!" cried Mrs. Upchurch, embracing her.

"We got here an hour ago, and I had to wait until the Judge had finished his breakfast. Why do men hate so to breakfast alone?"

"I don't know, darling, but is he still 'the Judge' to you?"

Annabel laughed. "I feel impertinent when I call him 'Gamaliel.'"

"Well, as long as he doesn't mind. Isn't it queer how conventions change? I remember, and I'm not so old, when no well-bred Virginia woman would have taken the liberty of calling her husband by his Christian name."

"That's one liberty I shouldn't fight for. Have you finished breakfast?"

"No, I was just taking my second cup. Have you had yours, dear?"

"Yes, but I'd like one of Altrusa's muffins."

"My darling child!" Though Mrs. Upchurch, who was natural only when she was artificial, could think of nothing more expressive than an ejaculation, she was genuinely moved by the return of her daughter. "Bring Miss Annabel a hot muffin, Altrusa," she ordered, and added with difficulty, "Come, sit down, dear, and I'll fix your coffee as you like it. Why, you look almost like an actress. I mean, of course, a very successful one— or perhaps an opera singer would be better. Well, I must say, I am never astonished at what marriage can do!"

"It isn't marriage, Mother," Annabel rejoined with the sincerity she had preserved beneath her external French artifice. "It is Paris and having so much money to spend."

Rising like a trout to bait, Mrs. Upchurch caught at the correction. "Well, I am still less astonished at what money can do."

"I've brought you the loveliest fur coat, Mother. Mink that will be so becoming to you and last for years. And I got you a dress in Paris. Black velvet, with a little ermine at the neck and sleeves. I bought presents for everybody."

"My dear, my precious child!" There was really nothing to add, Mrs. Upchurch felt, wiping her eyes. "My best gift will be your happiness. What have you done to your hair? Not bobbed it?"

"No, but I try to make it look as if I had. I was ever so keen to bob it, only men are so set in their ideas about hair. Old men especially," she added as an afterthought.

"All men are set, Annabel. But that little blue hat is adorable on you, and your furs are so becoming. I don't believe any of us realized before how lovely you are."

"Isn't it wonderful what clothes can do for you?"

"But you couldn't look so well if you weren't happy," insisted Mrs. Upchurch, who had not lost sight for an instant of the thing that she really wished to know.

Annabel raised her eyes from her plate and looked at her mother, while a smile that was gay, mocking, and a little wistful played over the rich curves of her mouth. From a fresh and pretty girl, she had blossomed, Mrs. Upchurch decided proudly, into a beautiful woman. Not so beautiful, of course, as poor Amanda, who was merely the wreck of herself now, but cer-

tainly more interesting. Everything about Annabel appeared to
be brightened by a shining glaze; her coppery hair, with its lustrous tints, which had been chestnut; her alabaster skin, which
had been merely pale and pretty; her radiant eyes, which had
become larger and deeper and mysteriously shadowed by her
darkened lashes. Yes, it was indeed wonderful, Mrs. Upchurch
mused, it was little short of miraculous, what money could do.

"Is anybody happy, Mother?"

Mrs. Upchurch shivered, for this was not what she had expected. "Not many, my child. Most people are afraid of the
word happiness; but I hope it is different with you."

Annabel shook her head. "I don't believe much in happiness.
People just pretend because they're ashamed not to, that's all.
But even money can't buy happiness. All it can buy is the best
substitute, and that's a sham like everything else."

"Oh, my dear baby," moaned her mother, "there are times
when you talk as if you'd lived always. You frighten me when
you are so serious."

"I'm not so serious; but I never wanted a sham, and sometimes
I think there isn't anything else in life."

"Is anything wrong? Hasn't your marriage turned out well,
dear? You needn't pretend to your mother."

Annabel pondered the question, while her winged eyebrows
fluttered together as they did when she was brooding. "To tell
the truth, it isn't so bad as I thought it would be," she answered,
and continued, after a pause in which Mrs. Upchurch beamed
encouragingly: "But there's too much fondling in it. I believe
marriage must be better in winter than in summer."

"Men are like that, even the nicest men. He may grow less
affectionate," Mrs. Upchurch added hopefully, "though at his
age you never can tell."

Annabel laughed, and the flippancy of her tone grated upon
her mother's delicate hearing. "I've heard you say a hundred
times, Mother, that youth and age never match."

"Oh, my child!" exclaimed Mrs. Upchurch, horrified beyond

words to hear herself quoted with such inopportune accuracy. "That was before—before——"

"Yes, of course, that was before I had an old husband."

"But, Annabel, the Judge isn't really old, you know. After all, sixty-six is only the prime of life for a man."

Again Annabel laughed. "And, I suppose, twenty-three is only the prime of life for a woman?"

It was all disquieting; it was all most unfortunate, Mrs. Upchurch meditated, with a smiling face but an anxious heart. Never, not even when her own husband was alive, had she felt so urgently the need of a strong moral support. Religion, yes, but even more than religion, she craved the efficacious belief in reticence, in refinement, in perfect behaviour. If the world continued to grow away, not only from God, but from good breeding as well, what, she wondered despondently, could be trusted to keep wives contented and the working classes in order?

"You will be happier after you are settled," she said in as sprightly a tone as she could assume. "We must try to make the house more cheerful, especially those old drawing-rooms, which I always thought depressing."

"But he is so particular, he doesn't want me to touch anything. He won't even give up those horrid lace curtains."

"Then you must go slowly." Mrs. Upchurch changed her advice quickly, though her tone was as animated as ever. "Be careful to go very, very slowly. So many second marriages are spoiled by the wife's trying to change too much."

"Oh, I don't care about that," Annabel rejoined carelessly. "He may choose to live in a museum of bad taste, if he pleases." She rose, and stooping over her mother's shoulder, kissed her lightly on the cheek. "I must show you my linen. I bought the most wonderful linen, and embroidery too. Now, I must run away because I promised to be back to kiss him before he goes down to his office at half-past nine. Could anything be more absurd," she demanded, with airy insolence, "than to be obliged to cross the street and walk two whole blocks just to keep a man in a good humour by kissing him before he goes to work?"

"Could anything?" Mrs. Upchurch echoed earnestly. Gazing after her daughter's flitting figure in the street, she finished absent-mindedly but emphatically, "Could anything be more absurd?"

ORTUNATELY, as Judge Honeywell found occasion to remind himself in the next few months, the waters of Vichy had enabled him to begin the winter with an improved digestion. Otherwise, how could he have survived the exhausting pleasure of dining out every night in the week? Recently, too, especially when a dance followed the dinner, he had fortified his spirit against boredom by drinking more champagne than was good for his joints. To be sure, he had always indulged his thirst with the grace of a Cavalier rather than the austerity of a Puritan, though he had wisely abstained from the more frivolous, or, as he thought of them, more feminine French wines. Now, however, he decided that the French, who had aged gallantly, knew what they were doing. Only champagne with a genuine sparkle provided the sprightly optimism required for an evening in the placid society of chaperons. Here also, he caught himself reflecting, was another advantage gained by his discreet retirement from the bench; for he could not have reconciled his conscience either to drinking while he judged others or to administering what he (being of independent means and superior to politics) could afford to regard as a caricature of the law. With the more affluent part of Queenborough society (which had reduced its fortunes but stocked its cellars in the uncivilized pre-war days, before the bootlegger had developed from an outlaw into an institution), he regarded prohibition, without fear and without hope, as a piece of paternal legislation, designed less for the benefit of inebriate wife-beaters than to satisfy the philanthropic thirst of modern Pharaohs of industry. "Prohibition without temperance may be a dangerous extreme,"

he remarked facetiously, "but dangerous extremes make interesting history."

In his dancing days, before he was married to Cordelia, who
had disapproved among other things of trying to stay young, he
had wasted scant sympathy upon the rows of indomitable ma-
trons flanked against the draughty end of the ballroom. But now,
while he suffered politely among them, he was moved to wonder
if they also had discovered that necessity is the reluctant mother
of endurance. On the floor, perennially flirtatious and recklessly
nimble, he seldom failed to remark several agile septuagenarians,
whom he had known as dashing blades while he was still a boy.
Watching their starved faces and their desperate trotting, he
longed passionately to be at home by his library fire; yet he refused to leave Annabel whirling among the dancers like a flower
in the wind. At their first cotillion, they had created between
them the sentimental fiction that it gave him pleasure to watch
her success with the inconstant youth of the period.

"Don't you get tired sitting against the wall, Gamaliel?" At
last she was learning to call him "Gamaliel."

"Not when I'm watching you, dear."

"But to watch me the whole evening! And at the cotillions
you can't even play bridge."

"Well, there aren't many cotillions. At the private houses I
can usually make up a game with other husbands or wives who
are in the same plight. I never noticed it before, but it appears to
be a familiar plight for husbands and wives."

"I wonder," Annabel said thoughtfully, "why women who
love to dance so often marry men who don't?"

"And men who like poker so often marry women who prefer
bridge?"

"Isn't there anybody you enjoy talking to? Cousin Amanda
comes regularly, you know, though she has given up dancing."

"Yes, but she was never a great talker." His face clouded, for
he shrank, without admitting it, from the thought of Amanda.

"She looks so sad. I'm afraid she is beginning to break," Annabel returned, with a worried frown. "Every one says she is the wreck of herself."

To this he made no reply; but finding himself beside his early love at the Christmas cotillion, he looked at her more attentively than he remembered looking in the last thirty years. Yes, it was true; she was simply, poor lady, the wreck of herself; and he wondered sadly, with that evasive idealism which had become a second nature to him, and indeed to the entire community in which he lived, if her numerous charities were not making too heavy demands upon her strength? Her fine silver-grey hair was thinner and appeared faintly yellow in the blaze of light; there were bluish hollows in her temples and beneath her eyes; and her complexion had lost its transparent glow and blanched to the colour of a withered rose-leaf. Worst of all, he felt, there was a look in her eyes that he could describe only as deserted. It couldn't be romance, he insisted defiantly to himself. For surely no woman approaching sixty would permit herself to cling to a romantic illusion.

"The dances have changed so much since our day," Amanda said suddenly.

He started, for her voice might have come from the past. "Yes, they've changed," he answered gently, almost tenderly, since tenderness was safe now. "But not, according to my taste, for the better."

"No, the old ones were certainly more graceful." She smiled, and he was pained to see the wrinkles about her mouth deepen like an impression in wax. "Except with Annabel," she added generously. "Annabel couldn't be anything but graceful."

While he listened to her voice, looking away from her after Annabel's rose-coloured skirt, which tossed and whirled and fluttered in accord with the music, he became aware that a pleasant sensation was permeating his weariness, as if he were enfolded in wings of beatitude. Just to sit beside Amanda, without seeing her changed features, just to hear the monotonous music of her voice talking of trivial things, restored to him, like a precious gift she had saved for this one moment, the security, the self-confidence that he had felt slipping away. Without an effort of his own, this soothing and beneficent influence enveloped him. Beside Amanda, he was no longer elderly, for his being old had never entered her faithful mind. Sitting there, while her muted tones rippled on, he felt that her sympathy filtered into his consciousness and pervaded his reverie. With her, he had not only a past but a future, because she had never thought of him, she could never think of him, as finished. Fragments of dreams, of defeated ambitions, started again to life in his memory. The book he had intended to write; the struggle for political freedom which had seemed so important; all the splendid lost causes of which he had once been the champion! If only it were not now too late! If only he could begin anew with Annabel by his side! If only this rhythm of precious influences could encircle Annabel instead of Amanda! For while he longed for the inspiration of Amanda's fidelity, he longed even more to have it flow through the delightful vacancy of Annabel's youth.

"I sometimes wonder," he heard his voice murmur, "if I might have amounted to more if I hadn't spent my life in a small place?"

"Amounted to more?" The lilt in her tone flattered him. "Why, what more could you have been?"

"Well, I don't know." This was true; for he had spoken in a twilight pause between waking and sleeping. Since he was not of an introspective cast of mind, he could not have told where circumstances had failed him, or where he had refused to yield himself to the adventure of life. A veiled motive, a wisp of idea, had prompted his words; yet beneath these vagrant shadows, so far below the surface of his thoughts that it groped there in a primeval void, he felt the quiver of some exalted purpose which had been frustrated before its birth. Was it possible that, in other circumstances, he might have made a larger or finer thing of his endeavour? After all, what could have satisfied this voiceless craving? Not ambition; not achievement; not marriage; not fatherhood. Though he had been successful, as men value success, he had never burned inwardly with that triumph over obstacles which is its lasting reward. Though he had loved three women, he had never thrilled to the Olympian ecstasy—or was it merely the Hungarian rhapsody?—of passion. Though he had begotten children he had missed (by how fine an edge? he wondered) the inalienable pride of paternity. Happiness, as he looked back upon it in this mood (and he was sensible enough to admit that his dissatisfaction was only a mood) resembled some trick of magic which had failed to work when it was tried.

Out of these subdued influences and emanations, he became aware that Amanda was still speaking.

"And you never wrote the great book on law we used to talk over." Thirty-seven years ago, and she had not forgotten! What long, what unconscionable memories women had for emotion!

"No, I never wrote it. I don't know why. Time passed, I suppose, and I was busy making a career. Sometimes I think that I have been too comfortable all my life. I've had two of the best wives in the world," he added dutifully, "and they have made me too comfortable."

"But you were happy?"

"Happy? Yes, I've had a happy life. Perhaps that is one of the reasons I didn't write my book. I doubt if a great book, even on law, was ever written by a really happy man."

"Well, I waited for it. I always hoped you would write it," she said softly; for she belonged to a devoted generation, and her only hold on life was to exist vicariously, as some pale ethereal fluid, in the lives of others. What had nourished her heart, he wondered sadly, since she had missed the vital joys of marriage and motherhood? And why had she never married when every unattached man in Queenborough for two generations had proposed to her as a part of his culture! Then, because he had never acquired the new habit of thinking of women as detached beings, he returned with alacrity to his own failure of purpose.

"I suppose there are few men who accomplish all that they dream of," he rejoined mildly. "Annabel has torn her dress again, hasn't she?"

The girl was dancing in their direction while she held up the ripped hem of her rose-coloured skirt. As she drifted toward him, with her loosened hair, her geranium mouth, and her winged eyebrows, which brooded over the virginal mystery of her gaze, his longing to put his hands on her was so sharp that he drew back as if he had been stung by her beauty.

"A RE you ready to go home?" he asked in a muffled voice. Peace had flown now, he realized dimly, without regretting his loss. He was snatched back from the harmony of Amanda's influence into a circle of vehement discords, and it seemed to him that this confusion in which he was so swiftly immersed flowed, not from his own nature, but from the magnetic current of Annabel's youth. He felt her radiant energy, her joy of living, her joy even of suffering, less as a stimulus to his mind and heart than as a dangerous intoxication of the nerves, a destructive yet irresistible stream of vitality.

"Not before supper? You aren't going before supper?" she asked in surprise. "Unless you're tired. If you're tired, I'll get somebody else to bring me home."

"Oh, no, I'm not tired. I'll wait for you," he answered. Nothing could induce him to leave her; nothing could persuade him to go home alone. Still he sat there, with stoical fortitude, though it seemed to him that he had never in his life before understood what fatigue could mean. Ever since his return from Europe, he had felt tired without relief, and now this exhaustion of the nerves was approaching a crisis. Abroad he had not been working, and there had been quiet days, and even nights, when he had had brief relaxations from uncongenial pleasure. But ever since his return, this incessant weariness had stolen over him like a lethargy. He desired nothing intensely but Annabel, and he desired her only in brief flares of emotion.

While she floated away from him now, Amanda inquired gently, "Do you grow tired of just watching?"

"Oh, no, it is a pleasure," he answered punctiliously, though his voice throbbed like an aching nerve in his ears. He had lost again the inspiring belief that life was not over, and he knew that it would elude him now until his mind was at rest. The unwilling chaperon on his right opened her bag, after a furtive glance in his direction, and turned to snatch a view of her hair in the long mirror on the wall. Looking over her shoulder, while he rose to return the scarf she had dropped, he saw the upper half of his own features reflected; and it seemed to him that a caged eagle gazed back at him from his bright dark eyes— a spirit, restless, craving, eternally unsatisfied, yet with a wild comedy in its despair. Perhaps, after all, the fault lay in himself, not in circumstances. Perhaps he had been too easily contented in his prime with the second best of experience. Perhaps he had skimmed too lightly over the glazed surface of inherited wisdom.

With a sardonic twist, while his eyes followed Annabel, his mind sprang back to Cordelia. It occurred to him as extraordinary that he could remember Cordelia with vividness only when he was indignant with Annabel. A flash of temper was the solitary gleam that illumined Cordelia's features, and this magic worked, he had discovered, only when the flash was directed toward the wife he now loved in her place. Singular, almost incredible, he mused, was the way Cordelia had become alive in his mind after that painful scene with Annabel over his wardrobe. A trivial episode. Over and forgotten in an hour, with nothing to remind him that it had ever occurred, unless his eyes fell by accident upon the fine emerald ring, which Annabel preferred even to her engagement ring with its magnificent diamond. He was convinced that the emerald had erased all resentment from her memory; and in his own mind it had left merely the wonder how he could have lived for thirty-six years and never quarrelled with Cordelia. Was it because she had been more tactful, or he had been less confirmed in his habits? She had given him, it was true, the handsome mahogany wardrobe, which Annabel had offended him by removing from his dressing-room, but he had scarcely remembered the association in his violent recoil from the strange object he had found in its place.

"What? What?" he had gasped at sight of the new cabinet

between the two side windows, where he liked to take one last look at his hair and beard before going downstairs. "Why, where are all my things? I must have my things where I can put my hands on them."

"It is a surprise for you," Annabel explained, flushed and excited. "I had it made after the one you liked at the Ritz."

"But that was at the Ritz. I didn't mean that I should like it for my own dressing-room. I didn't want it in my own house."

"Well, it's ever so much nicer," insisted Annabel, who, unlike Cordelia, could never be satisfied to regain by act what she had surrendered in argument. "Nobody uses those heavy old wardrobes any longer. You have plenty of shelves."

"It has always stood there." He was beginning to lose control of his temper; and Annabel, instead of holding firmly to hers, as Cordelia would have done, was rapidly approaching the point where she would burst into tears. "I want it here between the windows, where I can find my things when I need them. You must understand, once and for all, Annabel, that I cannot have my arrangements interfered with. A wife must learn, as well as a husband, to bear and forbear. I have borne patiently a good many things, and if our marriage is to be a happy one, it is time that you should at least begin to forbear. I have let you make as many changes as you pleased in your own sitting-room and even downstairs; but you must keep your hands away from my personal comforts. . . ."

Since he was just beginning to feel thoroughly wound up, he might have continued indefinitely in this strain, if Annabel had not choked with a paroxysm of rage, and cried out furiously that she did not want to be married, and that if he were unkind to her, she would go home to live with her mother. Her tears, even more than her words, which were too incoherent to be convincing, brought him to his senses; and when she fled from him into the guest-room and locked the door, he followed ignominiously, and protested through the keyhole that he had not meant to hurt her feelings.

A regrettable, a most humiliating occurrence! For the reconciliation, though it had restored the wardrobe to its sacred use, had endowed Annabel, not only with an advantage that she did not deserve, but with the emerald ring she had seen and admired upon her last visit to Tiffany's. . . .

It was two o'clock when they went home, and sitting with his arm about her, as they sped through the silent streets, he wondered how he could gather sufficient energy to face his work in the morning. A chill of depression benumbed his faculties, and he scarcely responded to the pale glow of Annabel's head against the light of the window-pane. He hoped, without intensity, that she would be affectionate or at least gentle when they reached home. After the tedious emptiness of his evening, he felt that he had earned a right to her tenderness.

When the car stopped, she alighted with a dancing step and tripped gaily into the house.

"Do you want anything, Gamaliel?"

"No, dear. I'll get to bed as soon as possible."

"Is your dyspepsia bad again? I can fix you some hot water and soda in a minute."

"I don't need that. I'm a little tired, that's all. Shall I put out the light?"

She had already reached the top of the steps, and by the time he had attended to the doors and windows, and followed her upstairs, she had slipped out of her gown into a flame-coloured kimono. When he entered the bedroom, her hands were busy with the jewelled band on her hair, and in a moment the short, bright curls were floating in a veil over her shoulders.

"I hope you had a happy evening, darling," he said tenderly. Could she, he asked himself, hear without sympathy the hunger that quivered beneath the guarded tones of his voice?

"Oh, I enjoyed it. It passes the time anyway," she answered, after a pause; and he felt that to her also the spoken words were as meaningless as leaves drifting on the surface of some dark stream of memory. He longed with all his suffering heart to draw nearer to her; his remoteness, while he stood there and watched her, was almost intolerable; yet he knew that no word, that no embrace, could bridge that dark current flowing between them.

"You don't think you are doing too much?"

She laughed. "Oh, no, but it is dreary for you. Why didn't you come home earlier and let some one else bring me back?"

He shook his head. How could he tell her? How could he make her understand why he had waited, why he had clung to that jealous sense of possession which tortured him when he saw her dancing with younger men?

"Oh, I like watching you dance," he replied, with a curious ache in his throat. "It is a very pretty sight."

She smiled back at him from the mirror; and it seemed to him that this reflected smile floated out from the glass and melted into his being with a burning radiance. Youth shone through her in the glow of some hidden flame; through her misty eyes, through her gleaming hair, through her ivory shoulders above the drooping sleeves of her kimono. For an instant his heart leaped, and the violence of the shock almost suffocated him. Then, in the very gesture of putting out his hand to touch her bare shoulder, the flash of desire went out of him like an extinguished light. He felt nothing but this inescapable loneliness, and the thought stabbed through him: "She will look this way when I am dead!"

Turning slightly in her chair, she folded the loosened garment over her bosom. "Do you feel better?" she asked sympathetically. "Have you got over the chill?"

"Oh, yes. I'm quite comfortable now." Of this inner frost, creeping like death over his mind, he said nothing. "All I need is a good sleep."

"Perhaps I'd better stay in the other room?" she rejoined quickly but softly, as if she were warding off a refusal by her gentleness. "I'm not ready. There's ever so much more to do before I'm undressed, and I don't want to keep you awake."

"But I love to have you near me. It is a comfort to know that you are there." His voice faltered because he could not put into words the way he had looked forward to the hours when he should have her alone in the friendly darkness. Only her unconquerable youth protected him from the fantasies that hovered in the twilight region of consciousness. Yet he could not put this into any speech that she would understand. "You don't know how much it means to me——" Assailed by a new suspicion, he broke off and added slowly: "Do you mean just for to-night?" Was it merely that she preferred to be alone, asked this sudden fear, or was the nearness that he found so comforting repugnant to her untarnished youth? Had he been repugnant to her from the beginning? He longed in an agony of suspense to know the reason of her avoidance; but he knew that it was a secret he could never discover.

"If you don't mind, just for to-night?" While she waited expectantly for his consent or refusal, a breathless hush dropped over her features in the mirror. Through this hush he felt—or was it only an imaginary torment?—the throbbing pulse of her aversion.

"I want you with me, but——" Could she fail to hear the cry of pain beneath the commonplace words?

"I'll keep you awake, and, besides, I must sleep late to-morrow." In her eagerness, there was no room for sympathy, no room for the thought of any longing except her own. With the unconscious cruelty of innocence, she devoured whatever crossed the flowery path of her egoism.

Wounded yet unresentful, he smiled down on her; and accepting his smile as an unspoken consent, she raised herself on tiptoe and offered him one of her light kisses, which brushed his eager lips with the wings of a butterfly. Then, as he made a despairing grasp at her, she slipped away from his outstretched arms and across the floor to the adjoining room. When she had passed out, she closed the door behind her, and an instant afterwards he saw an edge of light flicker dimly along the threshold. That edge of light entered his heart like a blade, and while the chill of age or of death crept over his senses, he walked to the front window and looked beyond the sleeping city into a darkness which was merely the shadow of his own isolation. In the street below, a car stopped, and he heard over vast fields of silence the ringing cadence of happiness.

"Good-night! It was so beautiful."

"I shall see you again soon. Good-night!"

"Good-night!"

"Good-night!"

A door opened and shut, and the car rolled on into the city. But for hours after he went to bed, those gay young voices echoed across the encompassing desolation.

N THE morning he awoke with a cough, and before night, Dr. Buchanan had pronounced his ailment bronchitis.

"You've been overdoing it a bit. Better stay in bed for a day or two."

"There are important matters at the office."

"No matter is so important as keeping well. You are falling a trifle below your standard, Gamaliel. This is what happens when you begin to neglect your golf."

"Yes, I got out of the habit last summer. Annabel plays tennis. It is strange the hold habit gets over you." Though he spoke cheerfully between his spells of wheezing, he felt tired and old —older than he imagined he should feel for the next twenty years. His features, above the youthful pink and white stripes of his pajamas, looked as if they were modelled in clay.

"Well, you mustn't let yourself get flabby. I never saw you in better shape than you were last spring. Europe didn't agree with you as well as it used to, eh?"

"No, the food was bad. All that French stuff is apt to upset you. You can't even order an egg and have it served as God or nature intended. I can't see where the French got their reputation," he added brusquely, for he had never been just to that interesting and versatile people.

Annabel, who had been arranging her hair for the evening, was wrapped in her flame-coloured kimono; and from her perch on the foot of the bed, she remarked brightly, "But Vichy did wonders for him."

At her voice, the Judge turned his head on the pillow, while a flush enlivened the sombre gravity of his face. "Oh, yes, I was all right after that," he assented. "You must break my engagements for the next few days, Annabel; but don't give up any of your parties just because I'm under the weather. It isn't anything to make a fuss about."

"I sha'n't mind a bit staying at home," she answered sweetly. "I shouldn't think of leaving you until you are able to be downstairs in your library."

The flush in the Judge's face increased to a burning red, which filled his eyes with a suffusion of happiness. There was pride in the glance he raised to Dr. Buchanan's jovial countenance. Had his old friend noticed how attentive his young wife was to him and how lovely she looked in her gay kimono, with the cloud of coppery hair on her shoulders?

"Oh, you needn't worry, Annabel," returned Dr. Buchanan, who was more encouraging than tactful. "You aren't going to lose him so soon."

"Yes, don't give up your engagements, dear," the Judge urged tenderly, consoled by the thought that she had offered voluntarily to stay at home with him. "As a matter of fact, I'm quite fit, but Buchanan is getting a bit fussy, and I may as well give in to him." He had learned by now that Annabel was one of those charming women who could make a smile or a single graceful gesture conceal a multitude of defects. Even to his uxorious mind, it appeared absurd that so trivial a sacrifice should make him contented just to lie in bed and remember, between spasms of coughing, how happy he was in his marriage.

For the next week, while he kept to his bed, he saw only, and that with feeble rapture, the best side of Annabel's nature. Though she was childishly incompetent as a nurse, the very brightness of her presence, the warmth and glow of her sympathy, made his sick-room more agreeable than it had ever been in the days of Cordelia's efficient care. Provided, of course, that he was not in danger, it was more beneficial, he felt, to follow Annabel with his eyes, while she moved about making mistakes, than to have his medicine administered at regular hours and his broth prepared by an angel from heaven, even though that angel were as capable as Cordelia. Discomfort, linked so long with unhappiness in his mind, made scarcely an impression upon his grateful serenity. Just watching Annabel when she ran in at night, after hearing him cough, with the flame-coloured kimono slipping carelessly away from her bosom and her rosy feet tucked into velvet mules—just watching her was better for him than the most expert attention.

While he remained an invalid, thinking first of his own health and making only the impersonal demands of a patient, Annabel was as kind to him as he could desire. All day she flitted about his room, intent upon her childish ministrations, forgetting to shut the door, though he had tried to teach her that it made a draught on his head when she left it ajar; reading to him in an interested voice all the parts of the newspaper he invariably skipped; reciting with animation the extravagant gossip she had heard over the telephone. It was natural, perhaps, since she had never been ill and Mrs. Upchurch was as remarkable for her constitution as for her character, that Annabel should not have learned what sounds and sights distract the nerves of an invalid; yet in spite of her too redundant vitality and the unnecessary noise she made in the room, she had never been more lovable to him that she was while he was dependent upon her care. In those few days he grew to understand her nature as he had never understood it, even in the hours when he had felt closest to her in affection. There are women, he had always known (having a wide theoretical knowledge of character) who, though virtuous by instinct, recognize no ultimate authority beyond emotion. These women, he had dimly surmised, might have their own exalted standards, however conflicting they appeared to a balanced mind where sober reason was in the ascendant. He was beginning now to suspect that Annabel, whose opinions were merely organized prejudices, might be led by her devious impulses to unerring decisions. But even when she was most moral in conduct, it saddened him to reflect how little abstract morality was contained in her motives. In the deeper phases of thought, she was, he perceived, occasionally noble but always unethical. The wisdom of the ages had left her, not only unimpressed, but defiant; and she still remained, after marriage, a pure experimentalist in behaviour. On the few occasions when he had been tempted to invoke the Stern Daughter of the voice of God, he had refrained because of a suspicion that duty was esteemed by her as little as Wordsworth was read. To Judge Honeywell, whose faith, however flexible, was triumphant over logic (who could recite the Apostles' Creed so long as he was not required to practise the Sermon on the Mount, and could countenance Evolution until it threatened the image of its Maker), to this perfect pattern of the conventional mind, it appeared that all women, except Cordelia, inhabited some misty area between inspiration and lunacy. Whenever he argued with Annabel (which was seldom, though not so seldom as he wished it had been) he felt that he was entangled in some exquisite cobweb of unreason. Yet, in her peculiar fashion, she possessed intelligence of a high order. He was astonished by the ease with which she contrived, in the absence of logic, to reach accurate conclusions. After forty years of social life and the law courts, where his acquaintance with human nature had comprised the standard types one encounters at dinner parties and at the bar of justice, he was scarcely prepared for the swiftness of Annabel's flashes of insight. Well, after all, it was not for her intelligence, it was not for her character, that he had loved her. It was not even for her kindness, though she had proved to him that, when he demanded nothing, she could be as kind as a daughter or a sister. What he loved her for was this unfulfilled promise of ecstasy which had become less a balm than a sword in his heart.

On the day when he came downstairs for the first time, Annabel's attentions began to wane, and after an evening or two with a book in front of the fire, he discovered that she was drooping from suppressed weariness. Reading was evidently better for one than for two, especially when the reading was so divided.

"You must begin going out again, Annabel," he said, after

a period of deliberation. "I shall probably be kept indoors for another week or so. If I am able to go down to the office for a few hours every day, it will be as much as I expect."

"But you will be lonely," Annabel protested, though she brightened visibly.

"Not a bit of it. I can always amuse myself. When I learned my letters, people were taught to read without skipping."

"How dreadful!" she exclaimed, and then, "Perhaps somebody will come in to play chess with you. I'll ask sister Edmonia to dinner." Animation sparkled in her eyes, and from a mood of depression, she kindled into liveliness.

"Oh, I can take care of myself. I shouldn't bother about Edmonia. She will drop in of her own accord when she feels like it."

"Then how about Major Bedgebury? He plays a good game of chess, doesn't he?"

"Average, only average. You needn't worry about asking him."

Even in his youth, Judge Honeywell had been a reserved man, of few intimacies, and after his marriage, Cordelia had never encouraged the casual caller at meal hours. There are not many friendships, he had concluded, that can be cemented without the durable bond of food and drink, or perhaps those he had formed had not been of that independent order.

"Well, how about Mother? You enjoy her."

"Yes, I can say truthfully that it is a pleasure to talk to a sensible woman like your mother."

The very thought of Mrs. Upchurch restored the lost flavour of life. He had spent an evening with her in front of the fire, while Annabel attended a rehearsal of the Little Theatre League, and that evening still shone with a tranquil light in his recollection. Cheerful, pretty, adroit in conversation and indefatigable in flattery, there could be no more delightful companion to a man who had left the vortex of emotion behind him. Unlike Annabel, she always agreed with his decisions, and, unlike Cordelia, she never failed to see the point of his jokes. For hours, she could twitter merrily in her discreet and entertaining fashion; for she was too wise ever to be original and too tactful ever to argue. To the Judge, who was tolerant of any views that were not brought into vocal conflict with his own, there was refreshment in a mind so sprightly that it was not troubled by convictions. It was comforting, too, he told himself, in this unwholesome and indecorous period, to find a woman who was neither infested with public virtues nor puffed up with repressions. Yes, when all was said, he had, however inadvertently, selected an ideal mother-in-law, one whose character was still as normal and trim as her figure.

"I'll see if she can come to-morrow evening," Annabel said, and there was buoyant relief in her tone. "Mary Percy is giving a dinner dance, and if you're sure you won't be lonely, I'd rather not disappoint her."

He smiled at her over his book, cheered by the change in her voice, even though his judgment warned him that it was dear at the sacrifice he had made. Over his lowered spectacles, he could see her burnished head, like November leaves in the sunlight, and beyond it a mirror disclosed his own blanched and silvery reflection, with the discoloured patches beneath the eyes and the corded and stringy throat between the high points of his collar. Was it only beside Annabel, he wondered, that he looked so much older, or had he really aged ten years since his attack of bronchitis?

"You must go, dear," he said. "You must not let me stand in your way." But he was thinking: "Exercise. That is what I am feeling the need of. Six months ago, when I got my golf regularly, I didn't come within years of looking my age."

A FTER all, it was the Judge's sister, and not Annabel's mother, who came to dine the next evening. Little dreaming that she might be needed, or that Annabel would think of going out, Mrs. Upchurch had accepted an invitation to play bridge; and so it happened that when the Judge measured out his thimbleful of old Bumgardner, the dauntless Edmonia seized the opportunity and begged to have her drooping spirit refreshed.

"I hoped that Constable might mix us a cocktail," she said, encouraged by the sight of the bottle with its distinguished label, "but this is a very good substitute. All the better because you don't waste it in a decanter."

Beneath his beetling eyebrows, the Judge's bright brown eyes slanted after the whiskey. "My gin gave out last year, and as I have scruples about bootleggers, I am holding on to my prewar whiskey. There! Be careful, or you'll spill it, Edmonia. Hadn't you better let me pour it out for you?"

Mrs. Bredalbane shook her head over the bottle. "I fancy, my dear brother, that my hand is still as steady as yours," she replied, with a laugh. "A little plain water, Constable, not soda. That is one of the things you learn in Scotland, Gamaliel, never to spoil the flavour of fine whiskey with charged water. Why, I've had the Duke of Dallmally take away his best whiskey and substitute a second best when he heard me ask for Apollinaris." She added a little plain water and raised the glass to her lips. "Yes, this has quality, there's no doubt of it," she remarked a moment later. "I approve of your scruples about bootleggers."

The Judge was surveying her with displeasure. "I may be old-fashioned, Edmonia, but in my day ladies in Queenborough were not supposed to drink whiskey."

Mrs. Bredalbane chuckled. "Your day was happily before prohibition, my dear brother, when you did not have to take anything for fear of losing everything. Yes, you are old-fashioned, if you don't mind my agreeing with you, but I can overlook your reactionary views in return for my appetite. This fish is particularly nice. I suppose you have still the same cook."

"Yes, we have had her for twenty-five years. Constable brought her from Ireland and married her the month after she came."

"That was sensible of Constable. I must say I admire your habit of holding on to the best. And that reminds me that I never saw Annabel looking so pretty. The child has learned how to dress, and that means a great deal. Poor Amanda, for all her fine figure, never knew what to wear."

Gazing at her disapprovingly but enviously over his frugal dinner, the Judge wondered whether or not it would be wise to afflict her with good advice. It was evident to him that any one who indulged herself as intemperately as Edmonia did needed good advice in abundance. Without delving into her character, there was, he felt, sufficient food for admonition in the recklessness with which she endangered her digestion. No man or woman could eat so heartily, to say nothing of the way she drank, and expect to remain well. That Edmonia, an exception to every rule, did remain well in spite of her greediness, was little less than an affront to his own abstemious diet. While he watched her, he longed to indulge in a veritable orgy of rebuke; but, being by judgment averse from importunate counsel, he contented himself with the implied warning: "For my part, I have always tried to remember Buchanan's formula for a long life: Trust in God and keep your diet light."

Edmonia nodded approbation over a second helping of Smithfield ham. "With your chronic weakness, I suppose you are wise; but it is unfortunate that you are obliged to deny yourself a taste of this ham. It has a delicious savour, and I hope Annabel has enjoyed it. After all, there is no better way to cook a ham than by that old recipe of Cordelia's which calls for plenty of Madeira and a dash of Worcestershire sauce."

"Is it possible that you will feel no bad effects?" he inquired with a tinge of asperity.

"Not a particle." Mrs. Bredalbane airily pooh-poohed the idea. "You must remember that, in the case of twins, there is usually a strong and a weak one, and, fortunately for me, I was the strong one of us two. Besides, as a girl I was obliged to consider my face and figure, as long at least as I had romantic aspirations, which are now comfortably over. Many a time, when I was trying to reduce, I have said to myself, 'age has at least two advantages: when you are old, you may eat as much and cry as much as you please.' "

For the first time, he looked at her with sympathy. An uneasy sensation assailed him, and he asked himself, with a sting of self-reproach, if he could have been unjust in his judgment of her?

"That reminds me that I have never seen you cry, Edmonia," he rejoined.

"And I hope you never will, Gamaliel. Before I felt it was safe to cry, I stopped feeling the need to. There doesn't seem anything left in the world worth crying over."

"I am distressed to hear that," he rejoined, innocent of satire. "Indeed, I was under the impression that you had, on the whole, enjoyed your life."

"Oh, I don't mean I haven't enjoyed it. I've had a good deal of fun, and there aren't many women, I dare say, who have managed to make a little happiness go so far. You know I always had what Mother used to call a pleasure-loving mind, and I never approved of the sour kind of duty you pretend to enjoy. On the contrary, I've always believed that happiness, any kind of happiness that does not make some one else miserable, is meritorious. That, my dear brother, is what you held against me in Queenborough. You Episcopalians may have made most of the history and all the mint juleps in Virginia; but you have left your politics and your laws to the Methodists and Baptists, and pleasure-baiting has always been the favourite sport of those earnest Christians."

"But, my dear sister!"

"Oh, you know, Gamaliel, that you could have forgiven my committing a sin if you hadn't feared that I had committed a pleasure as well. More than this, you resented the way I wasn't satisfied simply to stay ruined and to stew in the consciousness of sin for the rest of my life. It wasn't my fall, it was my being able to get up again, that you couldn't forgive——"

"Edmonia, I protest——"

"Well, wait a minute until I have finished. Now that Mother is dead, I may say what I think without fear of producing apoplexy in the family tradition. The trouble is that you are all tainted with Puritanism, even down here in Virginia, where, Heaven knows! you ought to have escaped the blight. But America is an anæmic nation, and the danger with national anæmia is that it runs to fanaticism in the brain. You are so harassed by the idea of indecency that, when you can't find fresh food for scandal, you resort to the canned variety. Could anything prove this better than the fables you invented about me?"

"Were they actually fables, Edmonia?" he interrupted hopefully.

"Mainly, Gamaliel, mainly. To be sure, I had that early fling, but, for the rest, I have lived what I suppose you would call a fairly respectable life with four husbands. I had spirit enough in the beginning not to be ruined, and, of course, that was an offence against your social tradition; but the way you hounded me—I don't mean you, Gamaliel, any more than the others—simply shows how indecent the imaginations of decent people become when the mob instinct is aroused in them. If I had been as timid as most girls, I dare say you would have destroyed everything except the historical scandal; but when the Lord let me be born in America in the nineteenth century, He gave me a skin thick enough to survive it."

"My dear sister!" Judge Honeywell exclaimed again, and he

added, after a pause in which he asked himself if there could be more than a vestige of truth in Edmonia's belated defence, "It pains me to think we may have been unjust to you."

"Oh, you needn't begin to worry about that," Mrs. Bredalbane responded cheerfully. "You enjoyed it, and it hasn't done me any harm that is worth speaking of. Only don't breathe a word of my confession to anybody. I value my fascination for the young too much to endanger it, and it isn't my actual virtues, but my legendary vices that draw the flies to my honey."

That was like Edmonia, he reflected gravely. Even as a girl she was her own worst enemy; she destroyed sympathy by her flippant and unregenerate—he had almost said, carnal—spirit. Yet, even while he meditated in this fashion, his cultivated mind, which worked by precedent alone, was stumbling through a baffling maze of conjecture. Was there a leak, after all, in his inherited system of prudential morality?

"But that is all over now," Mrs. Bredalbane had resumed in a vivacious tone, "and the chief thing, at our time of life, is to continue to find the world amusing. It isn't easy to keep amused when things have ceased to be serious. At least one important concern is essential to a cheerful life, and I feel sometimes that I have exhausted my interests. After love and travel, there isn't much left except religion and the pleasures of the palate, and of course social reforms, though none of these make any personal appeal to me. If my digestion gives out, I suppose I shall have to turn to the Church," she concluded, with a sigh of resignation; "that is the only thing I haven't tried; but it has always seemed to me to lack a sense of humour." She sighed more heavily, while her brother, inferring from the sound that her mood was dampened, kept a watchful eye upon his precious Bumgardner, which he had discreetly moved to the other side of the table.

To his relief, she appeared satisfied with the plum pudding on her plate; but over the dessert, with Constable out of the room, she inquired if he had any of that choice apricot brandy left in his cellar; and when he replied vaguely that there might be a bottle or two under the cobwebs, she remarked, with even more than her usual audacity, "After all, Gamaliel, your marriage has turned out better than I expected."

The Judge, who was cracking an English walnut, stopped long enough to stare at her through his glasses, which reflected the rays of the candles in a dazzling glimmer.

"Yes, it has turned out very happily, Edmonia. It was all I could do," he added, with an accent of pride, "to persuade Annabel to go out to-night and leave me alone."

Mrs. Bredalbane, who was inordinately fond of nuts, was sweeping the scattered shells on her plate into a neat pile. Before responding, she carefully selected a fresh supply of walnuts from the silver basket, which she remembered as one of a pair that she had given Cordelia and Gamaliel as a wedding present.

"Since she has settled down, I suppose it is all as it should be," she responded slowly, intent upon the nut she was shelling. "But if you had told me the marriage would turn out as it has, I shouldn't have believed it. Annabel seems to me to be the kind of woman that would turn any man's head."

"Well, as long as she is satisfied to turn mine!" he rejoined with mild acerbity.

To-night, he found Edmonia, who was always unwelcome, positively distressing. It distressed him to listen to her loose talk on serious subjects; and it distressed him still more to see her make the immoderate meal of an unbridled appetite. For thirty-six years Cordelia had permitted him two English walnuts after dinner, and since her death he had never exceeded his daily allowance. Having been for so long the master of his appetite, if not of his fate, he could only regard Edmonia's indulgence as a melancholy spectacle, though naturally of a piece with the rest of her conduct. For even the World War, which had varnished the reputation where it had failed to stiffen the virtue of so many soft-hearted women, had done little, he conceded sadly, in the case of his twin sister. The charge that he had misjudged her had been unable to survive the sight of her hearty pleasure at the table.

"Have you seen Amanda lately?" she inquired so abruptly that he was startled out of his moralizing.

"Yes, I enjoyed sitting beside her at the Christmas cotillion."

"Didn't you think that she looked the mere shadow of herself?"

"Why, no." He was direct but disingenuous. "I must say that I did not observe it. We had a very pleasant conversation."

"Well, that was like a man," Mrs. Bredalbane commented, and her tone was not flattering to his sex. How different, he thought, was the consummate tact of Mrs. Upchurch, who respected his feelings as well as his wine cellar. Next time, he must warn Annabel not to ask Edmonia to dine with him. If he must have some one in to take her place, he preferred Mrs. Upchurch, or any other woman who was too ladylike to indulge either in malice or in whiskey however old.

"She could hardly expect to say beautiful for ever," he said in a tone of remonstrance.

"Not beautiful, perhaps, but at least, poor thing, she might have been able to preserve her illusion. With her illusion unimpaired, she might have gone on being lovely as long as she lived."

"Her illusion? Did she possess one?" Though his tone was playful, he was attacked by a curious shiver, as if a snail were slowly creeping up—or was it down?—his spine.

"Doesn't every woman, my dear brother, possess one until she is wrecked? Woman lives not by love alone, but chiefly by illusions."

He laughed uneasily. "I never pretended to know much about women, Edmonia. I was fortunate enough to choose the safer and simpler subject of the law."

Mrs. Bredalbane nodded. "I agree with you, at least as far as Amanda is concerned. You proved that you knew very little about her."

"I knew she was the most beautiful woman of her time. When a man knows that, it is sufficient for him."

"Beautiful, yes. As far as features went, there wasn't anybody who could hold a candle to her. Her trouble was that she lacked charm. I suppose it takes a little sense to be charming, but beauty appears to get along better without it."

"I never missed intelligence in her. With a woman as queenly as that, all a man could do was to worship."

Mrs. Bredalbane went on placidly eating her walnuts. "It is pathetic the way fashions in beauty change."

"Yes, I am sorry to say, the queenly type appears to be as extinct as the pterodactyl. We run to the other extreme to-day. Do you realize, my dear sister, that nuts are the richest food you can eat?"

"It doesn't matter, Gamaliel. Unlike you, I am not hanging on to anything, not even to my husband. You will have no real freedom, my dear brother, until you cease to cling so tightly to Annabel. Human beings, especially youthful human beings, are not made to be clung to; it brings out their worst qualities."

Even the iron composure riveted over the Judge's soul by forty-odd years of the law was not impervious enough to keep his irritation from oozing into his voice. "I fail to understand, Edmonia, why you should imagine that you are entitled to give me advice." Unless to tell himself that her mind, never logical at best, was befuddled to-night by her unwise indulgence.

"I am speaking from greater knowledge of the world, Gamaliel. You haven't changed much in some ways since you were a boy, and I hope you don't resent my saying that you have never lost the proverbial innocence of a great intellect."

To this preposterous charge, which he resented as warmly as any man, young or old, could have done, he replied with scathing sarcasm: "Am I to consider you a judge of innocence, Edmonia?" Then, observing that she was reaching again for his Bumgardner, he added hurriedly, "I think we shall be more comfortable in the library," and rose from the table. Was it possible, he asked himself, that a Virginia lady could be befuddled with drink? Not only a Virginia lady, but a Honeywell, and his twin sister! This, he told himself, as he waited, with dignity, for her to sail ahead of him out of the room, was what happened in age to a woman who had forgotten her modesty in youth! For the belief that Edmonia was reprehensible had become one of the articles of faith in his Fundamentalist creed.

FTER Mrs. Bredalbane had gone, leaving him with the impression that she had held something back, though less, to be sure, than she might have held back with propriety, he sank into his favourite chair and gazed thoughtfully at the smouldering logs. The book he had intended to read, the fourth volume of the *Life of John Marshall*, lay near at hand; but, departing for once from his nightly custom, he did not open its pages. Gradually, as if he were sinking into some grey mist of contemplation, he began to muse upon the variegated pattern of life—of his own life in particular. Into these meditations Annabel rarely intruded; for nothing had astonished him more in a marriage that was rich in surprises than the swiftness with which her influence evaporated when he was once removed from the tantalizing delight of her presence. Though his passion for her glowed with a tardy florescence of youth, he had begun to realize that it lacked the deep-rooted strength of maturity.

Having replenished the fire, he leaned back in his chair and asked himself the inevitable question of the brooding mind: why when he had sought happiness should he have found only a fugitive pleasure? Did all men of sixty-six surrender to this ominous sense of futility, or did it mean that in his pursuit of joy he had mistaken a deciduous bloom for the everlasting flower of the soul? Would his life have been a broader and finer thing in a richer soil and a more stimulating atmosphere, with opportunity for his pampered intellect to renew its vigorous growth? Could he have grown old without this smothered resentment against fate, this lurking suspicion that he had been defrauded of perfect fulfilment?

Then, while he was still musing, his head dropped back on the cushions, and he drifted out into an unenclosed region of darkness.

When he started up (though not for the first time, since he retained a dim memory of having replenished the fire again) there was the sound of subdued laughter on the porch. A minute later, a latchkey was slipped into the lock, and he heard the front door open and shut.

Was it because he had been asleep that Annabel slipped in, as soft and radiant as his dream, and stopped to smile at him from the tremulous shadows of the firelight? Even to his still dazed faculties, there was a perception, scarcely stronger than the faint glimmer on the hearth rug, that the moment was charged with significance, that a magical change had come over her in the hours since she had left him. Not only was she lovelier than he remembered her, but there was a disarming tenderness, a suavity, in her smile, as if her gemlike lustre had melted in the vehemence of some inward flame. Her dance frock of palest primrose was half hidden by a scarf of amethyst gauze, which trailed from her bare shoulders to her small golden slippers. Yet it was not the colour of her dress, it was not the vivid beauty of her changeable face, which held him there, transfixed in a gesture of wonder and delight. What enraptured him was the discovery that happiness illumined her as if it were the fire at the heart of an opal.

"I have made her happy at last!" he exclaimed inwardly, with a sensation that was strangely flat and stale for pride of possession.

"So you're back," he said aloud. "Was it a nice party?"

"Oh, lovely!" She hesitated, as if she were struggling to collect her thoughts, and continued, after a long silence in which it seemed to him that he heard the fluttering of her heart—or was it merely the whispering of the flames?—"Every one missed you."

Her voice, always enchanting, was subdued to the melancholy strain of dream music. The firelight wove a pale nimbus about her hair; and he felt, with sudden anguish, that she was a symbol, not only of his lost paradise, but of all the burning desire of the world.

"It does you good to go out," he said, and wondered if she would shrink away from his caresses as she had done when they parted. Surely pleasure must have made her kinder, he thought, only in his own mind he used the phrase, "more womanly."

She moved toward him, and the shimmering amethyst scarf wound after her on the floor. "I adore dancing." Though her voice was caressing, it was so low that it might have floated across an immeasurable stillness. A faint dreaming smile curved her lips, and this smile, so rare, so blissful, so unutterably sweet, was like the eternal smile of legend. For all its wistful sweetness, it separated them as sharply as if it had been not a smile but a sword.

"Aren't you tired?" he asked, chilled by her ethereal remoteness.

"Tired? Oh, no, I am never tired of dancing."

"Would you like anything before we go up?"

"Oh, no. There was supper at midnight, but I wasn't hungry."

He glanced up at the clock. "Why, it is after two. I must have dozed all the evening while I was waiting. Yet I distinctly remember making up the fire once or twice and going to look out of the window."

"I wish you wouldn't sit up. There is really no need."

"Well, I sha'n't after this once. Perhaps I shall be able to go with you in a few days."

"In a few days?" she repeated vaguely, and added, with what he could not fail to see was an effort: "Was Sister Edmonia in good spirits?"

He frowned, partly because she had so lightly dismissed the prospect of his companionship, and partly because Edmonia was not a relative upon whom he could reflect with pleasure.

"The kindest construction I can place upon Edmonia's behaviour," he said, "is that she becomes unbalanced at times."

"Unbalanced?" With her musical echo in his ears, he asked

himself if she had heard only the last word of his sentence.

"Well, we'll go upstairs as soon as I put out the lights and lock up." As he spoke, she moved quickly across the room, and he watched the flutter of her primrose and amethyst draperies until she had ascended the stairs and disappeared into her dressing-room. The only reminder of her presence was a lingering scent, which he found agreeable though he instinctively disapproved of the pleasure it gave. Cordelia and her friends had never used any perfume more encouraging to the lower nature of man than bay rum; but, of course, as he reminded himself, Cordelia's friends had all been paragons of virtue, whose appearance and manner invited reform rather than seduction.

For the rest of the winter, Annabel remained silent, lovely, and inaccessible. He had never found her so kind, so considerate, so unapproachable. From the brightened lustre on her hair to her mysterious smile and her half-awakened gestures, she seemed to him more exquisite and more distant than she had been even in girlhood. At moments of rare insight, it occurred to him that she was living a hidden life—a life so vivid in happiness that its secret incandescence shone through her body.

"As long as she is happy," he thought a little sadly, and then, "Can it mean only that she has forgotten Angus at last?"

Now that his strength was returning, he had begun again to go out with her in the evenings. After the dreary hours he spent with chaperons, the feeling of her nearness on the drive home was almost a torment; and this awoke in him the sharp craving for sympathy, for tenderness, and above all for comprehension. But there were no words, he found, there were no caresses that could convey what he suffered. Only the old phrases came to his mind, and the old phrases hung like moth-eaten tapestries in the enchanted glow that surrounded her. He could not reach her; his voice could not penetrate the stillness into which her rapt and brooding spirit receded. Simply by withdrawing into her dreams, she placed the unconquerable vastness of the universe between them. . . .

"Have you noticed how happy Annabel is looking?" he inquired of Mrs. Upchurch one afternoon. "A little self-absorbed, but happier than I've ever seen her."

"Y-e-s," Mrs. Upchurch assented. Though she replied brightly, there was a troubled look in her face.

"I suppose," Judge Honeywell pursued, "that she has completely forgotten that young scamp."

"Y-e-s." While Mrs. Upchurch responded, three perpendicular lines, as fine as hairs, which she called playfully "lines of economy," appeared between her arched eyebrows. In her small but compact mind, she told herself that happiness like Annabel's, even a subdued and secret felicity, was not natural in a marriage of expedience; and these cryptic signs of beatitude had begun to make her uneasy. Yet, after all, where could one find better material for happiness than wealth, or a more suitable dispenser of it than an elderly and therefore indulgent husband? Nevertheless, she was obliged to acknowledge that Annabel's invulnerable calm was disturbing.

"Annabel has become very reticent," she continued presently. "You remember how we used to regret her lack of proper reserve? Well, since her marriage, especially in the last few months, she has closed up like a clam, and it is impossible to get anything out of her. I suppose this is the effect marriage has, and I must say that I think it is a commendable one."

"Quite so, quite so," the Judge agreed, for he felt no disposition to challenge her opinion. "Annabel, I am glad to see, is developing into a woman of character."

This was satisfactory so far as it went; and Mrs. Upchurch reflected hopefully that, since Annabel's husband was contented, there was surely no need for Annabel's mother to worry. It was possible, she argued cheerfully, that she had mistaken mere enjoyment of luxury for the symptoms of a more dangerous delight. Annabel, as her husband had just remarked, was becoming a sensible woman; and what truly sensible woman could fail to perceive the inestimable benefit of wealth and social position combined? Yet, with her usual ripe wisdom, Mrs. Upchurch paused to ask herself if her point of view could be prejudiced.

For, in her own experience, she had suffered so much more acutely from lack of money than from loss of love, that, as she would be the first to admit, she was scarcely a fair judge of their relative values. Though she was shrewd enough to realize that few women were so disillusioned, there were instants when she wondered whether she had become superlatively wise or was merely afflicted with the myopic vision of impoverished relicts?

"It is a great satisfaction to feel that she is happy," he said in a voice that trembled slightly.

"You are so wonderful." Mrs. Upchurch smiled at him with an archness that would have bewitched a younger man. "It is a satisfaction to me," she added, "to know that you are happy also."

"How could I be anything else with Annabel for a wife?"

Again Mrs. Upchurch smiled, but the archness of her look was brightened by a flicker of ironic amusement. "Annabel is devoted to you," she responded. "How could she be anything else?"

His face shone, and she was glad that she had been unscrupulous in giving pleasure. After all, though religion was a prop in calamity, there were occasions when she felt thankful that the right of private judgment had been safely established before she was left a widow and penniless.

"That is very gratifying to me," he answered. "I hope you are entirely comfortable. Remember that I wish Annabel's mother to have every luxury. I cannot separate your happiness from hers."

Her eyelids fluttered softly, for beneath her designing purpose there was a sound and grateful heart. "I cannot thank you enough," she said, and she spoke only the truth. "No one was ever more generous."

On this sanguine note, they parted gaily; and Mrs. Upchurch, hastening to the Woman's Exchange on the next block, ordered her favourite desserts with much of the pleasure and more than the recklessness of a bride, while the Judge strolled slowly to his house, where he was confronted almost immediately with the brittle nature of human happiness.

NNABEL was not in the drawing-room, though a fire was burning and the tea-table stood in front of the flames. A feeling came over him, as he glanced round the dignified room, that his wife had flitted away an instant before he entered. A savour of youth was wafted to him from the firelight, as if her fragrance were still interfused with the place she had left. At this subtle reminder of her power over him, his heart beat more rapidly and his senses ached with the familiar tremor of unsatisfied longing. With the eagerness of a young man, he turned back into the hall and went quickly upstairs.

Their bedroom was empty; but across the hall, in the little sitting-room which she had taken for her own use, and decorated in what seemed to him a grotesque fashion, he caught a glimpse of violet chiffon, and found her kneeling on the window-seat, with her eyes raised to a futurist sunset of black and red. Some poetic rhythm in her attitude, in the slant of her small burnished head and the drooping lines of her shoulder against the trellis of bared branches and the flaming background of sky,—some flowing harmony of mood and aspect recalled to him a dimly remembered picture of a Byzantine saint. She had not heard his approach on the carpeted stair, and while he stood watching her from the threshold, he felt that the past surged into his consciousness as the winter twilight flooded the deserted garden below. All that he had ever desired! All that he had ever relinquished! All that he had ever resisted! Nothing had changed between them; yet the clear contour of her head against the dark sunset and the hopeless despondency of her young figure, awoke, without a word, without a gesture, a sadness so profound that it was a supreme crisis of despair.

"Annabel, what has happened?" he called out sharply, in a voice which was charged with regret for something that he could not remember, for something that he had lost without ever possessing.

Her head turned slowly, as if she and the leafless branches and the vivid sunset and the dim world beyond were all under a spell. He watched the light slip from her gleaming hair to the twilight of her eyes, and from her eyes to the scarlet curve of her mouth and the straight folds of violet chiffon over her bosom. And while this ray of light glided over her, she looked at him with the mute disaster that he had hoped never to see again in her face. As he met the anguish in her gaze, he thought, with a miraculous flash of insight, "Only happy people can suffer like that!"

"Annabel!" he said again, holding out his arms, "has anything happened?"

She shrank away from him, and he repeated the question in a passion of sympathy. "My darling, has anything hurt you?"

If only she would turn to him for comfort! If only she would yield herself to his arms! So overpowering was his impulse to gather her to his breast that it seemed to him she must feel herself drawn by some irresistible influence. That he could love at last unselfishly, supremely, and yet to be incapable of bringing happiness to the beloved, appeared to him, while he waited there in suspense, to be the ultimate tragedy of the human heart. That love could not confer happiness! That love could not even bring consolation! At the moment, he felt that no other pang could equal the dull ache of his helpless despair, of his futile compassion. Yet he knew that she was submitting without a struggle to an agony which he envied even in his pity because it was the sharp anguish of youth.

"No, nothing has happened." Her voice was so low that he could barely distinguish the words, and beneath the subdued notes there was a tremulous longing.

"Are you ill? Are you tired?"

"Oh, no. I've been out all day. I just came in a little while ago."

"Are we dining out?"

"Yes, we promised the Dandridges."

"Would you rather not go out this evening? I will telephone that you are not well."

"No, there's to be a dance afterwards. I hate to miss a dance, and, besides, it is too late to disappoint Molly."

While she spoke in that strained low voice, and he asked these trivial questions in the hope that they might melt her frozen reserve—or was it aversion?—he heard around him, like a stealthy murmur, all the superficial sounds in the room; the singing of the flames; the fall of the ashes; the droning of the clock, with a curious jerking monotony, as if it were preparing to run down. And beyond the frosted panes, where the black boughs were etched now against a paling sky, he became aware that the wind had risen, and that bells were pealing far away, now loud, now faint, above the unquiet streets.

"If you have been out all day, hadn't you better rest before dressing?" (Did she hear, could she fail to hear, the stifled pain in his voice?)

"I was just going to lie down. Did you see Mother?"

"Yes, I met her by accident, and we stopped to have a few words. She is a wonderful woman, your mother."

Annabel looked at him with heavy eyes, which were encircled by violet rings, as if she had been weeping. "All women who have learned to be happy without happiness are wonderful," she answered wearily.

Was that borrowed wisdom, he asked, or was it uttered from the secret instinct of her own heart? He felt that he would give his life for her, and realized the next instant that his life was nothing to give. "So this is really love. I know it at last," he said to himself, while all other interests, all other pleasures, were scattered like straws. Only the joy of loving and being loved in return flamed against the desolate horizons of life. His heart, which had been an organ of uniform and temperate action, trembled like a leaf in the wind as she moved away from him out of the room.

A little later, while he fitted his studs with neatness and precision into the holes of his shirt, he found himself repeating aloud, after some reassuring maxim, "It meant nothing at all. It meant really nothing." A passing mood. Nerves, nothing more. Women, he assured himself, with satirical humour, were subject to moods, and even more unavoidably, moods were subject to nerves. Women, especially young or middle-aged women, were esaily agitated, as well as disposed by nature to vagueness and vacillation. To be sure, there was neither vagueness nor vacillation in Cordelia's character, which was, to say the least, flatly unequivocal. None the less, he found little difficulty in placing her also in the category of pure womanliness. For, like most lawyers and all vestrymen, he was able to believe automatically a number of things that he knew were not true. It was owing, indeed, to his proficiency in this exercise, which conservative people called "right thinking," that he had achieved his enviable position in an epoch when faith and facts did not cultivate an acquaintance. So, even while he adopted Cordelia's logical methods, he was able to meditate with comfort upon the nervous instability of women in general and of Annabel in particular. For example, what could be more vague than her manner at the Christmas cotillion, or more vacillating than her behaviour to-day? By to-morrow her mood might change and she might be herself again, he mused, skimming over the treacherous shallows of conjecture. How much in scenes like this one was genuine emotion, he wondered, and how much was instinctive drama? All modern youth impressed him as more or less theatrical, and Annabel was not devoid, he knew, of this spectacular twist, of this leaning toward the quickened movement of catastrophe. That absurd phrase, for instance, about women learning to be happy without happiness! Any one with an ounce of logic would recognize that as pure paradox; but the truth was, he supposed, that paradox, not reason, was the natural law of her being.

So he deliberated, and having deliberated, he finished his dressing and went down into Cordelia's front parlour, where he waited patiently with his eyes on the memorial designs in the

Brussels carpet. What would Cordelia think? he found himself asking. For more than a generation, he had asked this question in every predicament; and now, even though Cordelia was safe in heaven and a younger and more engaging woman occupied her place on earth, he still inquired from settled habit: "What would Cordelia think?" What would she think, indeed, of his second wife and her lack of all the essential qualities of wifehood?

This painful uncertainty was in his mind when Annabel descended the stairs, wrapped in an ermine coat, with her hair shining as if the afterglow had left a gleam in its waves; and as she came toward him, she diffused a radiance, a freshness, which captivated his senses. He had never seen her more brilliant; he had never seen her more gallant or gay; for her mocking smile invited while it eluded his tenderness. Well, he had been right after all, and the dangerous mood had vanished as quickly as it had come. His relief rushed to his lips; but the confirmed habit of a lifetime was stronger even than passion, and when he spoke it was merely to ask, as he had asked a thousand times of Cordelia, "Do I look all right to you, dear?" So fatuous was his state of mind that he hoped she would reply to Cordelia's verdict, "No other man looks so distinguished in the evening." But, to his disappointment, Annabel merely tossed back, without glancing over her shoulder, "Oh, you'll do very well. Nobody cares how you look, if you have money." He hoped in vain that she would turn and glance at him; for he had long cherished a favourite theory that Cordelia was right, and that the white and black of evening clothes set off to advantage his dignity, his slimness, and the patrician character of his features. To-night, too, he had taken unusual pains with his hair and beard, and it seemed to him that the glossy pepper-and-salt made a pleasing contrast to his bright dark eyes and to the air of belated youth that lingered in his expression. His appearance still caused him anxiety; and the fussiness about the fit and cut of his clothes and the colours of his ties and socks, which had occupied so many hours during his courtship, had never entirely disappeared.

But Annabel, unlike Cordelia, was interested in her own appearance and not in his, which she felt, with reason, made little difference one way or another at his venerable time of life. Humming a snatch of song, she folded her ermine coat (which he never saw without remembering how extravagant he had felt when he bought it) over her short velvet skirt, and tripped, in her silver slippers with scarlet heels, down the steps and into the car. Though she was as close to him as his own heart, she remained as inaccessible as the stars.

All the evening, seated among the submissive mothers of insurgent daughters, he watched her with an anxious solicitude which impressed his waning sense of humour as maternal. Fatherhood, he was sure, for he was both a father and a grandfather, contained none of these vehement alternations of pride and jealousy. Or perhaps he was mistaken, and it was not maternal anxiety, but some new dimension that love and despair had added to his spiritual nature. Certainly not for Cordelia, not for any child or grandchild that he had ever known, could he have endured so patiently these tedious hours of discord.

"If only I can make her happy!" he thought, attaining, in one brief exaltation, a selfless passion. "If only I can make her happy, I shall ask nothing else for myself. I will bear any discomfort."

In that moment, with the very act of relinquishment, there was a break in the clouds and light streamed into his mind. A faint, thin vibration, clear as the ringing of bells and luminous as the sunrise, quivered about him. Was something there? Was it light? he asked himself. Was it music? Was it ecstasy? Was it God? For a single point of eternity, beyond time, beyond space, beyond good and evil, he surrendered to this incorruptible harmony, to this cloudless substance of being. Light? Music? Ecstasy? God? Or merely a rainbow mist of illusion? . . .

The vision, which was not a vision, was gone before he had seized it, and the tumult of jazz was starting the old pain at the back of his neck. He thought with longing of his darkened house in the soundless night; but when at last the evening was over and they had reached home, Annabel flung off her ermine coat, and dropping on the rug in front of the fire, dissolved into tears. "It is nothing. Oh, it is nothing!" she repeated passionately. Though he pleaded with her until he was hoarse with fatigue and desperation, she would answer only, "Oh, it is nothing!"

A WEEK afterwards, when the perplexity had worn on his nerves, he went to see Mrs. Upchurch. Even the recollection of the faint pure harmony had died away in the darkness. He remembered it now only in flashes; nevertheless, he remembered it. For one instant of exalted vision, he had found a way out of despair.

"Has Annabel seemed to you—well, different of late?" he asked nervously.

"Different?" Mrs. Upchurch's tone was sympathetic but dubious.

"We were speaking a little while ago of her happiness——" Again he paused abruptly on a note of interrogation, and again she echoed with bright vagueness,

"Her happiness?"

"Have you observed any change in her since—since our last conversation?"

Mrs. Upchurch waited so long before replying that he repeated his question in a tone of exasperation: "I inquired if you had noticed any change in her recently?"

"I was just thinking——" she began, and trailed off into silence. Concerning truthfulness, as well as other rules of conduct, she was, by instinct rather than by theory, a pragmatist. In her own experience, she had found that few acts and still fewer reactions were either good or bad in general, but merely moral or immoral when applied to a particular circumstance. Falsehood, aversion from one's husband, divorce, murder—yes, dreadful as it sounded, even murder, appeared to her to be justified, or at least palliated, by certain extremities of desperation. And how much more excuse was there, she felt, for a conscientious objection to the naked truth.

"What do you feel about it?" she asked sweetly but firmly.

Turning away, he cleared his throat after a nervous habit that had always irritated her. Did it irritate Annabel also, she wondered, and were there other habits, confirmed by years, which were even more annoying to the capricious youth of the girl?

"I have been greatly disturbed," he began all over again, with an effort which she watched in alert sympathy.

"Disturbed?" After all, what was there to do but repeat his words like a parrot?

"Annabel has not been herself. She has seemed very——" He stumbled helplessly, and Mrs. Upchurch supplied, with an air of cheerful wisdom, the label:

"Nervous. Yes, Annabel was always of a nervous temperament."

"Then she has had these spells of depression before?"

"Oh, often. You must not take them too seriously. Girls are apt to be variable."

He made a slow affirmative gesture; but, after a brief pause in which he pondered her explanation, the harassed look appeared again in his face. "For the last week she has been listless and melancholy. Several times I have found her in tears when I came home, and I have heard her crying to herself in the night."

"I know. She tells me that she can't sleep, that she lies awake and thinks after she goes to bed." She sighed, hesitated, and added hastily, in a rush of courage over discretion: "I suggested to her that she had better try sleeping in the adjoining room. Indeed, Dr. Buchanan advised it."

When she had finished, she carefully looked away from him into the fire. Though she did not see his expression, his voice sounded lifeless.

"Yes, we've arranged that. Buchanan spoke to me." After a moment, he asked wearily, "Could there be a physical cause for her nervousness?"

"Oh, no. Annabel was always healthy, even as a baby. She has never had more than a day's sickness in her life."

"Yet she is frail looking."

"Not frail, but thin. It's the fashion to keep as thin as a rail, and she won't let herself take on an ounce. Girls are like that now."

Encouraged but unconvinced, Judge Honeywell gazed at his mother-in-law; and in a mirror over the mantelpiece, he caught a glimpse of two unfamiliar figures, which might easily have been the reflections of father and daughter. Had he ever thought of this obvious disparity in their ages, it would have depressed him; but his mind, a well-disciplined organ, refused stubbornly to admit the idea that Mrs. Upchurch was not an elderly woman. Only by regarding her as elderly, and therefore incapacitated for romance, could he maintain his suitable dignity as her son-in-law. And Mrs. Upchurch, who would cheerfully have worn a cap and mittens, if wearing them could have relieved his mind, abetted the charitable subterfuge to the best of her ability. "Are you sure it is nothing more serious?" he asked presently.

"Oh, perfectly!" she replied emphatically; for she was prepared, if he required it of her, to be sure of anything except downright immorality and the doctrine of evolution.

Again he cleared his throat before speaking, and again the hacking sound made her wince. "Have you heard recently of that young man?"

"You mean Angus Blount?"

She was playing so recklessly for time that she was scarcely aware of the asperity in his tone when he retorted with the question, "He was the only one, wasn't he?"

"Oh, yes." Of this she was fortunately convinced, and for this saving conviction she felt devoutly thankful. "She never cared a rap for anybody but Angus."

"I feel confident of that; but I suppose Angus is still living?"

"So far as I know. The last news came from his mother. I met her in market several months ago, and she told me that Angus and his wife had separated, and that he had gone to Russia for some newspaper." There was little certainty, if certainty was what he wanted, to be got out of this; but, as she hastened to remind him, with her natural aptitude for seeing the bright side, Russia is a country where anything may happen and frequently does. Russians appeared to her, indeed, to live in hourly expectation of the unexpected.

"Is it possible that she has heard from him?" he asked in a voice that trembled.

"From Angus? Well, I hardly think so. She told me just before her marriage that she had put the thought of him out of her life, and nothing has occurred of late to change her mind about that."

"No, nothing has occurred," he assented heartily. "However, he may have written to her, and that would naturally depress her."

"Yes, naturally." It was always easy to agree, and what agreement was more emphatic than a spirited echo?

"Is there any way," the Judge demanded abruptly, "that you could find out, of course without directly inquiring, what has become of him?"

She thought quickly but lucidly. "I might speak in a roundabout way to his mother."

"That is a good idea. Of course I have the utmost confidence in Annabel. The utmost confidence," he insisted sternly, as if Mrs. Upchurch had cast an aspersion upon her daughter's character.

"Yes, of course. The utmost confidence. We both have." It was all, she told herself furtively, in the best manner of conspiracy; and since she was clever at conspiring, and had resorted to it upon more than one occasion in the past, she felt that life promised to become almost as complicated as it had been when she was married.

"We must remember," he said, still sternly, "that we are trying to help her."

"I know. Dear child, she is the soul of loyalty, and she is devoted to you. There is only one thing more that I wish for her," she added, with a sigh, "and that is faith. During all that trouble with Angus, I felt it would have been so much easier for her if only she had had faith to fall back upon. My dear mother used to say that silent prayer was the best balm for any affliction; but there isn't any silent prayer in this age; there is only outspoken doubt."

"You are right, and it is most distressing," he rejoined, feeling as little inclination as usual to dissent from her opinion. Though he was not unacquainted with honest doubt, he was disposed to tolerate it only in a smothered condition. Smothered doubts, like buried sinners, were picturesque; but active and unashamed, they seemed to him as reprehensible as Edmonia. "The world has found nothing to take the place of duty, especially in a woman's life," he concluded sadly.

"Well, it isn't her fault that ideas have changed," urged Mrs. Upchurch, "and you must never lose sight of her devotion to you."

"I couldn't wish for a better wife," he responded fervently, and caught himself wondering if he had been untrue to Cordelia. Why was it that, in being true to the present, he was so often trapped into fear that he had been false to the past? "My life has been blessed by two good women," he added ceremoniously.

Impressed by his manner, Mrs. Upchurch was gazing at him attentively, though she had taken in scarcely a word he had spoken. In her busy mind, hemmed in by innumerable anxieties, she was trying to reason out why people are never satisfied with the troubles they have, but must be continually engaged in attaching new ones. With all the comforts of life to choose from, peace, prominence, wealth, security, why were Gamaliel (she was doing her best to think of him as "Gamaliel") and Annabel beginning so soon to turn from the sunny path of married happiness into the shady entanglements of a difficult situation? For Mrs. Upchurch, who lacked dramatic temperament and dreaded situations, except in novels, where she demanded them, was beginning to feel, as she expressed it precisely, at the end of her rope. After the stress of Annabel's unhappy love affair, marriage with an elderly man, a man who had passed the age that requires watchful waiting on the part of a wife, seemed to Mrs. Upchurch to be as safe as the grave, if almost as monotonous. And now it appeared that love affairs die as seldom as lovers from sheer disaster. Was Annabel even more foolish than her mother, who had little opinion of the child's common sense, believed her to be? Where was Angus? Well, wherever he was, it was natural, Mrs. Upchurch decided, to assume that he also was bent on making trouble.

"I'll find out all I can," she promised readily, "and let you know in a day or two. I shouldn't worry a moment if I were you. Never forget that Annabel is devoted to you."

Annabel is devoted to you! The words sang in his ears, sang in his mind, sang in his blood, while he strolled along the deserted blocks in the direction of home. Even the ceremonial procession of his thoughts rustled like wind-driven leaves, and took flight into golden air. The burden of age, that bitter sense of an increasing loneliness which he dreaded more than pain, more than tragedy, was consumed in this sudden liberation of spirit. While he remembered that Annabel was devoted to him, nothing else mattered in life.

As he approached the house, a car stopped at the door, and Annabel alighted and waved to him languidly. In the damp air her face was as fresh as a flower after rain, and there was a starry depth in her eyes. What was it? he wondered, what burning memory, what hope, what desire?

"You have been out," he said, and could think of nothing to add.

"Yes, I've been out." Her voice scarcely reached him, it was so low and so charged with an indefinable quality. Rapture? Pain? Passionate longing?

He put his hand on her arm, and beneath the mink coat she was wearing, he felt her flesh shrink away. As they entered the house together, she slipped past him and went upstairs alone, while he felt that the chill of desertion was penetrating his heart.

The next afternoon the voice of Mrs. Upchurch, floating over the telephone, requested him to stop by for a minute on his way back from his office. As he entered her drawing-room, she received him with the sanguine yet sympathetic smile which was irresistible to all men who were unhappily married but hoped for the best.

"Well, he's safe in Russia," she announced triumphantly.

"Safe?" Even to his disturbed faculties the word sounded far-fetched.

"Safe for us, anyhow. His mother heard from him last week, and he said nothing of coming back to America."

"There was nothing, then, that could have depressed Annabel?"

Mrs. Upchurch hesitated; but her hesitation sprang less from regret for the news she had to impart than from her firm belief that trouble came from telling men anything they did not wish to know. "Nothing," she said after a moment, "except that his wife has divorced him."

"Could she have heard that?" He breathed heavily, and she motioned to a chair while she dropped back on her sofa.

"Of course it is possible, but I doubt it. And even if she has heard it," demanded Annabel's mother, "what difference could it make to her now? After all, she is married, and," she pressed this point in as delicately as if it were a needle, "Annabel is devoted to you."

"Yes, I realize that." His tone was grave but far from emphatic.

"So even if she has been a little depressed, it doesn't mean anything. You must remember that Annabel has always taken things more seriously than most girls of her age. She never had light flirtations, and before her marriage she never gave a thought, I am sure, to any man but Angus. Now that she cares for you, you can trust her to put him out of her mind."

"I trust her absolutely. No man could ask for a better wife. If it is a question of patience——"

"That is all. Only have patience with her, and everything will be all right."

He promised solemnly, but, after all, it is easier to promise a virtue than to practise it. Day and night, he had suffered from a jealous suspicion, and now Angus, who had been as unreal as a bad dream, was as living as the pain in a tooth. For Judge Honeywell had been tormented, without intermission, ever since the afternoon when he had stolen upon his young wife while she watched the futurist sunset, and he was beginning to feel that the constant ache had worn on his nerves. At bottom he was an amiable man who wished harm to nobody; yet he felt, as he descended Mrs. Upchurch's steps, that he would cheerfully consign Angus to the nocturnal shadows of Russian freedom.

It was one of those early spring evenings when a mulberry-coloured haze floats in the air after sunset. A pale yellow light was still suffusing the west. Straight overhead, a solitary star was burning like a white fire in dim pastures of sky. Through the windy dusk, waves of memory ebbed and flowed in an invisible tide. Things he remembered in fragments. Things he had forgotten. Things he had never tried to understand in the past. He had the feeling, while he walked there alone, that if he could think of the right word to speak, if he could discover some secret key to experience, all his difficulties would become as simple and clear as day. The right word! But what was it? Had he lost it? Had it ever been spoken? Closing in about him, he was aware again of this universal rhythm of spirit. If only he could open his mind! If only he could let the harmony stream through his soul, like light, like peace, like that Sabbath without evening in which his father believed. But he knew that he was imprisoned mind, heart, body, in the mould of earth, and that he could not escape.

He quickened his pace, covered the last block, with what in a less dignified person would have been almost a springy step, mounted to the porch, inserted his key in the lock, and opening the door softly, entered the hall. Pausing an instant later to look in a mirror under the staircase, he saw, through an open door, the reflection of Cordelia's drawing-room, where Annabel was tearfully disengaging herself from the arms of a young man who was not Angus.

Fair, strong, well-favoured, the strange young man looked at him from the glass with a pair of singularly living blue eyes, while the fantastic thought sprang into the Judge's mind, "That is the son I ought to have had!"

RS. UPCHURCH sat thinking before her fire; and her thoughts, trim, bright, brisk, were combined with as much determination as would not endanger perfect tolerance and a desire to please everybody. In the last ten minutes, departing from Annabel's problem, she had considered the disadvantages, in man or woman, of an incurably amorous habit of mind. For it seemed to her that even the insidious irony of the modern point of view had scarcely damaged the popular superstition that love and happiness are interchangeable terms. Old and young and perennially middle-aged, she beheld the world enslaved by this immemorial illusion. Was she herself, she sometimes asked, the only person who had been able to maintain a true sense of values and an equilibrium of the emotions? Judge Honeywell with his law and learning; Amanda with her exalted character and her simple wit; Annabel with her artless sophistication; and now this young man who might have been but was not Angus—all this company of happiness-hunters appeared to be little better than a troupe of romantic comedians. Of them all, Amanda seemed to her the most innocent and appealing; for at fifty-nine, Amanda was still confiding enough to be betrayed. Annabel, of course, was too sophisticated for that; it put a strain upon Mrs. Upchurch's credulity when she tried to imagine Annabel in the earlier plight of Edmonia. Was it merely, she questioned, that ruined women, like fragments of Colonial architecture, "dated," as they say, a period in history? Or were all moral laws engulfed in some recent volcanic eruption? Well, whichever way it was, there was comfort, however cold, in the knowledge that there was nothing she could do about it, that there was nothing she could even be expected to do.

The relief she found in this reminder was dampened almost immediately by the thought of the strange young man, who was a stranger only in the part of a lover. She had known him quite well as Dabney Birdsong, when he was a little boy wearing knickerbockers, and with the most marvellous curls. It seemed to her only yesterday that his mother had wept over the inevitable sacrifice of those curls. "If only he were a girl!" the mother, meeting Mrs. Upchurch in market some twenty years ago, had lamented. And now, in so short a time by the calendar of middle age, Mrs. Upchurch was trying to think of Dabney, not only with a shorn head, but as Annabel's lover. Not her lover, of course, she mused hopefully, in the discreditable European sense of the word; merely her lover in the superior, though more tragic, American fashion. Why was it that Annabel, with all the wealth she could desire and an adoring husband, who lived but to gratify her whims, should have scarcely recovered from one painful affair before she was plunging with unslaked ardour into another? None of this would have happened if he had married me, thought Mrs. Upchurch.

As she had so often insisted to a conveniently deaf Providence, she had never been immoderate, she had never even been exacting, in her demands of life. All she had ever required of a second husband was that he should be comfortably, if not amply, provided for. Birth, youth, breeding, appearance, character, yes, even character,—all these agreeable perquisites of marriage she would have exchanged for the consolation of an established income. But Destiny, as she had not failed to observe was often the case, had granted her every opportunity except the one she urgently needed. As an engaging widow, armed with a disenchantment so profound that it was mistaken for softness of temper, she had been approached by youth without intelligence, by appearance without character, by character without youth, by birth and breeding without another redeeming attribute; but wealth, being the one and only gift she desired, had successfully eluded her grasp. In the end, since she was as amiable as is consistent with virtue, she had thankfully ceased her struggles, and had nestled into the less lucrative, and certainly less exacting, position of mother-in-law to a rich and generous man.

She was waiting now for her son-in-law, and in a few minutes she heard his ring at the bell, sharp, imperative, and not like Annabel's, a long-drawn-out jangle, which continued until Altrusa sauntered, tying her apron behind her, to the front door. When the Judge entered and held out his hand, Mrs. Upchurch saw that he was looking tired and old, older indeed than she had ever seen him. "If men could learn to give up like women," she thought, "it would be so much more restful."

"I've had a painful scene with Annabel," he began, roaming away after he had dropped her hand, and staring down into the small back yard, where he could see nothing more interesting than a few clotheslines. "I should not have mentioned it to you if she had not insisted."

"But it can't be worse than what I know already."

"If anything, she is more determined than ever."

"Determined? You mean to be miserable?" It was impossible for Mrs. Upchurch to keep a rasping note out of her voice.

"Determined to wreck her life. Determined not to give up this young man."

"And it isn't even the same young man!" wailed Mrs. Upchurch.

"No." He turned his blanched and stricken face away from the window. "But it is the same infatuation apparently."

"You mean she is obliged to have somebody?"

"I mean she thinks she is obliged to have somebody."

"But there's nothing really wrong in it. Annabel, with her upbringing, couldn't be anything but a pure woman."

"The terrible part is that she is without regret. I had almost said without shame." Fantastically enough, this sounded to Mrs. Upchurch like an echo, and she wondered wildly how long it had been since she had heard that word applied to behaviour. Had the label, like the fact, become so antiquated that nobody was ashamed any longer?

"I believe," the Judge continued grimly, "that if anything

were really wrong, she would not hesitate to tell me. She seems to have absorbed an idea that decent reserve is hypocrisy. She even boasted of the way she had brazened everything out instead of trying to hide it."

"Well, you can't deny that she is truthful. That means a great deal," protested Mrs. Upchurch, who had contrived, through a difficult experience, to preserve the major virtues by the sacrifice of the minor.

"It appears to mean everything in her case. But it is impossible to discuss it with her. It is like trying to argue in two different languages."

"I know," Mrs. Upchurch nodded with sympathy. "They see things so differently now."

"I fear that our marriage was a mistake. I fear for her," he added punctiliously.

"Oh, it can't be so bad as that. Give her time to recover. Have patience a little longer."

"I am willing to have all the patience of the ages," Judge Honeywell said, with sorrow in his voice, in his long white face, and in his silvery hair and beard, which had lost lustre. "I have done everything I could for her happiness. I cannot see where I have failed."

"You have been perfect," Mrs. Upchurch returned, and for once she was speaking sincerely. "I suppose her affair with Angus awakened her emotions, and that—and that——" Before the calamity in his face, she felt that she could not go on without weeping.

"How long has she known this young man?" he inquired, pausing in his restless roaming and sitting down in the chair on the other side of the wood fire.

"Oh, all her life. She used to play with him; but he's been away for a number of years. I believe he first studied engineering at Columbia, but after he went into an office in New York he seemed to feel he wasn't getting on, so he borrowed money and went to Paris to the Beaux Arts. He is doing quite splendidly as an architect, I've heard, and for the last two years, after he came back to New York, he has been making a reputation. You haven't forgotten David Summers, who used to live here, and then became famous as an architect in New York. He designed St. Stephen's Church, you know, and the Boynton Library. Well, Dabney has been in his office ever since he came back to America, and Summers sent him down to Queenborough about the design of this terminal station. There is nothing wrong with him—Dabney—I mean. Every one thinks he is a splendid boy, and that he has a brilliant future before him—and his mother says she doesn't believe he has ever looked at a girl twice——" She broke off in confusion, and continued hurriedly, after a breathless pause: "I haven't seen him since he was a child, but I remember that he had the most beautiful auburn curls. It seems only yesterday that I met his mother in market, and she cried when she told me she had had to cut them off because the other boys made his life a burden." Mrs. Upchurch was speaking with recovered vivacity, and before she had finished it seemed to her that she had offered something in extenuation, if not in excuse, of Annabel's conduct.

"It is a week now since——"

"I know." She seized his words before he had uttered them, so desirous was she of helping, of understanding. "You came straight to me."

"At Annabel's request. At Annabel's urgent request."

Mrs. Upchurch sighed. "You are the soul of chivalry."

"I have done the best I could."

"No man could possibly have done more."

Soothed but not consoled, he turned his grateful gaze upon her; and while these interchanges of flattery on one side and appreciation on the other continued, the fancy played in Mrs. Upchurch's mind: "How easily I could have managed him!"

Aloud, however, she remarked merely, "I cannot feel hopeless. Annabel is so young."

"Yes, she is young." Though he sighed as he answered, this glamour of youth enveloped his senses like an inescapable perfume. "She insists upon talking about it," he complained bitterly.

Mrs. Upchurch nodded. "I thought she had become more reticent. After all," she concluded sternly, "there is something to be said in favour of suppressions."

He assented drearily. "In my day, we should have thought so; but, I suppose, we are behind the times."

"I believe this goes no deeper with Annabel than her dramatic instinct. Some women enjoy unhappy love affairs, you know, though I have always felt that they are greatly overrated. But you must remember that Annabel makes drama wherever she is. I don't mean that she is to blame; but things just seem to happen about her."

She felt sincerely sorry for him. It was that unconquerable illusion again. In his own place and period, he appeared to be endowed with every requisite of happiness. As the survivor of an age of urbanity, he was more than impressive, he was even majestic. If he could but realize that each period of life has its own essential ardours and enterprises. "He is becoming an old man," she thought sadly, "and yet, in his own generation, beside Amanda, he would still be only middle-aged." Made wise by sudden vision, she beheld his disaster less as an individual revolt against nature than as a part of the universal striving to break through the stale crust of experience into some intenser reality than life had afforded.

"You will come and reason with her?" he asked, with a pathos that moved her more deeply than she liked to feel.

"Yes, I will come. Not that there is anything left to say. I have reasoned with her until I am worn out; but, after all, isn't she beyond reason?"

He dropped his head into his hands with a sound between a sigh and a groan. Could anything, she asked herself, be more un-manly than an elderly man in the clutch of an emotional crisis? With a fantastic flare of memory, she recalled his dry-eyed solemnity on the day of Cordelia's funeral. As an example of behaviour, she preferred the earlier manner, the manner of the circumspect 'eighties; yet she was just enough to admit that it was as difficult to be solemn as it was to be circumspect in a crisis with Annabel. And it was even more difficult, she divined, for an elderly husband to be manly in a crisis with a young wife. Though she felt deeply compassionate, she had been brought up on robust legends of the dominant male, and even while she pitied him with her heart, she despised him with her intelligence.

"I have wondered," she said thoughtfully, "if I ought to give that boy a good scolding. Do you suppose it would help?"

He raised his face from his hands. "Oh, I've talked enough. I said some things I don't like to remember. I'm afraid I lost my judgment for a few minutes. It isn't talk that is needed now. It is——"

Yes, she knew what was needed; but while she looked at his bleached and furrowed face, she preferred not to put this need into words. Everything but youth! Everything but youth, and the whole world thrown aside! "I ought to have known," she thought regretfully, "I ought to have known men! I ought to have known Annabel! Even more, I ought to have known life!" For it seemed to her that this undefeated error was the secret canker at the heart of experience. "You may count upon me to do all I can," she said aloud, "but our one need is patience. I am sure, I am perfectly positive that it will be all right in a little while."

He rose hopefully, almost with a spring of energy, and while he held out his hand, which felt soft and limp, a whimsical regret flitted again through Mrs. Upchurch's head. "If he had married me, how much happier he would be now." It was unrefined, she knew; it was almost an indelicate idea; yet it entered her thoughts with a definite sensation of triumph. "Try to remember," she implored him as they parted, "that the more violent a—a passion is, the sooner it blows over." For, comforting or not, that was what she had observed.

HOUGH it was after six o'clock when she crossed the street on her way to reason with Annabel, Mrs. Upchurch found, upon questioning Constable, that the Judge had not returned from his office. He was still walking the streets with his disturbed thoughts, she supposed, and reflected how much more sensible it would have been if he had accepted this blow as philosophically as he had accepted Cordelia's death.

"Is Mrs. Honeywell upstairs?" she inquired, and after receiving an affirmative reply, she slipped out of her sealskin coat (a gift from Judge Honeywell, who was of the opinion that mothers-in-law should wear only sealskin or mink) and walked sedately up the curving stairs to the second storey. While she ascended, she observed, as she had done at least a hundred times in the last six months, that nothing had been changed in the house since Cordelia lived here. Furniture, carpets, curtains, even Cordelia's portrait, hanging side by side with one of the Judge —all these solemn, commemorative objects were exactly where they had been before Annabel's marriage. "Men have queer ideas of loyalty," she meditated, and the deeper she meditated and the higher she ascended, the queerer they seemed to her. "I wonder if that could have anything to do with it?" she inquired suspiciously, and decided immediately that it had nothing whatever. No amount of loyalty to his first wife would have disturbed Annabel. "She would encourage, not only loyalty to the dead," Mrs. Upchurch mused, "but downright infidelity with the living." A minute later, as she opened the door of her daughter's room, she felt that she required all her patience and more for the scene that was awaiting her.

Annabel, who enjoyed tragedy in any posture but preferred

it lying down, declined now in the midst of luxuries which, her mother felt, she had procured, if not dishonourably, well, at least under false pretenses. Beneath a coverlet of peach-coloured satin decorated with garlands of roses, she was propped upon large, soft pillows, where lace and embroidery had banished the cool decorum of Cordelia's linen. Her bright hair hung free on her neck, and her nightgown of primrose crêpe was slipping from a shoulder that looked as if it were carved out of ivory. So young, so delicate, so transparently lovely, she appeared, from the bloom of light on her hair to her pale hands, which lay curled, like alabaster flowers, on the satin quilt, that Mrs. Upchurch caught her breath as she had done on the day when Annabel returned from abroad. Surely, by now, she should have grown accustomed to her daughter's enhanced beauty. Yet, whenever she saw her after a brief absence, she was startled afresh, just as she was when she glanced out on a flowering pear tree in the garden across the street. "She wasn't nearly so pretty as this when she was in love with Angus," she thought. "It shows what money can do. Her hands alone show what money can do." And her respect for wealth, which had been ample before, became inordinate while she drew a chair to the bedside.

"Annabel," she began in a tone which she tried to make as natural as it would have been if her child had remained poor and merely pretty, "isn't it time that you came to your senses?"

Annabel gazed at her with eyes that appeared enormous in her small, transparent face. "I've never been out of them, Mother."

"Have you forgotten that you are married?"

The girl shook her head, and all her coppery hair burned like flames about the head of a Christian martyr. "I wish that I could!"

"When are you going to get up?"

"To-morrow."

"Has that boy gone away?"

"He isn't a boy. He is twenty-six."

"When does he go?"

"To-morrow. He is going to Europe next week."

"Then, I suppose, you won't see him again?"

At this Annabel began to weep. "He is coming in the morning to tell me good-bye."

"That is very unwise, my child."

"I can't help it. I am obliged to see him once more."

Mrs. Upchurch looked at her severely. "What I can't understand," she said, "is the way you have got yourself so worked up over a boy you used to play with in the street. Why, I can't even think of him without auburn curls."

"Well, he's big enough now, and I haven't seen him for fifteen years."

"Only the other day you were just as wild about Angus."

Annabel shook her head impatiently. "Oh, that didn't mean anything. I thought it was real, but it wasn't. I got over that months ago."

"But it was just as real while it lasted, and it made just as much trouble for everybody else. Have you forgotten how you behaved when he married?"

"Well, even if I did, it didn't mean anything. I wanted something real. I am not like you. I can't be satisfied with shams."

"Can't you see that, if only you have patience and exercise self-control, this will pass away just as quickly?"

A furious sob answered her. "But I don't want it to pass away. Oh, Mother, can't you understand, even if you haven't any romance in your nature? If I can't have love, I'd rather die! I don't want to live, if I can't have love in my life!"

While she wept, her mother considered her gravely and in silence. With sentiments, even improper sentiments, Mrs. Upchurch was unhappily familiar, and of them she felt that she had no reason to be afraid; but confronted with a genuine passion, especially with a guilty passion, the kind that people enjoyed as well as feared, she was as helpless as a wren in a thunderstorm.

"How do you know——" she began, and broke off disconsolately. Though she had dragged her mind for an argument, she could find nothing more pointed than the Socratic method, which impressed her as threadbare from use and wont. "How do you know," she tried again more emphatically, "that this is really love?"

Annabel tossed back the drooping clusters of her hair and gazed at her mother reproachfully. "If you'd ever felt it, Mother, you would know without being told. It is like lightning when it strikes you. You don't have to wonder and hesitate, as I used to do when I thought I was falling in love with Angus. You are just caught up in a cloud of fire, and you can't help yourself. We knew it the very second it happened. It was the first night I went out to dinner without the Judge. Nothing has been the same since. Nothing will ever be the same again as long as I live. I'm in a dream all the time, except when I'm in despair. Oh, won't you try to understand, Mother? Won't you try to imagine what it means to me?"

Mrs. Upchurch sighed, while she struggled in vain to think of an answer. She had never heard the divine passion described so fluently; but, then, as she reflected, not many emotions were as articulate as Annabel's. Women of the past generation, however voluble over trifles, were seldom able to prattle intelligibly about love. While she listened to her daughter's impassioned voice, she recalled dolorously a phrase she had so often heard on the lips of her mother: "That is the kind of woman who is obliged to have a man in her life." To wives and spinsters of Victorian tradition that necessity had appeared indelicate; but it seemed to Mrs. Upchurch that nothing was indelicate any longer, not even the need of a man in your life. Was it really the war? she asked herself; for her conventional mind preferred to hold a world war, rather than original sin, responsible for Annabel's misguided behaviour.

"Well, I cannot see anything to do about it, my child," she said presently. "You will have to make an effort to be brave and think of your husband."

But this, it appeared, was the last thing that Annabel felt an inclination to do. "He has had his life," she replied, with an obstinate frown. "He has had his life, and I want mine." It was cruel, but, like so many cruel things, Mrs. Upchurch decided, it was true also.

"You must not forget, my dear, that you married him with your eyes open."

"I didn't, Mother. He knew, but I didn't. I didn't know how immoral marriage can be."

"Immoral? Oh, Annabel!"

"When you dislike a person. When you simply can't bear to have him near you."

"Hush, Annabel. You mustn't say such things. I won't listen to you."

"I know you would have lied about it, Mother, you and Cousin Amanda. You would have lied and pretended; but I won't. I won't be a sham all my life." With a sob of desperation, she rushed on: "I know I am unkind, I know I seem ungrateful. When I am away from him, I tell myself that I will be different. But as soon as he comes into the room, I can't think of anything except the fear that he will want to be affectionate."

Mrs. Upchurch moaned. "I tried to warn you, my child."

"Oh, you wanted it, Mother. You can't deny that you wanted it. But you shouldn't have let me do it. He shouldn't have let me."

"Are you reproaching me?"

"You oughtn't to have let me."

"But I did warn you. I told you that very few girls of your age could be happy with an old—with an elderly man. I tried to make you see that you would get a great deal in exchange; but I warned you that you would have to give up all idea of romance. You have had a great deal in your marriage, and have you forgotten already how absolutely you had finished with love?"

"I thought so. I thought so, but you must have known better."

"My dear, I finished with it more than twenty years ago, and I've managed to get on very well. Love isn't everything. I've tried it, and I know that it doesn't fill a very large place, as I once said to you, except in the lives of women who have never had it. If you only knew how much of its value depends upon its absence."

"You're different." Annabel's voice had risen above its plaintive melody to a key that sounded almost hysterical. "You can't understand, Mother, because you are not real. But he ought to have known better. He ought to have considered me more."

Mrs. Upchurch shook her head. "You have yet to learn, Annabel, that love makes most people, especially most men, inconsiderate."

"But how can he be in love at his age?"

"There isn't any age, my dear, when men can't be. I'm not sure about women, because it has taken a world war to make women begin telling the truth about themselves, and they haven't told half yet. As for men, I haven't a doubt that they can fall in love with one foot in the grave."

Annabel flung out her bare arm as if she were pushing the thought away. "Oh, Mother, I cannot live without love!" she cried, dropping back into her monotonous refrain. "If I cannot have love, I'd rather die!"

As she descended the stairs a little later, it seemed to Mrs. Upchurch that she still heard that changeless cry echoing from the other side of the world. Her visit had done no good. There was nothing that she could say, and, even if she had spoken words of wisdom, Annabel, in her desperation, would not have listened. It all came back, Mrs. Upchurch decided, to the lost idea of duty. "The Judge was right," she thought despondently. "You can't hold people in when you take the sense of duty away." And not duty alone, but remorse also, which she had found even more efficacious in unlawful love, appeared to have flown on wings of levity and ridicule. She remembered hearing once of an aunt on her mother's side who had been restrained from the fatal step by pondering Goldsmith's mournful advice to lovely woman. Well, if Goldsmith was a convenient household remedy in her grandmother's time, Mrs. Upchurch could only regret that the world had passed away from such simple antidotes to sin. But what, she asked, could be more deplorable than the swiftness with which the high tragedy of one generation declines into the low comedy of the next?

As she was putting on her coat in the hall, the door of the Judge's library opened, and, almost involuntarily, she turned and entered the room. She had hoped not to cross that threshold again until her mind was at rest; but, in spite of her sharp recoil from the meeting, she shut the door quickly behind her and spoke in a sympathetic and imperative manner.

"I think you have been wonderful. Yes, you have been simply wonderful. If you can be patient a little longer, I am sure the strain will soon be over. He is going away to-morrow, and you know how quickly youth forgets."

He flinched, and she saw that the reminder of youth was like the flick of a lash. Even her emphasis upon "wonderful," an epithet that she had found of inestimable value in dealing with men, appeared to have lost, in a measure, its potency. He looked seventy, she was quick to perceive, though six months ago, a stranger would have taken him for a man of late middle age. His skin had faded to the colour and the brittle texture of old parchment. There were inflamed pouches under his fine eyes, which had been so clear and bright for his years. Even his hair and beard looked as lifeless as scorched grass. This, she told herself with resentful bitterness, showed what that destructive passion could do even to the elderly, even to the well established in life.

"What troubles me most," he said in a hoarse whisper, "is the thought that I may have been to blame for it all. I cannot rid my mind of a feeling of self-reproach."

At this her tears gushed forth, and she fumbled in her bag for the handkerchief she had left on Annabel's bed. Not finding it, she wiped her eyes on her glove. "That is morbid. You must not let such an idea take hold of you. You have been perfect. Even Annabel says you have been perfect." Had Annabel said this? Well, if she had not, Mrs. Upchurch reasoned, it was what she ought to have said.

"Does she?" His face brightened.

"Don't think for an instant that she blames you for anything. How could she?"

"I am so much older that I ought to have known better."

"Nobody ever knows better when it comes to marriage. And if she had sought the world over, she couldn't have found a more indulgent husband."

"Perhaps not. Anyhow, it is kind of you to say that. But indulgent husbands, like so many other useful institutions, appear to have gone out of fashion. Nobody values them any longer."

"That is what girls think now; but just let them try fending for themselves as I have done. It is all a part of the loose talk the war released into the world."

He pondered this moodily. "It isn't, I fear, quite so simple as that. There has been a change, a readjustment of ideas, perhaps even of standards. We may have been too strict in our views; but the pendulum is swinging too far in the opposite direction to-day. The younger generation has caught hold of something different, and this difference confuses me. I have even asked myself if the wisdom of the ages can have been wrong."

"I think it much more likely that the younger generation is wrong," Mrs. Upchurch replied, with a tartness of which she was ashamed as soon as it had escaped her. "It looks to me like sheer immorality. I don't mean in fact, of course," she hastened to explain. "Annabel couldn't be underhand if she tried. She is as honest as the day."

"I am sure of that, and I am sure that you can't dismiss all this as mere immorality. Immorality we have had always with us, but it was different from this—this—I had almost said this revaluation of morals. Annabel has her point of view as clearly defined as we have ours. That is why we can't bring the old pressure of authority to bear on her. It is like the thunder of the papacy to a Protestant; it thunders as hard as ever but it fails to strike. The thing that has disturbed me most is that there seems to be some intellectual basis for the whole attitude. It may not be a sound one; nevertheless, it is there, and that lifts Annabel's motives above the plane of—of——"

"I know, I know." Mrs. Upchurch spoke emphatically, for she felt that this was one of the occasions when innuendo is the agent of delicacy. "You are too tolerant, too generous. I don't believe there is another man in the world who could be so—so" —she hesitated, swallowed hard, and then brought out with tearful urgency—"wonderful."

The effect this time was obviously beneficial, and before she could accentuate it with a firmer repetition, he answered in a trembling tone, "I hope I have not been unjust."

"You could not be," Mrs. Upchurch assured him; but she was thinking: "If he would act instead of moralizing, it would be so much more manly." Aloud, she said earnestly, "We both felt, we had a right to feel, that Annabel's first unhappy experience had made her older than her years."

"She may be older," he admitted, "but not in the way we thought."

"And, of course, she loves to talk about her feeling. Not that she has spoken of this to any one else. I am as positive as I can be that she has not breathed a word of this to a living soul except ourselves. She has promised me, and we can trust her absolutely."

"I sometimes wonder," Judge Honeywell said, "if I ought to have mentioned it even to you."

Mrs. Upchurch gazed at him through a mist of admiration. "To her own mother?" she murmured reproachfully. "Why, she made you. You couldn't help yourself, and, besides, she would have told me anyway."

"Yes, she insisted, and I am convinced it is better you should know."

"Oh, much better! What I am doubtful about is the wisdom of allowing her to see Dabney again. Couldn't you," she inquired in Victorian idiom, "put your foot down on that?" For there existed in her mind a tenacious belief that husbands were still invested with the weapon of authority; and, like all small women and nations, she respected violence more than a disarmed neutrality.

Judge Honeywell, who did not share this conviction, shook his head with a satirical smile. "I don't think it would do any good. Nothing I can say has the slightest effect upon her. I suppose it will have to wear itself out," he added gloomily.

"And that will be much sooner than we expect," Mrs. Upchurch responded, with recovered optimism. "With a temperament like Annabel's these things can't last but a few weeks. It is merely in her imagination, and as soon as she takes a little trip or begins planning for the summer, she will forget all about it. In the meantime, we must look on the bright side of things," she urged; for she had remembered her formula for a cheerful life, and the mere sound of the inspiring platitude braced her spirit. "Remember that you must not become morbid and reproach yourself. No woman in the world could have had a more devoted husband."

Already he looked better. How well she understood men, Mrs. Upchurch exulted, as she left the room and the house. How well, how perfectly, she understood men!

She had reached the pavement, and her feet were pointed in the direction of home, when there seized her like a flash of inspiration, like a divine call to duty, the feeling that, before she said her prayers and turned to her pillow, she must speak one last warning to Annabel. "If only I can make her promise not to see him again," she said to herself, while she wheeled about and retraced her steps to the door.

CHAPTER 14

ONSTABLE was still standing on the threshold, for he had his reasons unrelated to the domestic infelicity of the Judge for watching the street; and while he held the door open for her, Mrs. Upchurch brushed past him without a word and toiled wearily up the stairs. Her proper instincts, inured to the consecrated discomforts of matrimony, had already remarked with concern that Annabel had moved across the hall into a room two doors away from the marital chamber. Though Mrs. Upchurch's mother had been long in her grave, and was denied the stringent pleasure of admonishing a rebellious generation, the daughter could still hear her saying crisply, "When husband and wife begin to occupy different chambers, I expect trouble to follow." Well, trouble had followed here promptly enough to satisfy any moralist; and yet, though she yielded to no one, as she often said, in respect for the Spartan fortitude her ancestors had displayed in marriage, Mrs. Upchurch could not help wondering if they had ever really understood the value of privacy. Having suffered in her brief wifehood from the male sense of possession, which she regarded as excessive, she was inclined to accept the modern theory that both privacy and fresh air are beneficial in wedded life. Yet her mother, who had borne eleven children with little difficulty, and certainly with less complaint than women make to-day over one or two, had sternly condemned, not only separate rooms, but even twin beds as immodest. "And now it is exactly the other way," Mrs. Upchurch mused, impartial but keenly observant of revolving conventions.

The door of Annabel's room was closed, and as Mrs. Upchurch noiselessly opened it, she was distressed to hear the sound

of smothered weeping. The logs had burned down on the and-
irons, and the room was suffused with a melancholy light from
the green afterglow beyond the black fretwork of trees. In this
wan glimmer, which made sad things appear even sadder, as if
they were drowned in clear water, Annabel was kneeling beside the bed, with her arms flung out upon the coverlet and her
feet upturned on a white bearskin rug. Her gown of primrose
crêpe was one that her mother had made with fastidious care in
order to save the cost of a seamstress, and at sight of the pros-
trated garment, with its frivolous garlands of forget-me-nots,
Mrs. Upchurch felt a strange clutch at her heart and an almost
irresistible impulse to cry. This moment restored to her Annabel as a baby, and all the dreary years of widowhood—the bleak-
ness of genteel poverty, the shams and subterfuges and deceits
that had served her ends and destroyed her faith,—all these sordid and ugly facts were swept away by the flood of maternal
passion.

"My baby! Oh, my baby!" she cried, and dropping on the
fur rug by the bed, she enfolded Annabel in the sheltering
warmth of her sealskin coat.

Annabel turned her head, and her mother saw that there was
more than romantic drama, that there was genuine heartbreak
in her eyes.

"My darling child, what can I do? Tell me. Tell Mother."

"I can't live without love. If I can't have love, I'd rather
die!"

"You're so young, my child. Wait a little longer. Only have
patience."

"I can't wait until I am old. I want it now. I want my life,
Mother!"

"This will pass, dear. Think of other women."

"I don't care about other women. They were just shams.
They just pretended to be real."

"Oh, Annabel!"

"You were all afraid of life, and you called your fear virtue."

"My child, what are you saying?"

"I don't care. I'm not afraid. I want my life while I am young."

"But you have so much. Remember all your blessings. All the devotion. All the—luxury."

"I don't want it. I want my life."

"Have you forgotten what it means to be poor?"

"I haven't forgotten, and I don't care. I'd rather be poor. I'd rather beg my bread and have my own life again."

"You have never tried begging your bread, my dear," Mrs. Upchurch said solemnly. "I have, and I know how bitter the bread you beg can taste."

She held her daughter closer, trying to lift her into bed; but Annabel broke away from the clinging arms and sobbed wildly that she wanted her life again. "It will kill me," Mrs. Upchurch thought distractedly, more unhappy than she had been since Annabel was born. "It will kill me, but there is nothing I can do about it." For, in spite of her infinite resources, she felt, for once in her adroit experience, completely resourceless.

"Is it really this boy, Annabel?" she asked presently, unable to believe that so much suffering could be inspired by so inadequate a cause.

"If he goes away, I shall die, Mother. I can't live without him."

"It is easy to say that, dear, but, somehow, we go on living just the same. Look at all the women who lost their lovers in the war."

"But that was different. Oh, can't you see, Mother, that was different?"

"Yes, perhaps it was different." Though Mrs. Upchurch couldn't see how it was, she was willing to yield anything so long as it was only in words.

"That was different because it meant something," Annabel insisted. "At least they had life."

"You will have life too, dear. You are so young."

"But I want it now, Mother. I don't want to wait until I am old to begin to live."

Over and over. Was there to be no end to it? "If only you could see, Annabel, that love isn't all of life, that it isn't even a very large part of it."

"It is all I want. I don't want anything else."

"How can I help you? What can I do?"

"I want to be free. I don't want to be married."

"But you are married, my child."

"I don't want to be, Mother! I don't want to be!"

"Hush, Annabel. Have you no regard for your husband? It is as hard on him as on you."

"It isn't. He has had his life. All I want is my own life. That is all."

Mrs. Upchurch sighed with weary patience. "You must have pity on me, my child. I am worn out."

"Poor Mother. I know you are. Go home and go to bed."

"How can I leave you when you are like this? Won't you try, just to please me, to put it all out of your mind? Eat something and go to sleep. I'll tell Constable to bring some sherry with your dinner. Won't you try . . ." She turned over in her mind the different forms of persuasion she might employ, and found them all useless. Was it true, she asked herself, in sudden depression, that not duty, but the fear of living, had held back youth in the past? In the earlier generations, how many girls had married men old enough to be their fathers or grandfathers, and yet nothing disastrous had come of it, nothing, at least, with which husbands, aided by duty or the fear of living, had not been able to deal. Women had known then how to live without love, just as they had known how to live without beauty or happiness; but she realized now, watching Annabel's bleak despair, that it had been because they had something else to put in its place. Something abstract and ultimate! Something as unalterable and as everlasting as the Rock of Ages! Even if duty were merely a symbol—well, a symbol, Mrs. Upchurch decided, is better than an abyss to fall back upon. A quiver of weakness attacked her elbows and knees. It seemed to her that there were no longer any moral properties left in the world. Experience was reduced to the sum of pure egoism.

Bending over Annabel, she kissed her tenderly on the cheek. "Try to be quiet, darling, and remember that it is almost as important to look up to your husband as it is to be in love with him. Thank God, you are married to a man you can respect."

Annabel's flippant laugh answered her. "Oh, I could respect him just as much if he were still Cousin Cordelia's husband!"

"Will you let him come in and say good-night?"

A shiver of aversion trembled through Annabel's body. "No, I can't see him. I can't bear to see him."

"Well, you don't have to see him. Go to sleep, and I'll think what I can do in the morning. All I ask is that you will let me have one good night's rest."

But that warning shudder had spoken to Mrs. Upchurch more poignantly than any words, than any tears, could have done. "If it is really that, there is nothing we can do," she told herself hopelessly. "You can't bring moral pressure to bear upon a physical aversion."

She stayed until Annabel's dinner was brought and she had watched her sip the wine and eat the wing of a chicken. After a glass of the Judge's sherry, she felt that her own hardy optimism was beginning to show signs of revival. When, at last, she went softly downstairs and out into the street, she was able to assure herself that aversion, like so much else that is unpleasant in life, is often merely a matter of nerves. After the dose of veronal she had persuaded Annabel to take, a sound sleep and a good waking might work wonders. In the morning, Mrs. Upchurch concluded, everything, even the temporizing of the judicial intellect, would appear less melancholy. "It is a pity Gamaliel isn't just a little more—well, a little more masculine," she thought with a sigh; for, peculiar as it seemed to her, she felt exasperated rather than consoled by the Judge's magnanimity.

A little ahead of her, she recognized the stately figure of Amanda Lightfoot, wearing a coat trimmed with chinchilla, and an odd-looking hat, which was perched too high on her grey pompadour, after a fashion that had been much admired when she was young. In the glare of the huge electric light on the corner, the younger woman read, as if they had been hieroglyphics of lost illusions, the faint, innumerable lines that blurred Amanda's transparent skin. "She has suffered in her way more than Annabel," Mrs. Upchurch thought sadly, "but the difference is that she has learned how to suffer. She has made an art of unhappiness."

"I missed you at Mrs. Peyton's tea," Amanda said in a voice of faded sweetness. "You told me you were going, so I stopped to ask what was the matter?"

"Annabel has a cold, and I went to her instead. The Judge was obliged to be at his office."

"I am sorry. The dear child looked so lovely at the Easter cotillion."

"I am afraid that is how she caught her sore throat. I thought she'd better stay in bed for a day or two."

"Give her my love. As soon as my young people leave me free for a minute, I'll drop in to see her."

Mrs. Upchurch was gazing at her with genuine admiration. "You are so fond of children, Amanda, that you ought to have married. Some man missed an ideal wife when you chose to be a spinster, and I'm sure no other woman in Queenborough ever had so many admirers. Do you remember the way the men used to stand in line to watch you enter a ballroom? Only the other day, I came across an album with those verses Aubrey Dale wrote about dancing with you. Don't you remember the ones beginning, 'When Amanda's queenly form I press'?"

A flush passed over Amanda's perfect features; but it faded quickly, and the wrinkles, as light and intricate as the tracks birds leave in snow, were still visible.

"You wouldn't regret it, dear Bella, if you could see how useful and happy my life has been. I have so many brothers and sisters, you know."

"But they left you."

"Oh, no, I have them still. The children are with me every

day and I share all their pleasures. I am sure no woman in the world lives with the young more than I do."

Mrs. Upchurch smiled grimly. Living with the young had become for her, in the last week or two, a dubious blessing. Did Amanda, did any woman of mature years, really wish to sink her life and her interests into the grasping egoism of immaturity? Occasionally, perhaps, when she had slept well and was feeling composed in mind and body after a good breakfast. But not always, not to be perpetually obliged to attune every word, without merciful intermission, to a jazz orchestra. While she looked into Amanda's skilfully repaired face, she realized that the older woman's happiness was a mixture of fortitude and hypocrisy, and she realized also that Amanda was aware of her knowledge. "Well, she's safe with me," Mrs. Upchurch reflected; and she told herself that, notwithstanding the vast sex-lore accumulated by the researches of men, there are subjects upon which women do not give one another away.

"I'm glad you are busy, dear," was all she said. "Run in to see me whenever you have time."

"Indeed I shall, and I sha'n't forget Annabel. That marriage has turned out so beautifully. I can't tell you how happy it makes me to think that my dear old friend has youth to brighten his home."

Yes, Amanda had fortitude. Hypocrisy alone could not have carried it off with that accent of triumph.

After watching the majestic figure until it was lost in the shadows, Mrs. Upchurch turned away and entered her door with a dragging step. There was an edge of frost to the April air, and in her sitting-room a bright fire was burning. An amiable tortoise-shell cat was dozing before the flames; from his high-hanging cage by the window, a canary piped joyously; in the centre of the dinner table, where the candles were lighted, there was a blue bowl of pear blossoms; an aroma of herbs and spices floated in from the kitchen; the afternoon paper, secure from male aggression, lay still folded on a little stand beneath the reddish glow of the lamp. "And this," thought Mrs. Upchurch, while she gazed round her at the cheerful welcome, "is what they call loneliness."

Surrendering her coat and hat into the eager hands of Altrusa, she sank into the softest chair and stretched out her weary feet to the fender. Rest, rest and quiet stole gradually like an anodyne over her aching nerves. She sighed happily; there was no crisis here; there was no wild youth. She sighed more happily still: there was no sentimental age. There was nothing more agitating than the tranquil immunity of a mind that had finished with love.

CHAPTER 15

A T NINE o'clock the next morning, fortified by a solitary night and two cups of coffee, Mrs. Upchurch had recovered sufficiently to renew the struggle with youth.

"How are you this morning, my child?" she asked tenderly over the telephone. "Did you sleep well?" To her amazement, a bright voice answered her, "I'm all right, Mother. I wish you hadn't worried so yesterday."

Worried so! Was this the way the afternoon appeared in retrospect to Annabel? "Well, I sha'n't worry to-day if you are all right. I'll stop by after market."

For an instant there was silence; then, more brightly than ever, the voice responded, "Don't come this morning. I've made an engagement, and I've promised to lunch with Nellie Peyton. Had you forgotten her bridge party?"

"Yes, I remember. Are you really going?"

"Well, I ought to have telephoned her yesterday, but as long as I didn't——"

"Of course, if you feel like going, dear, I am delighted. It may do you good to get out again."

"There are to be eight tables, and then we're going to tea afterwards with Amy Ballard. I sha'n't be back till late. Not till after six anyway."

"Very well. I'll drop in between six and seven. But are you equal to that long strain? Have you sufficient command of yourself?"

"Oh, perfectly! There isn't a bit of use your getting excited about me, Mother."

The sheer audacity of this stunned Mrs. Upchurch, and when she had recovered breath, she exclaimed, with a touch of asperity, "Well, I like that! However, if you are entirely cured, I shall try to give a little attention to my own duties."

"Indeed, you ought to!" Annabel trilled gaily. "Come over this evening after you've finished everything you have to do. Good-bye, Mother darling!"

Had her ear deceived her, Mrs. Upchurch questioned the next instant, or had Annabel's voice broken with a sob on the last word? While she wondered, an impulse seized her to run over before she went to market; but immediately her artful judgment, trained to temporizing, curbed the motherly instinct. After all, it was better to leave the child to work out her own problem. Too much interference, in Mrs. Upchurch's experience, had invariably ended in trouble. Only weak characters needed constant support; and, for all her frail appearance, Annabel, as her mother had sad reason to know, was not without firmness of purpose. "There's a vein of iron in her somewhere," Mrs. Upchurch mused pensively. "That's what poor Mother used to say about me, and I suppose the child has inherited it. You may talk to her until you are hoarse, but, after all, talking never gets very far with anybody who is as determined and as fearless as Annabel. The only way is to let it wear itself out." She sighed as she left the telephone and began her preparations for market. "I believe these scenes take more out of me than they do out of her. In any case, I hope some of her cheerfulness has been saved for her husband."

While she attended to the automatic duties of the morning, and made a few purchases in the shops, she became gradually aware that a burden had been lifted, not only from her mind, but from her exhausted body as well. The sudden relief acted as a tonic upon her heart. Even now, she did not know what she had feared, merely that her nerves had waited for some impending disaster. In the tumultuous state of Annabel's emotion, undeterred as she was by the normal obstacles to a guilty love, Mrs. Upchurch felt tremulously that anything might have happened. That nothing had happened, she said to herself with vague thankfulness, was owing less to human ingenuity than to the divine mercy of Omnipotence; for at such moments her feeling overflowed in the orthodox forms of her youth. Tired yet rejoicing, she went through her uneventful day, and encountered nothing more depressing than the unwelcome sight of Mrs. Bredalbane on her way to the Judge's house.

"I am sorry to hear, Bella, that Annabel has been under the weather. I was there yesterday, but Gamaliel would not let me see her. I am sure I couldn't understand why."

"She is ever so much better to-day. I talked to her over the telephone this morning, and she said she was going to Nellie's luncheon."

"I'm glad to hear it. The truth is that I haven't been altogether easy in my mind about Annabel for the last few weeks. She hasn't been a bit like herself. What she needs is to get away from Gamaliel for a while. He is one of the best men in the world and born to be a husband; but that only makes him the more wearing in marriage. The theory that a man soon tires of his wife but a woman can never see too much of her husband doesn't thrive any longer even in male vanity."

"I am sure that Gamaliel and Annabel are very happy," Mrs. Upchurch protested, while her immovable smile felt as if it were a plaster on her aching face. "He adores her, and she has a deep affection for him."

"But don't you think it would be a good idea for her to go away?" Mrs. Bredalbane persisted. "I suggested to Gamaliel yesterday that she might spend the summer with me. Now, don't put on that startled-rabbit look, Bella. I assure you that I am even more than respectable, I am positively distinguished, in Europe. Anybody who can afford, not only to make bills, but to pay them, need never worry about her social position abroad. Why, in my day, which was both long and glorious, I have turned down, not only foreign dukes, but international bankers as well. Like Gamaliel, however, I have always preferred youth to wisdom."

"But, my dear Mrs. Bredalbane, I didn't mean to imply——"

"Oh, I understand, Bella. There is no need to apologize. I

suppose it is natural, after the things you have heard about me, that you should hesitate to trust Annabel to my discretion; but, if you take my advice, you will let her have a little needed vacation from marriage. It wouldn't hurt her to come away with me for a few months. I'd take the best care of her, and she could really see something of the world. As provincial as you are in America, it is hopeless to try to make you understand that behaviour as much as beauty is a question of geography, and that my respectability increases with every mile of the distance I travel from Queenborough. In France, my reputation is above reproach; by the time I reach Vienna, I have become a bit of a prude; and contrasted with the Balkan temperament, I am little more than a tombstone to female virtue."

Mrs. Upchurch's smile quivered into a pathetic contortion of her agreeable features. "That would be delightful for Annabel," she murmured, "but I am sure Gamaliel would never consent to her going away without him."

"I dare say you're right." Mrs. Bredalbane heaved a sigh over such uxorious folly, and then resumed, on a more cheerful key, "Well, I am relieved that the marriage has turned out this way, though it is hard for me to forgive Gamaliel when I look at Amanda."

Mrs. Upchurch's dissent was more lukewarm than it would have been the day before yesterday. "I suppose there isn't a doubt that she expected him to marry her, poor thing," she said, "but you know what men are, Mrs. Bredalbane."

"Oh, I know," Edmonia assented heartily. "None better."

"Constancy doesn't appeal to them as it does to women. The trouble is that Amanda has always lived in some world of sentimental invention. She has had absolutely no contact with reality."

"Well, we were all like that a generation or two ago. You can't blame her for not pricking the bubble when you remember the deluge of soapsuds that splashed over me. It took courage to face a ducking in those days, and so long as you were different from the wasp-waisted morality of the period, it scarcely mattered whether you were a saint or a sinner, for both got the same punishment, though, if anything, the saint got the worst of it. The venom with which they pursued me was nothing compared to the ribald mirth they showered upon poor Johanna Goodwin, who was as sexless as an amœba but had a mind of her own. She was the first suffragist in Queenborough, and that wasn't so long ago, my dear Bella."

"Yes, I remember. But she is one of the twelve greatest American women to-day. They put up a very small monument to her last year."

Mrs. Bredalbane chuckled. "Well, we can't deny that fame wears a sardonic smile! But poor Amanda, who chose the middle way, got neither four husbands nor a very small monument. She has fallen away to the shadow of herself since Gamaliel's marriage. Have you noticed that her mother's nervous habit of talking all the time in the same tone has taken hold of her?"

Yes, Mrs. Upchurch had noticed it, and she looked a little wan as she rejoined, "I wonder if she really believed love lasted like that?"

"It was more than love to her. It was a purpose in life."

"But she broke it of her own will." Mrs. Upchurch's tone sounded almost tearful, for even her elastic conscience had never been entirely reconciled to the part that worldly wisdom had borne in Annabel's marriage to Judge Honeywell.

"A lovers' quarrel, nothing more. But I happen to know—this is as secret as the grave of course," Mrs. Bredalbane lowered her masculine voice, "and I shouldn't like it to go any farther—that he fell more desperately in love with her than ever after his marriage. For a time he was threatened with a complete nervous breakdown, and the family thought that he would have to give up his career. I can't tell you how I heard it, but it came to me in the most direct way that he went so far as to ask Amanda to elope with him. Of course, she was the soul of honour, and she kept him true to Cordelia for thirty-six years. What she is enduring now," the fearless Edmonia concluded, "is almost the inevitable reward of virtue. But, for my part, I may say that, if she doesn't have one of those small monuments erected to her, it isn't because she hasn't deserved it."

A sensation of dizziness, to which she had become subject in the last trying months, swam through Mrs. Upchurch's brain. "I never heard that," she murmured in a flagging voice.

"You will never hear it from Amanda. She belongs to a generation that is sealed tight. I declare you are as white as a sheet, Bella. Here, take a whiff of my smelling salts. It is safer always to have a bottle with you."

"I'll go in now," Mrs. Upchurch remarked stiffly, as she declined the salts. Walking very carefully, for she was oppressed by an inclination to faint, just to give up and drop down quietly on the pavement, she went up one step at a time, and reached the door at the instant when it was opened by Constable.

"Has Mrs. Honeywell come in, Constable?"

"No, madam, not yet. But she told me to ask you to go up to her sitting-room and wait for her."

"Very well. She will probably be home in a little while."

She went up slowly, ascending with an effort, as if her feet were leaden weights, and at the top of the stairs, she looked into Annabel's sitting-room, which was decorated in black and orange, and saw a tea-table laid in front of the smouldering fire.

"I suppose I'm still feeling the strain of yesterday," she thought, while she sank down on the couch and slipped out of her coat. "And it was all so unnecessary!"

For a minute she closed her eyes to a swimming world and lay back on the cushions. When she raised her lids again, it seemed to her that every object in the room was intensified by the flickering firelight, and gazing through this tremulous glow, she saw, for the first time, a note placed conspicuously in front of the bronze clock on the mantelpiece. Rising, she groped her way toward it, and stopped to read the words "For Mother," with a sinking heart, before she tore open the envelope. Her trembling legs failed her, and she dropped into the nearest chair, while opaque patches floated before her eyes and her brain was filled with a slow humming like the music of distant bees. "I can't see," she moaned, fingering for the glasses she wore attached by a gold chain to the front of her dress. Even with the glasses on her nose, she found that these vague smears drifted before her eyes, and she struggled to see above and below them. Were the words really as incoherent as they sounded in her brain? Or was she the victim of some sudden delusion?

DEAREST MOTHER:

I am going away because I can't bear it any longer. There isn't any sense in letting one mistake spoil your whole life. I know now there has never been anybody in the world but Dabney, and he feels just the same way. We were made for each other, and we would rather starve together than be separated. Oh, Mother, you must understand!

I am not taking anything but a small bag, and if you feel that you can send me some clothes (my own old clothes) to the Hotel Blackwood in New York, I shall be ever so grateful. But if you feel that you can't do it, I'll manage with what I can get. We haven't much money, and it will take almost all for the passage, but don't worry about me. I am not afraid of anything but losing Dabney, and for the first time in my life, I am perfectly happy.

Your loving

ANNABEL.

There was a touch on her arm, and Mrs. Upchurch turned to stare vacantly into Judge Honeywell's face. Her lips moved, but no sound came, and the sheet of paper fluttered from her nerveless hand into his.

"Annabel!" she said at last, and choked over the name. "Annabel!"

He read the letter through, folded it carefully, and replaced it in the envelope. His face was leaden in its pallor and immobility; but while she watched him, she became aware that his weakness of purpose receded before an infusion of strength. Power had returned to him with the necessity for immediate decision. The crisis, which had enfeebled her resolution, had restored energy to his will.

"I'll go on to-night," he said. "There is time to catch the eight o'clock train." After a pause, in which she felt the shudder of his muscles, he continued dispassionately: "I cannot acquit myself of responsibility."

"You will bring her back." Her quavering voice was the voice of an old woman. "My baby! Oh, my little, little baby!"

"I will do my best. What more can I promise?" His manner was so wooden that for a moment she was tempted to cry out: "Why can't you forget yourself? Why can't you suffer as I do?" Then the mute anguish in his eyes pierced her despair, and she thought: "Yes, he suffers in his way. Only it isn't a mother's way."

CHAPTER 16

RAIN had fallen in the night, and a sharp wet wind was blowing when Judge Honeywell left his hotel the next morning. After a rest and a carefully chosen breakfast, for which he was astonished to find he had an appetite, he had hoped that New York would present a less gloomy appearance than the one he had seen on the short drive from the station. But he remembered that tumultuous centres of life are always depressing, except to the very young, who carry their sources of happiness within themselves.

As he walked slowly along the blocks in the direction of the small hotel on the West Side where Annabel was staying, he asked himself why he could no longer impose his stern but just will upon circumstances. "I must be getting old," he thought wearily. "Only youth enjoys a forlorn hope, and youth is a long way behind me." For it seemed to him that the actual boundary between youth and age is the moment when one realizes that one cannot change life.

The strong, wet wind, moaning like the deep tones of an orchestra, rushed past him; and he felt that the increasing violence hurled his thoughts down the long, drab street, where shop-keepers were opening shutters and children were thronging out on the pavement. He knew that he ought to suffer; yet this paralysis of soul was what he would have called in his younger days the opposite of grief. Vacancy? Despair? No, it was too inanimate for despair.

Still his thoughts raced ahead of him among a multitude of formless influences. And he felt that this dark wind, blowing through immeasurable silence, had changed into the inescapable loneliness of the grave. Around him there was eternal isolation of spirit. Not the human spirit alone, but the essence of all spirits. Spirits of men and women. Spirits of children. Spirits of animals. Spirits of plants. All immersed and drowning in loneliness. The loneliness of trees in tropical jungles, with roots coiling back into perpetual night; the loneliness of buried rivers stealing out of the earth and into the earth again; the loneliness of lost and frightened animals in stony deserts of streets; the loneliness of the dying in the wan glimmer of daybreak; the vast, frozen loneliness of stars over remote continents of ice;—all these invisible aspects of desolation crowded round him in the chill mist where his thoughts sped pattering like withered husks on the pavement. It was not pain that he felt. Any pain, if only it were alive, would have been a relief. What he endured, he told himself, with his gaze on the inclement sky, was the ultimate negation of being, the encompassing solitude of the end.

He went on slowly, and as he walked, a sound within his brain, far below in the dark emptiness, ticked like a clock that is beginning to run down: "Growing old. Growing old. Old—old —old—growing old." And over this abyss, on the frozen surface of his mind, the thought glided: "I'll take her to California next month. She has always wanted to see California."

Above a shabby front, he saw the name Hotel Blackwood, and he was about to turn in at the open door when a girl hurrying ahead looked quickly round, and he saw that it was Annabel. Annabel, vivid, rose-coloured, still wearing the sable toque and the mink coat he had bought for her in Paris. Yet she had asked her mother to send her "own old clothes"! Her absurd sacrifice, which was only a part of the irresistible variety of Annabel herself, moved him to a tenderness that was embittered by sardonic laughter.

"Oh, you!" she exclaimed, and stopped as she was entering the door. Her hands were full of parcels, and when she dropped one, he stooped to pick it up before he responded to her cry of amazement.

"You must have known I should come for you, Annabel," he

said, for her astonishment had seemed to him affected. "Where can I talk to you?"

She hesitated, while he thought that he had never seen her look so fresh, so guileless, so enchantingly lovely. Even the dampness from the moist wind that suffused her face was transferred by some hidden fire into the glamour of innocence.

"Come in," she replied reluctantly. "We've taken a little apartment upstairs. I can talk to you there. Dabney has gone to see about our passage. But it isn't any use," she added, with glowing obstinacy. "It isn't the least use in the world."

"Let me talk to you and see. I haven't come to argue with you—or—or to blame you. I can't rid myself of a feeling of responsibility," he explained, while the sense of his own generosity brought a tinge of moisture to his eyes. "I am older, and I should have known better."

For the first time she smiled, though not without a hint of impatience. "Well, it doesn't matter now," she answered brightly. "All that is over, and there's no need to begin worrying about who was responsible." The lilt of ecstasy in her voice was like the song of a lark.

She led the way, burdened with her parcels, of which he had tried punctiliously to relieve her, and he followed slowly into a hotel which smelled of unhappy yesterdays. Beneath a smoky ceiling, a dour-looking clerk sat examining his finger-nails. A decrepit charwoman was scouring a strip of tiled floor before an unappetizing restaurant. The lift rattled as it descended, and a drowsy negro blinked at them from the bars of the ramshackle cage. And Annabel, who had said that she would rather die than live without beauty, was apparently oblivious of the stale air, of the dirt and the dinginess.

In silence, he followed her into the lift, and in silence he waited until they stopped at the fifth floor and she alighted and nodded to him to come down the narrow passage. With the step of youth and joy, she flitted ahead of him, avoiding another charwoman and her bucket of soapsuds. At the end of the hall, which suffocated him with its close odours, she unlocked a door and passed into a small, musty room, where the electric light shone by day and the remains of breakfast had not been removed from the table. Beyond the stringy curtains of Nottingham lace at the window, there was a blank wall of discoloured brick.

She shut the door, placed her parcels on the hard sofa in one corner, and turned reluctantly to look at him. Her manner of calm efficiency surprised him even more than the absence of regret or contrition in her sparkling gaze. What he had expected he scarcely knew, but he had looked for something different from this. Hesitation, uncertainty, sadness; not this unruffled confidence in her perilous adventure.

"I wish you hadn't come," she said gently. Taking off her sable hat, she tossed it on the sofa and ran her fingers through the gleaming waves of her hair.

"I had to come, Annabel. What else could I do?"

"There isn't anything to say. I can never go back."

"You don't realize—you can't realize what it means. It is not fair to me. It is not fair to your mother."

"Poor Mother. Of course she will be hurt, but she will get over it presently. She always gets over things."

"She has never had anything like this. Can't you see that you are bringing disgrace upon us all? Upon yourself more than all the rest?"

She shook her head with a gesture that would have been superb, he thought, in a nobler cause. "I am sorry about Mother," she answered. "If she had ever lived, she would be able to understand; but she doesn't know what it means to be famished for joy. I suppose it is because she has never known what joy really is. I am sorry for you too," she added, with an afterthought. "I tried not to hurt you. Oh, I did try, but you will never believe it."

He bowed his head, while he felt his face blanch and wither beneath her brilliant eyes. "I at least ought to have known," he replied. "This is why I can't rid myself of the blame. This is why I shall assume the responsibility."

"You can't. You are kind and generous, but you can't do

that." A smile as faint as a shadow wavered and died and wavered again on her ardent lips. Was it a cruel smile, he asked himself, or merely the smile of brooding wisdom?

"If only you could realize," he urged passionately, "what it means to a woman to defy convention."

"Conventions don't matter. Love is worth everything."

What a child she was still, he thought, and asked immediately, "Do you love this—this boy like that?"

Her laugh entered his heart like a curved blade. "He isn't a boy. He is twenty-six, and taller than you are."

He winced. "But a year ago you loved Angus."

"Oh, that was a year ago! And besides, that wasn't real. I was only pretending because I was hungry for life. I was just looking for something I didn't have. If you can't understand, it is hopeless to tell you."

"And you think this is more serious?"

"It isn't serious. It is—it is solemn. I love him until it—it is like pain. Do you know what I mean?"

Yes, he knew. He knew because he had once been young and had loved Amanda that way—until it was pain.

"If you will come home with me, I will promise anything. I will give you anything."

"There isn't anything that would make up for it. There isn't anything in the world. You can't understand, you and Mother. You will never understand." There was a running flame in her words, and he felt that they scorched him with the smothered vehemence of her passion. "It isn't only that you are not young. It is that you live in a different world, and life doesn't mean the same thing to you that it does to us. You believe that it is right to be unhappy, but we know that it is wrong to suffer. We know you aren't really yourself, that you aren't even alive when you're unhappy. So many women chain themselves to their own fears, and pretend they are being noble. They call the chain they have made duty; but, after all, they are not noble; they are only afraid of life. Poor Cousin Amanda! All her virtues are rooted in fear.

Never once has she dared to be herself, and she hasn't dreamed that courage to be yourself is the greatest virtue of all."

Delusion? Sophistry? The modern mania for self-exaltation? Or merely the unconquerable audacity of youth—of youth defiant, intrepid, absurd, and indestructible! With sudden penetration, he realized that this new wild spirit of to-day was merely the cry of an immemorial longing for joy! Are the young ever afraid of the future? Do the old ever escape from the fear of shadows?

"I didn't come to argue with you, Annabel," he said, knowing that her words were folly but that her spirit was unanswerable. "I came to ask you to wait a little while—to wait just a little longer."

She shook her head. "I want my life while I am young. Life won't wait."

With a sigh, he looked away from her to the blank wall beyond the lace curtains. Nothing in the past had prepared him to meet such a crisis. There was no help in reason; there was no support in philosophy; there was no comfort in precedent. He could not any more than Victorian tradition become vocal in the presence of triumphant guilt.

"I'll make any arrangement, Annabel. I'll agree to any conditions," he pleaded helplessly. "I'll take you to California in May. You've always wanted to see California. I'll give you anything you may ask." It was fatuous, he knew; it was abject surrender of every masculine prerogative.

"But you can't. There aren't any conditions. I want to live. I want to struggle. Oh, can't you see that money, that having things, isn't happiness—it is only a substitute. Now that I have what I want, nothing else really matters. Not being poor, not being hungry, not going without——"

"You haven't tried it," he answered, and uttered, he felt, the only sensible words that had been spoken. She was both foolish and wrong, and she deserved, he told himself, all the punishment that would come to her; yet, while he watched her in despairing silence, he saw that her guilty passion enkindled her being. Not as a flower, but as a jewel, she was alive. The glow of prophecy and vision was in her face, and he realized that the ancient mysteries of earth were using her ecstasy as a vessel of life. Dawn and sunset and moonrise had melted into the gemlike radiance of her youth. Never in the years that he had known her, never in the months of their marriage, had he seen her transfigured by love.

"You can't fight life," he thought. "You can only endure it." He felt suddenly that he was slipping back, back into a bottomless void, and, against his will, his despair cried out: "But think of me, Annabel! Think of me with everything gone! Think of me with nothing to hope for, with nothing to live for!"

Her face quivered and paled. "I am sorry," she answered. Only that. "I am sorry."

For an instant, it seemed to him that he was suffocated by his anguish, by this encompassing void without light or sound. Then he recovered strength and said slowly, "Of course I shall give you your freedom."

She smiled triumphantly. "I *am* free."

His head ached from weariness. Had his journey to New York —had his whole life been a failure? "You have a great deal to learn. But what I can do, I will. At least I can keep you from the worst hardship. I can keep you from poverty."

"You're kind," she replied, genuinely touched. "You have always been kinder to me than I deserved."

"I shall still be kind. I may be doing wrong, but I shall be kinder than I have ever been."

However mistaken the impulse of benevolence might prove in the end, he felt, while it exhilarated his mood, that his frozen will was dissolving in light. For one moment, so swift that it was gone before he had seized it, he was thrilled again by that ineffable sense of divinity—or was it only seraphic illusion? Then the light faded; the miraculous visitation was over. After all, life was as fluid as time or as memory. It was impossible to distil its essence into a more permanent form than a glow, a perfume, an ecstasy.

"Yes, I shall still be kind," he repeated before they parted; but the exalted impulse had vanished, and there was only a dull emptiness where the radiance had flickered and died.

CHAPTER 17

I N T H E street, soft, fine rain, scarcely heavier than mist, was driving before the wind. He was without an umbrella, and while he walked on, looking for a taxicab, the dampness penetrated his overcoat and soaked through his flesh as through paper. Though he was chilled and wet and miserable, he felt a dull astonishment at the blunted edge of his grief. His world had fallen in ruins about him; yet he could wonder why there was no sharper pang in his suffering; he could think dispassionately, "If I can reach home and find my easy chair, my fire, and my whiskey, I shall be able to regain fortitude."

At the corner of Broadway, he found an empty taxicab, and shivering with cold, he directed the driver to his hotel. There was a train leaving for the South within an hour, and all his energies were bent upon reaching the station in sufficient time to find a seat disengaged. Still shivering, but fearful that he should be forced to delay his return, he hurried into the hotel, and coming out almost immediately, started again for the station. Everything was driven out of his mind by this desperate craving for physical comfort, for the inestimable consolation of habit.

The train was not crowded, and after he had settled himself, with a footstool and the morning paper, the nervous tension of his mind slowly relaxed. He was strained to the breaking point; he felt immeasurably tired; and he knew that the last twenty-four hours had extinguished forever the flickering impulse of youth; yet the numbness of his emotions had robbed old age, not only of its terror, but of its repugnance as well. Even decay appeared more desirable than a futile striving for happiness. Though he was a temperate man by instinct and education, he would have exchanged, at the moment, all the elusive pleasures of love for one drink so strong that it could banish the aching chill from his marrow. Since hot tea was the only substitute, he went back to the dining car and returned slightly sick but very little warmer. Leaning back in his chair, while the bleak landscape rushed past in glimpses of earth and sky, he sank into spiritual apathy. Pain was drowned in its flood. Even the recollection of pain rose merely in fragments to the troubled surface of thought. Nothing was permanent; nothing was complete; and through this impermanence and this incompleteness there was an escape from the conflict of thwarted desires.

All day he dozed in snatches of sleep and waking. When the chill had passed and the heat of the train had dried the dampness of his clothes, his head became heavy with stupor, and it was pleasant to drop the burden of existence and drift on and out into nebulous space. Waking now and then, he would think dimly, "When you have done the best you can, there is no use in worrying"; and then, while the unfinished thought was still in his mind, he would close his eyes and yield his will to the impalpable tide. All his life he had been a conservative character, as volatile as a judge, as adventurous as a vestryman; but in this hour of necessity, he was aware that the fortifications of faith had crumbled to dust. In one of his brief spells of consciousness, he found himself asking drearily, "Why is there no help in religion? Have creeds killed the Christ in Christianity?" Only by reaching beyond husks, beyond creeds, beyond forms, beyond self, could one, he had learned, apprehend the spirit of life. Did divinity reveal itself only in flashes of light, not in crystallized forms? "If I could grasp and hold that revelation," he thought, "it would be worth every loss, every sacrifice"; but he knew that the gleam had fled, and by no effort of will could he recover the vision. "Even if it were an illusion, it is better than any reality." But was it an illusion? Again he asked himself, Was it light? Was it ecstasy? Was it God?

At Washington, he kept awake long enough to send a telegram to Constable; but when a man he knew stopped to speak to him, he found that words were almost unintelligible. Afterwards in Queenborough, when he was warm and his head was clear, he would begin to think and to feel again. Afterwards, but not now, not until to-morrow, when a good night's sleep had enabled him to collect his faculties. . . . Not now, but to-morrow . . .

It was ten o'clock when he reached Queenborough, and he emerged, bewildered and shivering, into a swift, fine rain which was changing rapidly into snow and sleet. It seemed a hundred years since he had gone away and left budding leaves on the trees; but that century was shrouded in a fog of forgetfulness. Since yesterday, he had become an old man, and spring had slipped back into winter.

When his chauffeur appeared and took his bag from the porter, he called the man "Granger," though Granger had left him the year before Cordelia died. Alone in his car, wrapped in the fur robe, a chill shuddered through him, and when he reached his door, the man, whose name was King, was obliged to help him across the sleety pavement and into the house. Here he was taken in charge by Constable, though he had a confused impression, as he entered his library, that Cordelia would come in a few minutes to bring him hot whiskey and water. He was tired; he was chilled to the bone; and he was older than eternity.

"I've mixed you a hot Scotch, sir," the solicitous voice of Constable breathed through the fog in his ears. "It was the way you used to like it when you caught a cold."

Yes, he had liked it that way in another life, in that life which he had once lived with Cordelia, and which had suffered now a painful resurrection in time. Though he remembered that Cordelia was dead, he still glanced with vague uneasiness toward the door, as if he half expected her benevolent apparition to enter and begin the work of caring for him where she had left it off when she fell ill. Poor Cordelia, how devoted she had been to him, and how unequal was the affection he had been able to give her!

"Thank you, Constable. I am glad you thought of it."

Like warmth, like blessedness, like the indestructible peace of eternity, he felt the hot drink pervading his body and spirit. Though he still shivered so violently that Constable was obliged to hold the glass to his lips, he told himself that he was cradled in physical ease. The shock, the chill, the long bleak day, and that suffocating depression which was worse than shock or chill—these images of pain melted in the glow that saturated his being.

"I took the liberty, sir, of telephoning for Dr. Buchanan," Constable remarked out of the surrounding film of contentment.

"That was right, Constable. You did quite right." Yes, it was fortunate, he reflected, that Constable was gifted with an infallible instinct for what was correct in an emergency.

"He told me he would step over at once. Shall I help you upstairs to bed before he comes?"

"No, I'll sit here. I always miss this chair when I'm away."

How he had missed it! How he had longed for it during that intolerable day in the train! A passion for comfort, for bodily ease, for the unruffled velvet surface of luxury, possessed him now like the craving of love or of appetite. Though he had lost the fire of youth, he saw that the comfortable embers of age were still warm. His favourite chair, his open fire, his cherished books, his few precious cases of old Bumgardner, his wholesome meals, which were prepared with discretion and eaten with imprudence; his friends, his bed, his pipe;—all these solid pleasures of age would become, he surmised, a not unworthy substitute for the imponderable delights of youth. And then, suddenly, through the fog in his brain, he heard the liquid music of Annabel's laugh and felt the thrust of a curved blade in his heart. Was it yesterday? Was it last year? Or was it in some lost dimension beyond time and space?

"Here is the doctor, sir," murmured the soothing tones of Constable out of the humming around him.

Swimming like a gigantic fish through the firelight, he saw the huge shape of Dr. Buchanan bending over his chair. Was it really his friend and physician? Or was it only a vague dream of him, which quivered and vanished against the unconquerable desolation of life?

"So you're back again with a chill." The doctor was beginning with his suave and superficial complacency. "A bad chill, I'm afraid. A very bad chill. We must get you to bed."

"I waited up for you." He answered through the whirling haze of his thoughts.

"There, there, don't move until I've looked you over. A bad chill, nothing more, but with your bronchial trouble, it is better to be on the safe side of the fight. We shall have you well in a few days, but you must keep in bed and not run any risks from exposure. Who is here to look after you? Where's Annabel?"

"She is not here, but I have Constable. Constable is a host in himself."

"Oh, Constable is all right for the day, but you need a nurse to look after you in the night. I'll send one who can fix you up and give you your bath before she goes in the morning. As long as you are running a temperature, you must not get out of bed. Now, Constable and I will move you upstairs."

In his dreamy condition, yielding to the smooth authoritative voice was bliss. All the long, quiet years when he had yielded himself to the capable ministrations of Cordelia were gathered in his surrender now to a luxurious vacancy of mind. No slow judicial process; no firmly drilled reasoning; no logical necessity. Merely a shimmering void of sensation into which his spirit sank as a wounded bird sinks in the afterglow.

Wrapped in warm blankets and solicitously supported on either side, he ascended one step at a time to his bedroom, where a cheerful fire was burning and his soft bed was already turned down. While they undressed him with gentle hands and slipped his blue and white pajamas over his shoulders, the doctor purred encouragingly to Constable.

"Hot-water bags. Yes, and plenty of blankets. Is the bed ready for him? I'll leave a prescription at Barclay's as I go by. Until the nurse comes on, you'd better not leave him alone. This chill will be followed by rising temperature, and he must be kept closely in bed. Nothing serious. In a few days, he will be all right; but at his age a touch of influenza ought not to be trifled with. Remember, he is not to get out of bed until I see him to-morrow. . . ."

The warm wool of his pajamas made him shiver slightly as it passed over his skin. Yes, it was pleasant to be cared for; it was pleasant to be home again. All the troubles and perplexities of the last twenty-four hours dispersed in the agreeable ruddy glow that enveloped him; and into this glow the memory of Annabel receded and vanished with other unfulfilled dreams of his youth. His head dropped on one of Cordelia's pillows, and, with a sigh, he lay back, warm and comforted, between fragrant sheets and fleecy blankets, while the doctor's urbane presence hovered over him like an embodied image of congenial habit.

CHAPTER 18

WEEK afterwards, when young leaves interlaced the declining sunbeams, Mrs. Upchurch sat beside Judge Honeywell's bed, and told him, in the cooing notes of a king's mistress, that he was the most wonderful man in the world. Withered, she added to herself, in one of her brief but cutting flashes of parenthetical honesty, withered and parched and brittle as a dead leaf; yet, when estimated by moral values, which are of course the only permanent values, a most wonderful man.

"There isn't another husband in the world who would have been so generous," she murmured, and added, wiping her eyes, "My poor misguided child!"

It was agreeable to be told this in such caressing tones. It was more agreeable still to feel that by his magnanimity he had merited her praise.

"I cannot acquit myself of responsibility," he answered in a weakened voice, while Mrs. Upchurch wiped her eyes again and listened respectfully. "It may seem that I am condoning her act, but I cannot, at whatever cost to myself, let Annabel suffer. She shall have her freedom, and I will provide for her future as long as she needs it."

Mrs. Upchurch sighed as she placed her small, plump hand on his arm. "If it is the last word I ever speak, Gamaliel," she answered, while her voice broke with a sob, "you are the truest Christian I know. If the fault had been yours," she added, sincere in feeling though slightly confused in logic, "you could not be more magnanimous. I can only hope my poor child will never realize all that she has lost."

"I can't blame her. She was obeying the law of her nature. If she had loved Dabney before Angus, we should probably have been spared that tragedy also. There is no doubt, I suppose," he concluded generously, "that Dabney is the man who was meant for her."

"They are desperately in love, if that is what you mean," Mrs. Upchurch responded, in a tone of moral indignation which increased with his tolerance, "but she ought to have sacrificed feeling to duty, as women used to do when we put religious principles before personal emotions. I should never have believed that Annabel had this in her," she continued sorrowfully. "The truth is that too many women are losing all respect for the sanctity of marriage."

She waited for a rejoinder; but the Judge was attacked by a bronchial irritation which enabled him to cough instead of replying. Thirty, even twenty years before he would have felt with her that the sanctity of marriage was worth all the sacrifices that had been made in its name. Now, however, since his illuminating passion for Annabel, he had become suspicious of any effort to condense life into a formula. "Well, I can't blame her," he repeated, when he had recovered his breath. "She was made for love if ever a woman was."

"It is because you don't blame her that I ought to," Mrs. Upchurch sighed. "But you must not let this spoil your life, Gamaliel," she urged, with tenderness. "You are too fine a man to have your future ruined by any woman. There ought to be years of happiness ahead of you yet. After all, you must remember that you are only in the prime of life." As she finished, she thought of Amanda, and the recollection suffused her charming features with a faint flush of hope. Was it possible that Amanda's long-awaited hour was dawning at last?

"I feel that my life is over, Bella. I have one foot in the grave already."

"You'll feel differently as soon as you're up again. Your life isn't over yet by many years, and you will have the thought of your noble—of your wonderful generosity"—she softly accented the word—"to sustain you in the future. It is my poor, unhappy child who will suffer pangs of remorse."

Her tears overflowed, and turning away, she gazed through the window toward the dark splendour of the sunset. After all, unless the doctrines of piety, unless the precepts of morality, unless the sanctities of virtue and the sacredness of marriage,—unless all these consecrated beliefs were merely illusions, she told her trembling heart, Annabel must reap the inevitable whirlwind of her betrayal.

Rising and still wiping her eyes, she bent over the Judge. "Promise me, Gamaliel, that you will not reproach yourself."

For a moment his response was inarticulate. Then he murmured gratefully, "I promise you that, Bella. I have done the best I could. When you can honestly say that of yourself, nothing else really matters."

"Hold fast to that thought, my dear friend. I shall see you to-morrow. If there is anything that I can do for you—if there is any little delicacy that I can make to tempt you—ask the nurse to telephone me before she leaves in the morning. Good-night. I hope you will have the sound and peaceful sleep you deserve." Leaning over, she touched her lips to his forehead before she turned noiselessly away and went out of the room.

The staircase faced the south, and the light from the western sky tinged the drifting clouds with the colour of fire. Unutterably sad, she felt; yet, even in her sadness, her brave and buoyant spirit could find consolation in the hope that Amanda's hour was dawning. How mysterious was the intricate pattern of life! It was amazing, it was miraculous, she told herself valiantly, as she descended the steps, the way that all the worst things (of which existence appeared to contain more than its share) work together for good to those who love God and keep His Commandments. Surely no one deserved better of Providence than poor Amanda, who had been unfalteringly pious and chaste without reward for so many years. And what could bring home more poignantly to Gamaliel the beauty of long faithfulness than his experience with the impetuous cruelty of youth? Already,

Mrs. Upchurch could see in imagination the stricken look fade from Amanda's delicate face; she could hear—oh, how thankfully!—the hysterical tension relax in that mellifluous voice. Yes, it was selfish, it was unchristian to think only of one's own affliction. The brave and noble way was to mourn for Annabel, but to rejoice with Amanda. After all, did not this prove how mistaken people were when they denied the law of compensation in life?

CHAPTER 19

EACE, soundless peace enveloped him, while his spirit brooded in silence as if it were his native element. Between waking and sleeping, in some inviolable sanctuary of dreams, he lay with his eyes on the flaming sunset beyond the green mist of the trees. Out there, in the close of day, thundered the breathless rumour and burden of life; but here, in this still place, beneath the wavering pattern of the firelight, he was anchored in a serene haven. Here was the deep below the deeps of experience; here was the changeless beatitude beneath the shifting cycles of birth and death. Beyond this refuge of dreams, he was aware that time was flowing onward into eternity. Swift, fragmentary, glimmering between snatches of light and darkness, his past life rushed by him on the waves of an immense stream of illusion. The touch of fever still clouded his brain; but in the pervading apathy there was an effortless calm. His life moved beyond him while he himself was unmoved. He saw his childhood drift past on these bright, dark pulsations of memory. He saw his mother, whom he had passionately loved, and whom he remembered as immortally fair and young. From her dissolving image there emerged and dissolved again all the women he had ever desired or might have desired in his life. Unmoved, he watched them as they drifted out of time into emptiness. Amanda with her tedious fidelity; Cordelia with her unbridled virtue; Annabel with her elusive charm and her unconquerable aversion. Then other faces so fugitive that they vanished to mist in the very act of assembling. Women in the street whose glances had stung his senses awake; the French maid to whom he had barely spoken a word in spite of her furtive advances; the mulatto girl he had watched making his bed. Inchoate impulses which had shuddered out of life even while he resisted them. Though they had died in the flesh, he realized now that they must have lived on in some submerged jungle of consciousness. Well, they were finished now; they were over. There was no emotion toward life left in his heart; there was no longing even for Annabel. Like all the others, she had existed as a ripple on the current of that profound egoism, which is the secret source of both desire and regret, and like a ripple she also had subsided and vanished.

He had done the best that he could. Over and over the soothing refrain occurred in his thoughts. He had done the best that he could. Not only in the end, but in the beginning as well, he had done the best that he could. All his life he had resisted evil; he had kept the law; like the Apostle, he had fought with beasts and he had conquered. With a moderate concession to human frailty, he could afford to look back, not unworthily, upon an upright and, within reason, a religious life. He had earned his rest. He had earned fairly, by a well-spent prime, the long reward of a ripe and seasoned age. Yet he would have yielded it all in return for the briefest gleam of that lost, irrecoverable nearness of God. . . . A cloud was floating over the west; on the window-panes the flickering design of the firelight was like the trail of a glowworm; flames were lapping the fresh logs in the fireplace. For a few quiet moments, sleep stole over him like an enchantment through which vague, delightful images were drifting. . . .

So profound, so blissful, was this immersion that, when he opened his eyes again, he felt, for an incredible instant, that he had plunged back among the vivid perceptions of youth. In that dreamy interval, before his faculties awakened completely, it seemed to him that his mother was stirring softly in the warm firelight, which glistened on her white dress and on the chestnut-brown of her hair. Just as he used to do when he was a child, he waited drowsily for the sound of her footsteps on the carpeted floor by his bed and the familiar scent of lavender in her rustling clothes. Not until the remembered fragrance brushed his face, and the vision was bending over to smooth his pillows, did he awake sufficiently to realize that it was not his mother but the nurse whom Dr. Buchanan had sent to him. Strange that he had never before observed her so closely! Strange that this resemblance had never occurred to him until she stooped over him in the firelight and the ruddy gleams were reflected in the brown waves of her hair. Younger than his early memory of his mother; younger even than Annabel; the merest slip of a girl, he saw now, when he looked in her face. Fresh, spotless, and womanly, in her white uniform, with the competent hands of a physician and the wise and tender touch of a mother. Those beneficent hands and that infallible touch, he supposed, had made him dream that he was a child again. After all, was there any grace, any beauty, any virtue, that could compare with tenderness in a woman? Gentle and young! Young from her small, round head, where her short brown hair curled like the petals of a sunflower beneath the starched band of her cap, to her slender ankles, in white stockings, under the neat hem of her skirt. Swifter than light, swifter than inspiration, while he followed her with his eyes, the thought darted into his mind: "There is the woman I ought to have married!" There, sympathetic and young, obeying her feminine instinct in every exquisite gesture, was the woman he ought to have married.

The vagrant thought came and went. After all, life was over. Or was it never over until one had gone down into the grave? There were men who had begun their best work, who had won their supreme happiness, only when the prime of life was well past. Beyond the warm room and the flickering firelight, the vital sap had risen again; flowers were already putting forth from the green earth. "Spring is here," he thought dreamily. "Spring is here, and I am feeling almost as young as I felt last year."

Suddenly, beneath the dark sunset, an apocalyptic light rained from the sky, and in this light all the tender little leaves of April were whispering together.

*This world is a comedy to those that
think, a tragedy to those that feel.*

HORACE WALPOLE

ELLEN GLASGOW, an excellent critic of her own work, wrote
to Bessie Zaban Jones in 1935 that "as a comedy of manners,
I feel (why should I pretend to false modesty?) that *The Romantic Comedians* has never been surpassed in the novel
form."[1] Critics have concurred with Glasgow's high ap-
praisal of the novel. Most reviewers praised the book in generous terms when it was published in 1926. Gerald W. Johnson in the Baltimore *Evening Sun* called it "almost a
novelist's novel" and "high comedy, the sort that walks delicately upon the verge of tears." Writing for the *Saturday
Review of Literature*, Christopher Morley observed that it is
"one of those phenomena curiously rare in America, a really
witty book." Dorothea Lawrence Mann suspected it was
Glasgow's "most brilliant" book in a review for *Bookman*;
and Carl Van Vechten called the novel "witty, wise and delicious" in his review for the *New York Herald Tribune Books*.
Harry Esty Dounce in the *New Yorker* proposed that it "is a
really fine novel worth dozens of its author's *Barren
Ground.*"[2] Readers agreed with the reviewers. The Book-of-
the-Month Club named it their major selection for November, and according to William W. Kelly, sales topped
100,000 copies.[3]

Time has not lessened the extravagance of early critical
assessments. Later critics have agreed with Glasgow's own
high evaluation: Blair Rouse calls *The Romantic Comedians*
"the masterpiece among [American] novels of manners,"
and C. Hugh Holman claims it is "unsurpassed as an Ameri-

can comedy of manners."[4] In a letter to Allen Tate in 1935, Glasgow explained that "Until I wrote *The Sheltered Life* I liked *Barren Ground* best of my books, and after that I liked *The Romantic Comedians*," suggesting that she herself placed this comedy of manners among her three finest works.[5] Julius Raper seconds Glasgow's assessment, explaining that "this totally enjoyable comic vignette is clearly superior" to other of her novels and "stands with *Barren Ground* and *The Sheltered Life* — a very high niche indeed."[6]

The Romantic Comedians was written during the most exciting time of Glasgow's career, the decade of her fifties, when she experienced creatively miraculous years. Between 1925 and 1932 her very best work was published. Her first novel, *The Descendant*, appeared anonymously in 1897, and she continued to publish novels regularly, approximately one every two years. In 1925, when she was fifty-two years old, her fourteenth novel, *Barren Ground*, was published and received splendid reviews. Then followed her trilogy of tragicomedies: *The Romantic Comedians* (1926), *They Stooped to Folly* (1929), and *The Sheltered Life* (1932)—all receiving excellent reviews. During this period, too, the first collected edition of her works, the Old Dominion Edition of the Works of Ellen Glasgow—eight novels, including *The Romantic Comedians* — was published (1929–33).

After she had completed *Barren Ground*, Glasgow explained that she felt "the comic spirit struggling against the bars of its cage" (viii–ix), and *The Romantic Comedians* "bubbled out" in a year.[7] She had been immersed in the tragic life of Dorinda Oakley during three hard years of work on *Barren Ground*, the novel she wrote to show the betrayed woman as triumphant. The writing of this novel seemed to serve as a cathartic experience for the novelist as she poured her heart and soul into the life of Dorinda Oakley, who overcame her lover's betrayal in her youth to succeed as a farmer and landowner. Dorinda realizes at the close of the novel that "love was irrevocably lost to her"; she would find her happiness in "the serenity of mind which is above the conflict of frustrated desires."[8] It is almost as if this sensitive writer, who had personally learned to live behind a mask of irony and gaiety, felt purged of the pain of her own great disappointments in love and life after writing *Barren Ground*. She then turned to a comic novel, using her intellect to focus with irony and satire on the "happiness-hunters" in Queenborough (187).

The Romantic Comedians holds a distinctive—a singular—place among Glasgow's nineteen novels. Although wit and satire are present in all her work, *The Romantic Comedians* is the only novel that is almost pure comedy. Glasgow cautions the reader that "the ironic overtones may seem, occasionally, to deny the tragic mood of the book. For there is tragedy in the theme, though it is tragedy running, like the 'divine things' of Nietzsche, 'on light feet'" (xiv). She called this book and the two that followed, *They Stooped to Folly* and *The Sheltered Life*, her trilogy of tragicomedies. This first one is more comic than the other two; her tone darkened as she wrote these three novels, and *The Sheltered Life* is the most tragic of the three. In analyzing the comedy in the three novels, Kathryn Lee Seidel proposes that Glasgow employs "Horatian satire—tolerant, comic, tender" in *The Romantic Comedians* and *They Stooped to Folly*, but "works with the features of Juvenalian satire—bitter, vituperative and final" in *The Sheltered Life*.[9] Glasgow's use of satire and her choice of style and the voice of the narrator in *The Romantic Comedians* combine to produce her most comic work.

Glasgow wrote this novel in one year, probably less time than any of her other novels, and the text is shorter than sixteen of her works of fiction; only her first two novels, *The Descendant* and *Phases of an Inferior Planet*, have fewer pages in the first editions than *The Romantic Comedians*. Critics had repeatedly complained about the length of her novels; *The Battle-Ground*, *The Deliverance*, *Virginia*, *Life and Gabriella*, and *Barren Ground* all had more than five-hundred pages.

The text of *The Romantic Comedians*—shorter by more than 150 pages than many of her novels—is beautifully constructed with a style in which no word is wasted.

The Romantic Comedians is notable for its technique and form and craftsmanship. Glasgow explained that "every word in that book . . . was carefully chosen."[10] The style is witty, epigrammatic, and economical. Pithy, memorable quotations sparkle on every page. It is a classically unified novel—taking place in one year, involving a limited number of characters, and set in Queenborough except for brief scenes on shipboard and in New York City. The plot is an old one: old man marries young woman and is cuckolded. Part 1 tells the story of the attraction and courtship; Part 2 depicts the failure of the marriage. However, Glasgow makes something new out of this ancient material that Chaucer used so effectively in both "The Miller's Tale" and "The Merchant's Tale."

The voice of the narrator gives consistency to the text. Distanced, urbane, witty, and sophisticated, this voice maintains the satiric and comic tone of the novel. In fact, the voice sounds very much like Ellen Glasgow, the practiced novelist, who has observed human nature for fifty-two Aprils and, for the first time, taken an almost wholly comic view of the romantic foibles of men and women. The voice seems to be well above the action—as if the narrator, like James Joyce, were off paring her fingernails somewhere while her characters carry out their destinies, guided, not by the author manipulating puppet strings, but by their own characters and drives.

The preface indicates that Glasgow had moved away from the kind of notebook realism she had used for her books of social history. She had often done serious research, going to the place where a novel was to be set and studying the area. For the writing of *The Battle-Ground*, for example, which is set during the Civil War, she visited the Valley of Virginia to study the landscape, read diaries and letters, and kept with her during the writing of the novel full runs of three newspapers for the years 1860 to 1865. For *The Romantic Comedians*, however, she chose a different approach: "In my social history, for example, I had been careful to call every spade a spade and every molehill a molehill; but in this comedy of manners, I have not hesitated to call a spade a silver spoon or a molehill a mountain." Nor did she hesitate "to make two trees grow in my Queenborough where only one was planted before me in Richmond." She had decided that sound psychology "was more important, and incidentally more interesting, than accurate geography" (viii). In this decision she was wise, for the text of the novel sparkles with wit and satire, directed at both persons and place. She has moved away artistically from focusing so much on background to write about subjects she knows well: a place, Queenborough; a time, 1923; and familiar characters and themes.

According to Glasgow, Queenborough is "the distilled essence of all Virginia cities," but it is identifiably Richmond. When the novel opens, Gamaliel Bland Honeywell is in Hollywood Cemetery, where Ellen Glasgow now lies in the company of twenty-five Confederate generals and countless other distinguished Virginians. As the Judge drives home, he passes a "plebeian park, where the best taste of politicians was commemorated in concrete walks and triangular beds of canna," obviously Monroe Park. He looks down "the once aristocratic and now diminished length of Washington Street merging into the ostentatious democracy of Granite Boulevard"; Washington Street is Franklin Street, and Granite Boulevard is Monument Avenue. Lined with statues of Confederate heroes and the Confederate Monument, this avenue is now considered one of the most beautiful streets in the United States. Glasgow saw it in the 1920s as "grandiose," representative of "The Age of Pretence, The Age of Hypocrisy, The Age of Asphalt" (9). The Judge passes Saint Luke's, which is probably St. James's

Episcopal Church, located at Franklin and Birch streets. Though St. James's suffered lightning strikes and a devastating fire in July of 1994, much of it survived, including most of the Tiffany windows; it will be rebuilt. As the Judge passes the church, Richmonders are still on the street after Easter Sunday service; he recognizes familiar faces in the crowd and sighs, "Where else on earth . . . could people know so little and yet know it so fluently" (9)? He then arrives at his own house, "of which he was inoffensively proud; a collection of brownstone deformities assembled, by some diligent architect of the early 'eighties, under the liberal patronage of Queen Anne. In front of the stone steps, as they flowed down from a baptismal font of a porch, he recognized the heavily built figure of his twin sister" (12). This house with the "baptismal font of a porch" has been identified as once located on the southwest corner of Franklin and Foushee streets (now a parking lot).[11] Changes have been made in Richmond during the almost seventy years since the publication of *The Romantic Comedians,* but the city of Richmond is still recognizable as Glasgow's Queenborough.

Queenborough is provincial and patriarchal, its comfortably rich upper class governed by tradition and a strict social code. It is a sheltered life with citizens who naturally practice evasive idealism, most preferring allegiance to romantic illusions about life to reality. Life for the affluent aristocrats includes regular attendance at the Episcopal Church, invitations to Christmas cotillions and other frequent entertainments, large houses tended by servants. It is a perfect setting for Glasgow's comedies of manners, as C. Hugh Holman has described the genre:

> It [the comedy of manners] is a form that asks that its characters be placed in a sharply definable social situation, usually one that is elegant and sophisticated, and that the manners, beliefs, and conventions of that society be the forces that motivate the action. Its style is witty; its thrust satiric.

It usually places in its fable an emphasis on the "love game" and centers on at least one pair of somewhat immoral lovers. The comedy of manners on the stage and in the novel also demands a highly developed craftsmanship and a delight taken by author and audience alike in finished artistry, in conscious and successful artifice.[12]

Queenborough is the ideal place for Glasgow's romantic comedians: the unlikely lover, Judge Honeywell, "conventional to the core," who muses that "orthodox beliefs and conventional standards were safest" and comfortably recalls his own father's saying, "If there is anything wrong with the Episcopal Church or the Democratic Party, I would rather die without knowing it" (78, 8); his ever-loyal first love, Amanda Lightfoot, who "belonged to that fortunate generation of women who had no need to think, since everything was decided for them by the feelings of a lady and the Episcopal Church" (101); and the young Annabel Upchurch, Glasgow's "youth in arms against life," who rejects her elders' values as hypocrisy and sham (xi). With a protagonist, a representative and remnant of the old ways and old values, who falls in love with a young woman who is an emblem of the changing values of the 1920s, the reader experiences the clash of manners and customs—and a generation gap wider and deeper than the James River, on which Richmond-Queenborough sits.

Although *The Romantic Comedians* is set in a provincial southern city, it is a contemporary novel set squarely in its time—the 1920s. When the Judge is musing that perfectly normal women, like Cordelia, were neither "temperamental nor demonstrative," and because marriage is a practical arrangement, temperament, like Annabel's, was a troublesome matter in marriage, the narrator speaks: "Though he had married in the post-war period, he still thought in the primitive terms of a world which, like the Garden of Eden, was unaware of its own innocence" (126). To a large extent the

Judge still lives in the world of the 1880s, an innocent who does not take into account that the world has changed after World War I. The central conflict in the novel depicts the painful clash of the old values and empty forms dutifully observed by the old guard with the new values of the 1920s expressed and acted out by Annabel and Dabney Birdsong. Echoes of T. S. Eliot's wasteland theme permeate the text, beginning and ending with a clear message that April is, indeed, the cruelest month. Prohibition affects life in Queenborough; the Judge no longer enjoys going to his club now that no alcohol is served, and he savors his supply of old Bumgardner, jealously monitoring Edmonia's intake of his spirits. And the Judge's flighty fancies are liberated at Annabel's birthday party with the encouragement of provocative jazz rhythms.

Judge Honeywell, the protagonist, is the center of consciousness through the first ten chapters and remains at the center of the novel even after the narrator moves around to focus on other characters, Annabel, Amanda, and Bella. He is a good and decent man, a public figure respected for his position in the community and for his wealth. The reader, however, gets behind that public mask to find a man who has repressed his desires and settled for a proper life. He did not marry the woman he loved passionately, but Cordelia, a humorless woman who took care of him for thirty-seven years, catering to his comfort and his digestion. He realizes he had never told Cordelia he loved her and that she cared more for him than he for her—an unequal relationship. Most telling is that he thinks "the worst of all possible worlds would be one invented by good women" (56).

As the symbol of the patriarchy, he espouses all of the chivalrous myths about women, insisting that older women are not interested in love, that a man is only as old as his instincts, that some young women prefer old lovers to young ones. His sheltered mind allows these delusions about women as it allows him to delude himself. Caught in his obsession with the young Annabel, he disguises his motives to himself in buying her a dress and in offering to help her start a landscape business. He tells himself it is his duty to take care of Cordelia's favorite poor relative. More importantly, he insists to himself that he looks twenty years younger than his sixty-five years—an absurdity highlighted by his twin sister Edmonia, his hedonistic double, who "had been born with the courage of her appetites" and has energetically married four men and grown large with eating (13). After a discussion with Edmonia, who points out that Amanda is seven years younger than they are, the narrator describes the Judge's response: "Not only did he dislike an unprofitable comparison of ages, but he disliked even more the cheerful inaccuracy with which Edmonia assumed that he was as old as she because they had been born twins" (57). He is particularly vulnerable to Bella Upchurch's flattery, but Edmonia's reaction to this vulnerability is on the mark: "A great lawyer but a perfect fool" (29).

His own appetites have been kept in check. Amanda's virtue saved him when he appealed to her after his marriage to run away with him. And the temptation to submit to the charms of a French maid was successfully controlled. But now, with Cordelia gone, those long-submerged desires envelope him. He is moved by a powerful desire to touch the mulatto maid; he dreams of young and slender girls, "the glimmering ivory shapes of nymphs, who danced on rose-white feet to the music of running water" (34); he becomes obsessed with Annabel. These feelings are not calculated. At a party he resents having to dance with Amanda and longs "to dance with those images of fire and snow, without corsets and without conversation, who melted to wisps of tulle over soft little bones and wisps of gold or brown hair over soft little minds" (40). And then the narrator takes us into his psyche: "Not deliberately . . . would he have harboured such impulses; but, secret, strong, and brooding, this wish, which was more an instinct than a desire, welled up from the deep below the deep in his consciousness" (40). Not only is he a victim of his unconscious, but he is also pursued by the furies. In bed one night he is overcome by "the glimmer of ivory forms" that attack him "like a scattered flock of amorous furies" (52). He chases them away by taking up Cordelia's Bible on the bedside table.

Driven by his feeling "that he has missed the secret of life" (71), a passionate ecstasy that had eluded him, he reaches for Annabel, the symbol of youth and desire. Again, he deludes himself about Annabel, thinking she is marrying him because she cares for him and assuming that the spirited and selfish young woman will move into his house and into Cordelia's bed and become his companion. But his bride pursues her own social agenda, and he finds her unresponsive and emotionally cold, and he finally realizes she has an aversion to his physical presence. He longs for her presence, "for the sight and touch of her fragrant youth, of her dewy freshness" (117), but, like Tantalus, he is forever desiring but never satisfied. He begins to descend into despair and to experience epiphanies, realizing "he had been abandoned by youth while his thirst for life was unsatisfied"; he has experienced a "fruitless regeneration" (130). He suspects he bears the responsibility for his pain: "Perhaps, after all, the fault lay in himself, not in circumstances. Perhaps he had been too easily contented in his prime with the second best of experience. Perhaps he had skimmed too lightly over the glazed surface of inherited wisdom" (144). And he understands his misery, an understanding that goes to the heart of the book: "That he could love at least unselfishly, supremely, and yet be incapable of bringing happiness to the beloved, appeared to him . . . to be the ultimate tragedy of the human heart. That love could not confer happiness! That love could not even bring consolation" (172)!

The reader feels a measure of sympathy for Judge Honeywell—a victim of the values of his culture as much as Glasgow's tragic women figures, and also a victim of human nature, driven to his foolish behavior by fear of old age and death. But he remains a comic figure, nowhere more ridiculous than in his realization that love does not confer happiness. With a chorus of women characters who voice their views of love, Glasgow maintains the comic tone of the novel. And she rescues the temporarily defeated Judge by giving him an attentive young nurse to reawaken his springtime desires.

Gamaliel Bland Honeywell may be the perfect mold of the patriarchy, but he lives in a thoroughly feminine world. He has a butler, a chauffeur, a doctor, and he belongs to a men's club, but the men in his life play fleeting parts. Living in the city of Queenborough, doubtless named after Queen Elizabeth, he is surrounded in his daily life by women. His late wife, Cordelia, is a living presence in the text; his twin sister, Edmonia Bredalbane, visiting from France, interferes in his life and wickedly punctures his chivalric notions about men and women; Amanda Lightfoot, his first love, with her public loyalty to their early romance, makes him uncomfortable; Bella Upchurch, his late wife's poor cousin, coos and flatters and pours the "oil of adulation over him" (29). Bella's daughter Annabel completes the ensemble of women that spans three generations. Glasgow's brilliant depictions of these women are as fine in this comic novel with a man as the protagonist as they are in her books with women protagonists. Some of these women remind us of earlier and later characters in her work, but one, Edmonia Bredalbane, is unique in the Glasgow canon.

Edmonia was a belle in the 1880s as was Amanda Lightfoot and provides a contrast to her much as Susan Treadwell serves that function with Virginia Pendleton in *Virginia*. While Amanda stayed home in Queenborough and grieved over her failed romance with Gamaliel Honeywell, Edmonia lost her virtue and decamped to Paris, "regarded in Queenborough as little better than an asylum for determined profligates," where she lived a life devoted to pleasure (7). She loves fine food and red wine, and she "feared to be stout in age as little as she had feared to be scandalous in youth" (13). She is rich; she has been widowed three times and is married for the fourth time to Ralph Bredalbane, "an impecunious young mooncalf," "a stubborn fugitive from monogamy" (8, 58). Gossip in Queenborough had exaggerated her sins and attributed countless lovers to her, but those stories "were merely apocryphal" (13). Her physical presence was formidable: "Large, raw-boned, with strong, plain features, where an expression of genuine humour frolicked with an artificial complexion, and a mountainous bosom, from which a cascade of crystal beads splashed and glistened" (13).

Edmonia's very presence makes her brother uncomfortable, but her blunt talk and truth-telling terrify him. She silences him by talking "incessantly of things that were unmentionable among delicate-minded persons" (38), and she reminds him "that, in the case of twins, there is usually a strong and a weak one, and, fortunately for me, I was the strong one of us two" (158). Edmonia is a party-goer, and the Judge explains, "The inquisitive youth of the period . . . treated her scarlet letter less as the badge of shame than as some foreign decoration for distinguished service" (60).

But for all the real importance of Edmonia as a comic character, she is more than that. She provides a vivid contrast to both her twin brother and Amanda. She has keen insight into her brother's response to her: "You could have forgiven my committing a sin if you hadn't feared that I had committed a pleasure as well" (159). She understands both men and women. At first she encourages Gamaliel to attend to Amanda and not marry the young Annabel. She reminds him that "there is no fool like an old fool" (62). However, after Annabel and the Judge are married, she attempts to save the troubled marriage by inviting Annabel to visit her in Europe. Edmonia Bredalbane is unique in the Glasgow canon—a character who broke the rules and paid no price, a hedonist who is humane and compassionate, a happy person.

Amanda, however, has followed all the rules and survived on "fortitude and hypocrisy" (210). She has spent her adult life waiting, suspended in time, and now that her former lover is a widower, he sees her as a relic of the past with her "embalmed perfection," "a pressed leaf that has grown faded and brittle" (10). She had been the loveliest belle in the city and had received countless proposals from eligible men, but she chose to be true to her early engagement to Gamaliel Honeywell. Still wearing the colors of blue and lavender that he favored in his youth, she is unaware that he now likes red and green. She retains the carriage and full figure of the beauty of the 1880s, and she personifies "the traditional feminine virtues—patience, gentleness, moderation, reserve" (41), but the Judge feels no desire for this silver-haired woman: "He was still in love with Amanda; he would be always in love with her; but it was with an ageless Amanda of the mind, not with the well-preserved lady of the tarnishing years" (11). Amanda is now a burden to him: "Though he respected Amanda as deeply as he respected the memory of his mother or the Ten Commandments, he could not dismiss the thought that neither the memory of his mother nor the Ten Commandments insisted upon being romanced about as well as respected" (39). After the Judge marries Annabel, Amanda revealed publicly the price of giving up her "world of sentimental invention" (215); she appeared to others to be broken and aged.

In other novels Glasgow shows the destruction of both the perfect lady, wedded to convention, and the fallen woman, who breaks the rules. In this comedy she uses the two figures to show that Amanda paid a terrible penalty for following the rules of society and becoming the perfect lady—her static and barren life—and that even a lady's fall from virtue does not mean everlasting penance. Edmonia has outlived her disgrace and finds herself happily at home in Queenborough society of the 1920s.

Bella Upchurch, without the wealth of Amanda and Edmonia, has fewer options. She is forty-eight, younger than both, "a cheerful and pretty widow, with a cooing tongue" (28). She survives by renting rooms in her home and "nursing the vanities of her own and her late husband's male relatives" (13). She is the voice of common sense, who has suffered "an unhappy marriage and a disappointing widowhood" (28). Her level of expectation is low; she would have given up "birth, youth, breeding, appearance, character, yes, even character,—all these agreeable perquisites of marriage she would have exchanged for the consolation of an established income" (188). She is an astute observer of the human comedy, and she is aware of the disadvantages of an "incurably amorous habit of mind." She calls the notion "that love and happiness are interchangeable terms" a "popular superstition," an "immemorial illusion." And she seems to be speaking for the author herself when she, like Isabel Archer, sits thinking before the fire: "Was she herself, she sometimes asked, the only person who had been able to maintain a true sense of values and an equilibrium of the emotions? Judge Honeywell with his law and learning; Amanda with her exalted character and her simple wit; Annabel with her artless sophistication; and now this young man [Dabney Birdsong] who might have been but was not Angus [Annabel's former lover]—all this company of happiness-hunters appeared to be little better than a troupe of romantic comedians" (187). Bella Upchurch understands the comedy being played out before her, and her own disillusionment with love and life has led to a kind of cheerful, pragmatic wisdom. She sounds two feminist notes in the novel. When Annabel decides to marry the Judge and abandon her plans to start a landscape business with the Judge's financial support, her mother regrets that she herself had never learned "some useful pursuit" in her girlhood: "If I were Annabel, I'd think twice before I gave up landscape gardening for the richest man in the world. Whatever you earn honestly is money in your pocket, but in these days even rich men are not to be depended upon as providers" (112). Later, after a scene with Annabel over Dabney Birdsong, her young lover, and then an awkward encounter with Amanda, Bella Upchurch arrives home:

> There was an edge of frost to the April air, and in her sitting-room a bright fire was burning. An amiable tortoise-shell cat was dozing before the flames; from his high-hanging cage by the window, a canary piped joyously; in the centre of the dinner table, where the candles were lighted, there was a blue bowl of pear blossoms; an aroma of herbs and spices floated in from the kitchen; the afternoon paper, secure from male aggression, lay still folded on a little stand beneath the reddish glow of the lamp. "And this," thought Mrs. Upchurch, while she gazed around her at the cheerful welcome, "is what they call loneliness." (210–11)

She takes off her coat, sinks into a soft chair, and stretches her feet to the fender: "Rest, rest, and quiet stole gradually like an anodyne over her aching nerves. She signed happily; there was no crisis here; there was no wild youth. She sighed more happily still: there was no sentimental age. There was nothing more agitating than the tranquil immunity of a mind that had finished with love" (211). This quiet scene, described with such loving detail, shows the most sensible character in the novel and suggests the futility of the search engaged in by the rest of the happiness-hunters. Bella Upchurch has found peace, tranquility, and pleasure in spite of her relative poverty and because of her abandonment of the myth of romance.

If Amanda is the embodiment of the ideal of the lady, Edmonia the rebel against the values of her culture, and Bella the practical realist who observes outward forms but maintains an inner truth, then Annabel is the rebellious young woman of the 1920s. The reader sees her through the Judge's eyes as he is enthralled by her presence, but as time passes, he is inclined to measure her character and her actions ever more severely against the standards of his generation. Glasgow's satire is double-edged in depicting Annabel—she is satirizing the Judge as he comes to terms with Annabel's shortcomings, but she is also revealing with devastating clarity that this new generation offers no satisfactory substitute for the old values.

The reader first sees Annabel through the Judge's eyes in a shower of nature imagery: she has a "small heart-shaped face, with its faint golden freckles and geranium mouth"; her green and brown frock reminds him of "fields and streams"; "her nut-brown hair" reflects the "coppery glow of November leaves in the sunshine"; her voice is like "the sparkle of rippling water"; her eyes are as "gray-green as an April mist." Her eyebrows are "winged," and her body fragile: "As light as a swallow, he thought, with poetic imagery, as light and graceful as a swallow in the air" (15). He sees Annabel as nature herself, a force, but not a person. Annabel is "like some vision . . . that is as transparent as sunlight and as unattainable as ideal beauty" (63). She is "youth itself," but she is a most unlikely candidate for his affection. Not only is she slight in figure as opposed to the queenliness of the beauties of his generation, but she breaks all the rules of Virginian propriety. She tells her personal business to everyone, revealing her lack of pride, repeating the story of her heartbreak over the broken romance with Angus Blount. She tells the Judge that "I haven't many virtues . . . but I hate shams. . . . I despise the poor and I cannot endure the sight of the sick. All I really care for is beauty—well, and perhaps joy, if you could ever find it" (49). She also confesses to the Judge that she has no "moral sense, but I have a heart" (66). He later has "the feeling that she was not only childish, but ungrateful as well" (76). On their honeymoon, the Judge discovers that Annabel reads "rubbish" and that her mind is "obstinate" (116). He observes that she wanders aimlessly "through a labyrinth of blind impulses" (121). He also sees that she rejects any allegiance to the idea of duty. He finally comes to suspect that Annabel's opinions "were merely organized prejudices," that she "still remained, after marriage, a pure experimentalist in behaviour" (152–53).

But the reader can also measure Annabel by her actions. She is impulsive, self-centered, irresponsible, devoted to pleasure, and lacks any coherent moral code. In the midst of heartbreak over Angus, she impulsively accepts the Judge's proposal, a purely economic decision. During the three-month honeymoon in Europe, Annabel seems oblivious to the increasing exhaustion of her new husband. After they return home, she continues to lead the social life of a belle, out every evening dancing and dining as her husband becomes more and more fatigued, finally becoming ill. She falls in love with a young architect, Dabney Birdsong, and says to her mother, "I don't want to live, if I can't have love in my life!" (196). When Bella reminds Annabel of her duty to her husband, Annabel retorts, "He has had his life, and I want mine" (198). Annabel refuses to take responsibility for her actions and blames her mother and the Judge for the marriage, claiming that they "shouldn't have let me do it" (198). Her mother blames the problem on the war, which has changed morality; the narrator explains, "for her conventional mind preferred to hold a world war, rather than original sin, responsible for Annabel's misguided behaviour" (197). The Judge refuses to blame the war, and he has his own theory: "There has been a change, a readjustment of ideas, perhaps even of standards. We may have been too strict in our views; but the pendulum is swinging too far in the opposite direction to-day. The younger generation has caught hold of something different, and this difference confuses me. I have even asked myself if the wisdom of the ages can have been wrong" (201). For the Judge the "wisdom of the ages" doubtless refers to the Virginian code of manners, but he withholds judgment of Annabel's behavior and generously lets her go with her new lover.

Each of these major characters in *The Romantic Comedians* is a type, but Glasgow has made them into complex characters, rounded and believable. They participate in action that focuses on the relationship of the sexes and especially on love and marriage. Frequently one character serves as a foil for another, as is apparent, for example, in an early discussion between the Judge and Edmonia as the Judge explains "that a man remains young longer than a woman of the same age" (20). Edmonia replies, "I wonder what lascivious old male first invented that theory?" (21).

The narrator guides the reader through the story with comments about the relationship between the sexes. When Bella Upchurch is musing about what a good marriage prospect the Judge would be for her, the narrator explains, "But the idea of marriage, which has brooded through the centuries over the narrow field of woman's prospect, had not risen above the horizon of Judge Honeywell's consciousness" (30). The Judge sees Bella Upchurch, who is seventeen years younger than he, as an older lady of good character, "whose love life was well over." The narrator tells the reader that the Judge's view was "entirely a product of the chivalrous interpretation of biology" (30). And to a great extent the novel is about this gentlemanly view of sex as it led the Judge to a loveless first marriage, an imprudent second, and perhaps even a foolish third.

While the Judge shows what an older man thinks of women, the women surrounding him offer a range of views of the relationship between men and women. Edmonia and Bella both express the opinion that the value of marriage is exaggerated and yearned for by women who have never been married. Although Bella thinks one should marry for love the first time, she has come to view marriage as an economic exchange. Amanda has spent her life waiting, while Edmonia has seized pleasure whenever possible. Annabel simply follows her impulses. Glasgow explained that the idea for the book came out of her weariness "with having men write what they know or don't know about dangerous ages in women."[13] She chose a male protagonist at a dangerous age and anatomized his romantic views of women, but she placed those views in the context of various women's views of men. Thus she portrayed the great gulf between men and women with respect to the understanding of love and marriage.

Glasgow portrays her characters through description, dialogue, their internal thoughts, and the words of the implied author. In addition, she fills the novel with memorable scenes. The opening and closing scenes reflect each other and are deliciously ironic, setting the tone for the text and closing the text on similar notes. Edmonia's and Gamaliel's verbal sparring in chapter 3 reveals those characters and sets up a theme that will continue in the text: the conflict between romantic idealism and realism. The scene in chapter 7 between the Judge and his housekeeper, Mrs. Spearman, is richly comic. Each has the measure of the other: the Judge sees her as a "withered and incorruptible woman who had lost everything but virtue and clung firmly to that," and he wonders "where she found room to hold her suppressed desires"; Mrs. Spearman is suspicious of the Judge, "for anything less permanent than widowers she had never encountered," and she is anxious to find a new position—preferably with a gentleman "whose wife was hopelessly deranged but harmless" (53–54).

The scene between Annabel and Amanda in chapter 12 is a small masterpiece. Before accepting the Judge's proposal, the naive Annabel confronts Amanda to find out if Amanda wants to marry the Judge. Annabel asks personal questions, and Amanda gives appropriate, if less than truthful, answers. Annabel cannot judge the sincerity of those answers, "for the virtue of perfect behaviour lies, not in its rightness, but in its impenetrability" (105). Then Amanda, "noble in thought and attitude on a hard Victorian sofa," terminates the visit by instructing Annabel on proper etiquette for a "nice woman": never ask questions or talk about your personal affairs, govern your mind and control your temperament (105).

Not only is the closing scene memorable, it also provides a perfect ending for this comic work. In a number of her novels, Glasgow seems to lack the courage to take the end of her work to its appropriate destination. James Branch Cabell is not alone in criticizing her final paragraphs. After detailing his problems with the close of five of her novels, he summarizes: "Thus, time upon time, does Ellen Glasgow, after having evinced no parsimony in supplying her Virginians with trials and defeats and irrevocable losses, yet almost always manage to end, somehow, upon this brave note of recording her people's renovated belief in a future during which everything will turn out quite splendidly."[14] *Virginia*, for example, ends on a note that has provoked much discussion. Virginia Pendleton Treadwell, who has devoted her life to her husband and children, finds herself alone in her forties, abandoned by her husband and suffering deep despair, which she is unable to overcome. She feels that her life is over, and, indeed, the book portrays the bleak results of this woman's victimization at the hands of her family and her culture. But the novel ends with a telegram from her son, telling her he is leaving Oxford University and coming home. It is not clear whether this is a happy ending or a very temporary bit of good news. It may well mean Harry is coming home to give his life to his mother, suggesting that he will become another victim of the ideals of the culture.

In contrast, the ending of *The Romantic Comedians* is hilariously comic, believable in terms of the protagonist's character, a surprise for the reader, and a completion of the novel's circular structure—bringing Judge Honeywell back to the very first page of the novel. In the beginning, he is placing lilies on his late wife's grave on an Easter Sunday in April. The narrator tells us that for almost forty years he has "endured the double-edged bliss of a perfect marriage," but he is having a problem recalling his wife's face. "I am a bird with a broken wing," he thinks sentimentally (1). Then he feels the stirrings of spring and rebirth and resurrection as his "broken wing" tries "to flutter." In the end, the Judge is debilitated physically after his adventurous year—his courtship of Annabel, their marriage, and her abandonment; he is ill and lying in his bed, when he is suddenly attracted to his tender young nurse—younger than Annabel: "the vital sap had risen again" and "all the tender little leaves of April were whispering together" (240). The reader realizes in an instant that Gamaliel Honeywell has learned nothing from his experience with Annabel; he is not going to die nor will he succumb to marrying Amanda; he is off on another adventure. As Glasgow explains in her preface, "It was, indeed, this concluding paragraph that accented the rhythm and placed the final tone of the book" (xiv).

Critics have long suggested that Glasgow's model for Judge Gamaliel Bland Honeywell was the distinguished Richmond attorney Henry Watkins Anderson. Anderson was a successful lawyer, having done much work in the areas of utilities and railroads that earned him a national reputation. He had been mentioned for the Supreme Court during the Harding and Hoover administrations and served both of those administrations and Coolidge's. A brilliant man, he was self-made and noted in Richmond for his elegant style of living—a British butler, for example, and a chauffeur who drove his large town car furnished with fur lap robes in the back seat. When Glasgow met Anderson at a luncheon on Easter Sunday of 1916, she was at a low emotional ebb, living in the big Glasgow house on 1 West Main Street, alone except for her secretary-companion Anne Virginia Bennett, in the house where her large family once were together, haunted by the recent loss of her father and also by the ghosts of other beloved family members—her mother, her brother Frank, her sisters Cary and Emily, and her brother-in-law Walter McCormack.

She tells the story of her long relationship with Anderson in two chapters of *The Woman Within*, where she calls him Harold S— and explains that their love affair endured for only part of the time: "For seventeen months out of twenty-one years we were happy together." When they first met, they felt an immediate attraction and began seeing each other regularly. But in July of 1917, Anderson volunteered to head the Red Cross in Rumania during World War I, and he and Glasgow became secretly engaged before he traveled to the Balkans. There he was dazzled by the queen of Rumania and, though he apparently worked very hard for the Red Cross, found the time for a romance with the queen. When he came home to Richmond in June of 1918, he and Glasgow quarreled, and she took an overdose of sleeping medicine. This romance, which Glasgow may have felt was her last chance for love and marriage, was profoundly affecting. Yet when she had first glimpsed Anderson at the Easter luncheon, she claims that she wondered "whether he could be used effectively in a comedy of manners."[15]

Ten years later Anderson did provide the seeds of Judge Honeywell's character in *The Romantic Comedians*. Glasgow's early notes for the novel reveal some material that describes Anderson, and some of it is close to what she later wrote about him in her autobiography. As she is randomly jotting down ideas, she writes of her projected protagonist's questionable family background for acceptance into Richmond society: "He had found it easier to impress people in New York or Washington, where what Virginians of richer blood but simple manners called his 'antecedents' were unknown." His service for the Red Cross in Rumania during World War I with the title of Colonel is attributed in these preliminary notes to Col. Godfrey Plummer Bullfinch, an early name for Honeywell, who "had won his title as a Red Cross decoration and retained it as a political asset" (260). Other ideas in the notes for the protagonist of the novel that seem to be taken from Anderson's life are a relationship with the queen of Berengaria and his awe of British lords and ladies, his philandering with married women, his public display of his Red Cross medals, his seeing himself "in the robes of a Justice," his attraction socially in old age to young people, his affectation, hypocrisy, and selfishness. Also interesting is that there are brief notes on Violet, who seems to be the love interest and is identified as a poet. Glasgow refers to her briefly with these words, "Irony humor of Violet."[16] She seems to be a surrogate for Glasgow herself.

Three separate pages of names show Glasgow searching for the right ones. One list begins with these names: Blackledge, Bullitt, Goddard, Hardaway, Holladay, and Bullington.[17] When she tries Honeywell, she lists Philip Byrd Honeywell, Fitzhugh Byrd Honeywell, Gamiel Byrd Honeywell. Although Glasgow in one list selected masculine, powerful, sexual names such as Bullitt and Hardaway and also considered Virginian aristocratic names like Byrd and Fitzhugh, she settled on Gamaliel Bland Honeywell. This evolution in naming suggests the creative evolution that occurred between her initial plans for the book and the finished product. She gained distance from her disappointment and her anger as a result of the relationship with Anderson, and her view softened to amused irony. Judge Gamaliel Honeywell was conceived as a surrogate for Anderson, but he was born a quite different character. His name suggests he is game, bland, and a well-of-honey—no longer associated with such words as *black, bull, God,* or *hard.*

Glasgow's projected titles for the book also show a change in emphasis. She first noted "The Romantic Myth: A Comedy of Illusions," a title that is close to the final one. Later she tried "Bulfinch: In Search of Importance." Then she noted "A Red Cross Knight" with "Godfrey Plummer Bull-finch" on the next line and then later on the page "A Comedy of Cautiousness."[18] Fortunately, she settled on a title not in her preliminary notes. *The Romantic Comedians*, quite perfect for the novel she wrote, is less abstract than her first idea and broader in implications than the last two, which seem to focus on one person.

Fortunate, too, is that she dropped the character of Violet, and she ultimately did not use most of the material that specifically described Anderson, though there are vestiges of those early notes in the text of the novel. And she slyly suggests Anderson occasionally in the text. When the Judge's twin sister proposes to Bella Upchurch that she take Annabel away with her to Europe for a few months so that Annabel could have "a little needed vacation from marriage," she assures Bella that she is "respectable" in Europe: "As provincial as you are in America, it is hopeless to try to make you understand that behaviour as much as beauty is a question of geography, and that my respectability increases with every mile of the distance I travel from Queenborough. In France, my reputation is above reproach; by the time I reach Vienna, I have become a bit of a prude; and contrasted with the Balkan temperament, I am little more than a tombstone to female virtue" (215). Anderson—and others—could not have missed that wicked allusion to Queen Marie of Rumania, whose "Balkan temperament" precipitated the end of Glasgow's engagement to Anderson. And, too, Anderson had a twin sister, who has been described as dominating him throughout his life![19]

That this splendid novel has been neglected for many years is puzzling. Other work of Glasgow has been more widely read and studied, while *The Romantic Comedians* has languished, long out of print, known only to Glasgow scholars. It is an excellent choice for the classroom—for courses in the American novel, American women's writing, the 1920s, American humor, satire, and others. The reader who wants to be delighted will also be instructed about many topics. There is not really a comparable or similar work in American literature.

It may not have received appropriate recognition because it *is* a comedy, and American literature—with the exception, perhaps, of Mark Twain—does not take comedy, and certainly sophisticated comedy, as seriously as other forms of writing. Too, it has an old man as the central figure, unusual in the canon of American writings; one has to ponder deeply to come up with the names of any classic American novels that feature old men. And, of course, the book has not been read because it has not been available in print.

A sophisticated book, an adult book, *The Romantic Comedians* calls for a mature reader—of any age. It rewards that reader on many levels—among them, thoughtful laughter, social criticism, and insight into the relationship between the sexes. It was timely when published in 1926 with the background of World War I, prohibition, and the wasteland theme of other works of the period. It is still timely in its treatment of romantic myths, of evasive idealism, of the painful conflict of a man facing old age, and of the romantic differences between men and women. All of these subjects are treated with humor and satire.

Ellen Glasgow distanced herself from her material in this novel in a way she was unable to in many of her other novels, and with the use of an Olympian narrator depicted her romantic fools with satire, but with deep understanding, compassion, and affection. She wrote with her mind and not her heart in control, with her thinking and not her feeling ascendant. She produced a comedy of manners, a masterpiece in the genre.

Dorothy M. Scura

1. Ellen Glasgow, *Letters of Ellen Glasgow*, ed. Blair Rouse (New York: Harcourt, Brace, 1958), p. 193.

2. All quotations of reviews are found in Dorothy M. Scura, ed., *Ellen Glasgow: The Contemporary Reviews* (New York: Cambridge Univ. Press, 1992): Johnson, 274; Morley, 284; Mann, 284; Van Vechten, 278; Dounce, 282.

3. William W. Kelly, "Struggle for Recognition: A Study of the Literary Reputation of Ellen Glasgow," Ph.D diss., Duke University, 1957, pp. 238–39.

4. Rouse, Introduction, *Letters*, p. 17; C. Hugh Holman, "The Comedies of Manners," in *Ellen Glasgow: Centennial Essays*, ed. M. Thomas Inge (Charlottesville: Univ. Press of Virginia, 1976), p. 110.

5. Rouse, *Letters*, pp. 134–35.

6. Julius Rowan Raper, *From the Sunken Garden: The Fiction of Ellen Glasgow, 1916–1945* (Baton Rouge: Louisiana State Univ. Press, 1980), p. 117.

7. Citations to the preface and to *The Romantic Comedians* in this Afterword refer to the current edition and will be placed in the text; Rouse, *Letters*, p. 90.

8. Ellen Glasgow, *Barren Ground*, Old Dominion Edition of the Works of Ellen Glasgow (Garden City, N.Y.: Doubleday, 1933), p. 524.

9. Kathryn Lee Seidel, "The Comic Male: Satire in Ellen Glasgow's Queenborough Trilogy," *Southern Quarterly* 23 (Summer 1985): 16.

10. Rouse, *Letters*, p. 90.

11. Ruth Jones Wilkins, "Ellen Glasgow's Virginia: The Background of her Novels," M.A. thesis, University of Richmond, 1951, p. 70.

12. Holman, "Comedies," p. 110.

13. Rouse, *Letters*, p. 90.

14. James Branch Cabell, *Let Me Lie* (New York: Farrar, Straus, 1947), p. 237.

15. Ellen Glasgow, *The Woman Within* (New York: Harcourt, Brace, 1954), pp. 227, 224.

16. All quotations in this paragraph are from Notebook 3, Ellen Glasgow Collection, University of Virginia, pp. 263, 260, 263. For

permission to quote from this manuscript material, I thank Ellen Glasgow's literary executor, Ms. Margaret Williams, director, acting for the Society for the Prevention of Cruelty to Animals, Richmond, Virginia.

17. Glasgow, Notebook 3, p. 261.

18. Ibid., p. 260.

19. Anne Hobson Freeman, *The Style of a Law Firm: Eight Gentlemen from Virginia* (Chapel Hill: Algonquin, 1989). p. 103.

Suggestions for further reading
in addition to items cited in the notes.

Ewing, Majl. "The Civilized Uses of Irony: Ellen Glasgow." *English Studies in Honor of James Southall Wilson*. Ed. Fredson T. Bowers. Charlottesville: Univ. of Virginia Press, 1951.

Godbold, E. Stanley, Jr. *Ellen Glasgow and the Woman Within*. Baton Rouge: Louisiana State Univ. Press, 1972.

Hall, Caroline King Barnard. "'Telling the Truth about Themselves'": Women, Form and Idea in *The Romantic Comedians: Ellen Glasgow: New Perspectives*. Ed. Dorothy M. Scura. Knoxville: Univ. of Tennessee Press, 1995.

Holman, C. Hugh. "April in Queenborough: Ellen Glasgow's Comedies of Manners," *Sewanee Review* 82 (Spring 1974): 264–83.

———. *Three Modes of Southern Fiction: Ellen Glasgow, William Faulkner, Thomas Wolfe*. Mercer University Lamar Memorial Lectures, no. 9. Athens: Univ. of Georgia Press, 1966.

McDowell, Frederick P. W. *Ellen Glasgow and the Ironic Art of Fiction*. Madison: Univ. of Wisconsin Press, 1963.

Rouse, Blair. *Ellen Glasgow*. Twayne's United States Authors Series. New York: Twayne, 1962.

Scura, Dorothy M., ed. *Ellen Glasgow: New Perspectives*. Knoxville: Univ. of Tennessee Press, 1995.

Wagner, Linda W. *Ellen Glasgow: Beyond Convention*. Austin: Univ. of Texas Press, 1982.